The Changing of the Guard

Lesbian and Gay Elders, Identity, and Social Change

D0855169

The Changing of the Guard

Lesbian and Gay Elders, Identity, and Social Change

Dana Rosenfeld

 Temple University Press
Philadelphia

Temple University Press, Philadelphia 19122
Copyright © 2003 by Temple University
All rights reserved
Published 2003
Printed in the United States of America

Library of Congress Cataloging-in-Publication Data

Rosenfeld, Dana, 1958–
    The changing of the guard : lesbian and gay elders, identity, and
social change / Dana Rosenfeld.
        p.   cm.
    Includes bibliographical references and index.
    ISBN 1-59213-030-5 (cloth : alk. paper) – ISBN 1-59213-031-3 (pbk. :
alk. paper)
    1. Aged gays–United States–Interviews.   2. Gays–Identity.   3. Gay
rights–United States–History–20th century.   I. Title.
HQ76.3.U5 R68   2003
306.76'6–dc21   2002043552

2 4 6 8 9 7 5 3 1

Identity is available for use: something that people do which is embedded in some other social activity, and not something they "are." . . . The important analytic question is not therefore whether someone can be described in a particular way, but to show *that* and *how* this identity is made relevant as ascribed to self or others. . . . If there is one defining principle displayed in this kind of analytic approach, it is the ethnomethodological one that identity is to be treated as a resource for the participant rather than the analyst. –Widdicombe 1998, p. 191

If I am in a straight group, [like] when I was a hairdresser, I would never try to pass as not being gay, but I certainly would not be coming out like I was flaming, like I am gay and I am proud. I was never proud to be gay, I don't see what there is to be proud about. Really, I don't know what gays have done that is so great. –Henri

While sociological approaches to the life course can be found at purely macro- or micro-sociological levels, *it is the intersection between these levels that represents the most exciting juncture for the study of lives.* –Settersten 1999, p. 21

Honey, being so damned old now, I've seen it. I've seen it all, you know when they didn't like us, and then they started accepting us. It's going to be acceptable more and more as time goes by. –Constance

Contents

Acknowledgments

CERTAIN PEOPLE stand out as particularly supportive throughout this project, especially in its early, dissertation, stage. The University of California-Los Angeles Center on Aging funded the initial research, for which I remain grateful to this day. Melvin Pollner, my advisor throughout my graduate career at UCLA and a personal friend of many years, is the person to whom my development as a sociologist owes the most. Without his keen eye, impeccable insight, thorough knowledge of the discipline, clear direction, and good humor this project would not have been done. I am forever grateful to him. I am also greatly indebted to the rest of my dissertation committee—sociologists Robert Emerson and John Heritage, and anthropologist Peter Hammond—for their encouragement and feedback; to other members of the UCLA Department of Sociology, particularly Nicky Hart and Steven Clayman; and to Jay Gubrium, who was the first to publish my work.

Other sources of help, financial, critical, and emotional, emerged as the book began to take shape. The National Institutes of Health, which funded my work for two years through a Post-Doctoral Fellowship (National Research Service Award MH15730 from the National Institute of Mental Health), and the Department of Behavioral Science at the

University of Kentucky College of Medicine, which hosted and supported me while I worked on it; Eugene Gallagher, my mentor at Kentucky; the Colorado College Department of Sociology, where I am now proud to hang my hat; and the Colorado College Social Sciences Executive Committee, which funded the preparation of the manuscript–all of these played important roles in the lengthy and often frustrating process of producing the book.

I owe my thanks to the editors at Temple University Press, who saw the promise of the project early on. Micah Kleit was as helpful and supportive an editor as any author–especially a first-timer–could hope for, and those who copy-edited the manuscript exhibited an enviable eye for fluency. The anonymous reviewers solicited by Temple were both theoretically and structurally on point, and I hope they can see their hands in the finished product. Any and all glitches and weaknesses are, of course, my own.

When I first began formulating the project, a number of naysayers told me that I would never find lesbian and gay elders willing to talk to me. Needless to say, I did, and I remain grateful to them for their time, insights, life stories, and, most important, their honesty and trust. I remember them all quite vividly, even after all these years, and can only hope that they feel I have done their stories justice. I extend my gratitude to those I interviewed whose narratives do not appear in the book, and to other members of the Los Angeles lesbian and gay communities who helped and encouraged me throughout the data collection process.

Lastly, of course, are those patient people who fed, listened to, supported, and put up with me as I limped through the writing process. To Ben and Teri Whittaker, Joanne Moran (who got me started in the academic business, whether she knows it or not), Diane Girer, Greg Miller and Beth Lapides, Nicky Hart (again), Gary and Pierre Silva, all three Grillos (Brian, Paul, and Dominique), Valarie Schwann, Darin Weinberg, Maggie Kusenbach, and, of course, Missy Kelly: thank you, for everything. To my family—my mother, Judith Shepard Rosenfeld (an invaluable editor in her own right); my brothers Michael and Joel; Beryl Howell; Jared, Alina, and Calla Howell-Rosenfeld; my father, Alvin Rosenfeld, who would have done all that the above-mentioned folk have done, and more—and to my other family, the Blancs: this is for you.

The Changing of the Guard

Lesbian and Gay Elders,
Identity, and Social Change

Introduction

The Distinctiveness of Lesbian and Gay Elders

OLDER GAY men and women came of age in an era of unprecedented surveillance, legal prosecution, and social persecution of homosexuals, and moved into a workforce that was unparalleled in its overt hostility to them. In the 1930s, the post-Prohibition politics of the United States worked to shut down the veritable carnival of gay expression and association that had emerged in cities in the first third of the century, and criminalized homosexual association in virtually any form. Particularly in the 1940s and 1950s, gay men and lesbians were systematically harassed, jailed, fired from their jobs, and subject to involuntary incarceration in mental hospitals. Until gay liberation, riding the wave of the radical politics of the late 1960s, galvanized a nascent reformulation and representation of homosexuality, cultural depictions of homosexuality as anything other than a shameful, pathological condition leading to isolation and misery were censored and hard to come by outside certain (usually urban) areas. As a consequence, the most readily available homosexual identity was a stigmatized one; moreover, while the homosexual subculture, which thrived in many cities and

1

barely survived elsewhere, offered gay men and lesbians some respite from an isolated and insecure existence, it too was driven by the language of stigma. That "overt" homosexuals were discriminated against on almost every level was a constant reminder of the futility of leading anything other than a secret and secretive life.

Members of this group also lived through the gay liberation (in Mary Bernstein's [1997, p. 2] words, "the quintessential identity movement") and lesbian-feminist movements of the late 1960s and early 1970s during middle age, having spent their youth and much of their adulthood establishing relations with self and others in an exclusively stigmatizing context. At the brink of this movement, the homosexuals I interviewed (who were over the age of sixty-five[1] in 1995, when I collected my data) ranged in age from thirty-nine to sixty-three; for many, their stigmatized homosexual identities had been adopted and enacted within a distinctive nexus of relations for decades. For almost all, relationships with friends, family, and co-workers had been fashioned around passing as heterosexual, and relations with other homosexuals were often furtive, circumscribed, and complicated by the desire for association on the one hand and the threat of guilt by association on the other. Equally important, relations with self were shaped by an understanding of homosexuality as a potential danger to personal safety and, often, as a source of personal shame. Gay liberation bracketed stigmatized homosexual identities, condemned them as invalid and oppressive, and constructed those who continued to enact them—including the then-middle-aged—as ignorant and/or morally weak, implicating them in the radical rejection of a stigmatized homosexual identity and in its moral crusade to create a new one based on the open display of pride in transgressing traditional sexuality. Indeed, Steven Epstein's (1990, p. 9) assertion that neither gay, lesbian, nor homosexual identity "appeared in writing by or about gays and lesbians before the mid-1970s" suggests that the new gay activism that emerged in the 1970s was pivotal in making homosexual *identity*, rather than the homosexual *condition*, a phenomenon in its own right.

Clearly, then, the gay liberationist and lesbian-feminist movements that emerged in the late 1960s and early 1970s changed the symbolic and practical terrain on which gay men and women negotiated their identities and their daily lives. This change is evident in my respondents' accounts of their past and present lives, although often in unimagined ways. The commonsense expectation that Stonewall was a "shot heard 'round the world" was not borne out by my data—indeed, few of my subjects mentioned it, and several had never heard of it. The assumption that those who did not jump on the gay liberationist bandwagon declined to do so because of shame or fear of being recognized as homosexual was not borne out either. On the contrary, in keeping with Lee's (1987) and Adelman's (1990) findings that the homosexual elders they studied found passing as heterosexual to be "adventuresome and special"[2] and key to building a "positive self-image," respectively, many of my informants exhibited pride in having passed as heterosexual throughout their lives, and in having conducted their lives with skill, grace, and self-control. But the new formulation of homosexuality that emerged in the late 1960s and early 1970s, one that constructed it as a positive, essential, and authentic self that could only be honored through public proclamation, did affect all those I interviewed. It did so by challenging the integrity of those who continued to treat homosexuality as a private aspect of self best honored through its exclusively private enactment, and who shunned its public proclamation—and others' insistence upon it—as a dangerous, ridiculous, and insulting practice that threatened the tenuous standing homosexuals had managed to create. Thus, although many both within and without academia divide the homosexual world into pre- and post-Stonewall eras, both "eras" continue to exist within a lesbian and gay world that remains riven by competing claims about the nature of homosexuality, its consequences for self, and how it is best handled in public and private life. As this book will show, these assertions constitute not only intergenerational tensions, but intragenerational ones as well.

These claims are not merely background noise. On the contrary, they shape my subjects' assessments of their own past and present lives. For most, if not all, of my informants, the claims they make are matters of personal honor, and those that others make are matters of annoyance, even moral outrage. These claims are such important features of their talk that they became evident to me even when I wasn't looking for them, emerging through my analysis rather than my research design. It was through these claims that my informants constructed a world, and through which they produced themselves as competent actors appropriately responding to it. For many, producing themselves as competent in the context of the interview involved casting their past actions and interpretations as incompetent. In short, it was through these claims that they engaged in *identity work*– the situated work actors do to produce social categories and to affiliate themselves with or disaffiliate themselves from them.[3] This identity work is conducted in the context–and through the invocation, manipulation, and application–of available discourses, or mutually reinforcing statements about the world. Capturing the identity work of homosexual elders–their production of homosexual identities in general and their own homosexual identities in particular–thus involves appreciating their self-location in the discourses of sexuality to which they had access. As this book will show, the identity work of the lesbian and gay elders whose accounts figure here was strongly shaped by these discourses. While these informants treated the properties of these discourses (that of homosexuality as a stigma, and that of homosexuality as a source of status) as more or less salient at different points in the interview, they clearly displayed their understanding and assessment of them as unique and unmistakable features of competing ideologies. In short, they treated these discourses as ideal types, recognizable as such to anyone versed in the details and contingencies of gay life.

Data Collection

In 1995, I set out to interview[4] twenty-five gay men and twenty-five lesbians over the age of sixty-five living in the greater Los Angeles area. Conducting research in Los Angeles has many benefits, not the least of which is an internationally recognized organized lesbian and gay community, and finding groups of older gay men and lesbians was as easy as opening the *Gay and Lesbian Community Yellow Pages*, which listed the Coalition of Older Lesbians (COOL) and Rainbow, a group for older gay men and women. I attended their meetings and events, which included panels, picnics, dinners, parties, and book sales, as well as funerals and memorial services for members of COOL. While talking to these groups' chair people, I learned that the city of West Hollywood was organizing the West Hollywood Gay and Lesbian Aging Task Force, which I promptly joined. Several members of the task force were over sixty-five and active in these groups, and I cultivated relationships with them, asking their advice, interviewing them, and relying on them to introduce me to other potential subjects.

Soon after I began my research, the task force put on an event for lesbian and gay seniors. I helped organize the event, which was heavily advertised, and the task force included a description of my research in the questionnaire it distributed at the event. This yielded approximately forty potential subjects, half of whom I interviewed (the others were too young or were unavailable). Because they saw me at a variety of events, some overcame their initial distrust and consented to be interviewed. Abby, for example, had put me off several times, but told me that she had changed her mind once her friend Marilyn told her I had interviewed her and that it "was fun." Two or three refused to be interviewed, stating that they were closeted, and no amount of assurance about confidentiality would sway them. Most, however, agreed, expressing their happiness that someone was documenting the experiences of their homosexual generation, and were helpful when I asked if they knew of others I could interview.[5] This "snowball sampling" technique (Bailey 1994) provided me with fifty subjects, fourteen of whom do not figure in the book, for a variety of reasons. Some of the tapes were unintelligible in whole or in part, and, because I didn't want to misrepresent informants' statements, I withdrew them from the study. Some interviews were never completed (sometimes because of death), one was withdrawn by the subject, and others were either unsuccessful as interviews (i.e., due to memory problems) or proved, upon review, to offer few, if any, accounts of direct relevance to the book's focus (the range of identity practices in which homosexual elders engage). These practices, my analysis showed, are firmly grounded in the discourses of homosexuality that emerged over the course of the twentieth century and through which respondents identified as homosexual.

The Discursive Terrain: The Historical Revision of Homosexual Identity

Homosexuality as Stigma

The shift from sexuality as a function of gender to a function of sexual object choice has been well documented.[6] It was not until the middle of the century, when this version of homosexuality was imposed by the World War II-created psychiatry-state alliance (which "continued into the post–World War II era as the national state and local social control agents fiercely policed the moral and political landscape in the McCarthy era"), that same-sex desire, rather than gender and a range of other cultural codes that had informed gay culture, became "essential to group status" (Valocchi 1999, p. 213). This new discourse, while imposed from above, was also embraced from below, as middle-class gay men and women worked to distance themselves from the dominant image of homosexuals as gender inverts. (See Chauncey 1994.) The new gay identity that emerged from this middle-class aversion to public sexualized personas posited homosexuality as a benign yet stigmatized condition that required the homosexual to avoid heterosexual persecution by passing as heterosexual in public. Passing, in turn, required homosexuals to avoid recognizable homosexuals–in other words, recognizable gender inverts–and to condemn their public identification as unnecessarily legitimizing stereotypes of gay men and women that invited the persecution of all homosexuals. As Nardi (1994, p. 11) wrote, "for many in the 1950s, the debate to organize 'a highly ethical homosexual culture' centered on assimilation, either to seek respectability within the framework of the dominant ideologies or to recreate alternative socio-political structures."

This was particularly evident in early homophile organizations such as the Daughters of Bilitis (DOB) (the first lesbian organization in the world and founded in 1955), designed as an alternative meeting place to bars, where butch/ femme relations often prevailed and where lesbians often served as a "floor show" and were vulnerable to police raids. The DOB was committed to encouraging and shaping the adjustment of the "sex variant" to society;[7] indeed, its statement of purpose[8] declared its aim to be the "education of the variant, with particular emphasis on the psychological, physiological, and sociological aspects, to enable her to understand herself and make her adjustment to society . . . by advocating a mode of behavior and dress acceptable to society" (Daughters of Bilitis 1956, p. 4).[9]

As Goffman (1963) noted, the implications of this stigmatizing discourse for the identities and relationships of those who adopted it should not be underestimated. First, it posited the achievement of a heterosexual persona not only as the sole available key to safety, but as the only way to exhibit a respect for the "natural sexual and gender order." Second, those adopting this discourse would use what Goffman termed "recipes of being" to construct and understand homosexuals, including themselves, as stigmatized persons, and hold them to that discourse's standards of conduct for such persons. Put simply, members of their stigmatized category could either do the work required to keep their homosexuality a discreditable characteristic, or fail to do so and thus transform this characteristic into an actively discrediting one. Since the failure of one can easily redound to the status of all, the latter course of action threatens the tenuous safety that other homosexuals have managed to achieve. Any desire for affiliation with other homosexuals must, therefore, be balanced, if not weakened, by feelings of distrust; indeed, stratifying other homosexuals on the basis of the obtrusiveness of their stigma (see Goffman 1963, p. 107) resonates as a central aspect of my informants' homosexual identity work.

Out of the Closet and into the Streets:
Homosexuality as Status

Although riven by internal differences regarding their goals, methods, and stance toward the existing gay subculture,[10] the political movements that emerged in the aftermath of the Stonewall uprisings of 1969 agreed on a radical rejection of the stigmatized discourse of homosexuality and of the assimilationists' adoption of it, and on the replacement of this discourse with one constructing homosexuality not as a discreditable aspect of self best handled by passing as heterosexual, but as an accrediting political identity to be openly enacted in public as well as private arenas. Central to this construction was the insistence upon coming out as a crucial step toward achieving their individual goals, which diverged along the lines of the nature of homosexual identity on the one hand and the scope of the desired social change on the other.[11]

This shift toward the public proclamation of homosexual identity reflected a critical refashioning of homosexuality from a relatively private matter enacted within a circumscribed, relatively private social arena into an essentially political matter to be hashed out in a public, political one. The new gay activism redefined and politicized the term *coming out* and made it the movement's central and most immediate goal, claiming that the voluntary, public disclosure of homosexual desire would undermine heterosexual society's grip on homosexuals, which centered on a fear of discovery and forced gay men and women to pass as heterosexual–a practice that, in this new formulation, hardly resonated as benign. On the contrary, passing was seen not as a protective masking of an aspect of self, but as the denial, even suppression, of the authentic self. Given the "true" nature of homosexuality as a valid and validating essential and political identity, its "denial" in interaction with others was also a denial of the true, authentic self and an obstacle to the liberation of all homosexuals, even, to some, of all humans. Coming out would not only provide an immediate sense of personal well-being, but would constitute a social and political force for change.[12]

Despite these changes, stigmatized understandings of homosexuality are oriented to by gay men and lesbians living today as constituting a way to live or a way *not* to. Stigma thus remains a conceptual keystone of homosexual identity politics and identity work, clearly present in the discourse that formulates homosexuality as a stigma, and in that which formulates it as the opposite of stigma, as a source of status.[13] These discourses supply actors with the tools to construct, contest, maintain, and assess their own and others' identities, and provide their own scripts for constructing and evaluating the self, and for enacting it in interaction with others. In short, discourses call up particular sorts of selves: in the case of the discourses of homosexuality, a stigmatized or an accrediting one.

From Identity Discourses to Identity Cohorts

Once I started analyzing the transcribed interviews, I found significant differences between respondents' accounts and concerns, differences that were not based on traditional demographic variables such as age, race, socioeconomic status, and the like. Rather, they were based on the *type of homosexual identity* informants had adopted, which was, in turn, linked to the *historical era* in which they had identified as homosexual. The central fault line seemed to be the emergence of the accrediting homosexual discourse in the late 1960s and early 1970s, dividing the era in which homosexuality was exclusively constructed as a shameful stigma from a new one in which it was constructed as a positive political identity. This division complicated the array of options through which those I interviewed could understand and pursue their desires. Informants varied in their response to this discourse, some embracing it as an interpretive frame, others declining to do so. Consequently, while these respondents came of age in the same historical period and encountered the same stigmatizing discourse of homosexuality at more or less the same time, their identity careers are significantly different. Specifically, while some identified as homosexual well before the late 1960s and thus did so through the properties of the dominant stigmatizing discourse of homosexuality, others identified as homosexual during or after the late 1960s through the properties of the emerging accrediting one.

Types of identity careers shaped by the acceptance and enactment of different versions of the homosexual self thus emerged, and I began to think of these subjects as members of what I termed *identity cohorts* (see Rosenfeld 1999), composed of actors who identified as members of a particular category of person (in this case, a homosexual one) in different historical periods with distinctive, historically specific ideologies of self and other. My informants fell into one of two identity cohorts: the *discreditable* one, consisting of those who adopted a homosexual identity before the late 1960s and thus through the properties of the stigmatizing discourse, and the *accredited* one, consisting of those who adopted a homosexual identity during or after the late 1960s and thus through the properties of the accrediting discourse.

The implications of membership in one cohort or another would be wide. Theorizing identity cohorts requires us to take seriously the emphasis on the interrelated production of the homosexual self on the one hand and the world in which the self makes sense and in which it acts, interprets, and evaluates on the other. After all, as Jenness (1992, p. 72) has written, identification as homosexual "arises out of a partial reconstruction of the social world, including ourselves, as type constructs. . . . *In essence,* [homosexual] *identities are simultaneously products of and resources for social categories*" (emphasis added). Accordingly, informants would use the discourses through which they and other members of their identity cohort construct their identities to understand and construct a range of related realities, and to position themselves among them.[14] These realities include categories of others, and distinctive standards of action for (and evaluation of) self and other. In exploring the identity work of homosexual elders, then, this book examines these constructions within the context of sociohistorically anchored discourses to which these elders relate in distinctive ways by virtue of identity cohort membership.

Outline of the Book

Chapter 1 begins the daunting task of making sense of subjects' voices and experiences by tracing their identity careers–their self-understanding and self-identification as homosexual (or not) over time and in the contexts and constraints of their personal lives. It does so by considering their same-sex desires, experiences, and understandings before they actually identified as homosexual. This chapter begins the search for informants' construction of homosexual identity over the life course and within the context of prevailing discourses–lifelong projects I call *identity careers*–through which they came to understand the nature and implications of their desires, and determined (in the sense of understanding *and* creating) their quality and social standing. Chapter 2 continues to trace these careers, documenting the process of identifying as homosexual. The third chapter sums up and theorizes these identity careers, showing that they vary according to the historical era in which subjects came to identify as homosexual and thus according to the discourse of homosexuality through whose properties they construct themselves as homosexual. Chapter 4 begins to explore the influence of identity cohort membership on informants' understandings and practices by documenting their accounts of the world and their position in it as re/constructions informed by the discourse of homosexuality through which they identified as homosexual. Chapters 5 and 6 are devoted to the impact of these understandings on how each identity cohort managed its homosexuality in the context of the threats described in Chapter 4, and on subjects' evaluations of their own and other homosexuals' management practices. The final chapter discusses some methodological challenges and opportunities the research provided, and summarizes the book's main points, situating them in the relatively recent debate about the nature of identity in postmodern society. The book's appendix is a "cast of characters," presenting demographic information and key moments in subjects' lives to provide a coherent overview of their past and current circumstances.

1

"I Didn't Have Identity"

Same-Sex Desire and the Search for Meaning

It's funny, when I think back now, I can remember other instances in my life where I realized how attracted I was to women. I didn't act upon any of it, but I always had this thing in the back of my mind. —Abby

Before they can see themselves as homosexual, people must realize that homosexuality and homosexuals exist, learn what homosexuals are actually like as people, and be able to perceive similarities between their own desires and behaviors and those of people labeled socially as homosexual. —Troiden 1988, p. 269

Awareness of Difference

When recounting their identity careers, some respondents described always knowing that they were different. Those who always knew spoke of being attracted to members of their own sex during their early years, often in childhood, in strong terms, emphatically linking the significance of their sense of difference to the earliness of its emergence. A central theme was the development of a nonerotic homosexual gaze: a growing but as-yet-nonsexual fascination with watching members of their own sex. Dan (70), for example, "just felt good looking at men," and viewed this fact

14

as evidence that he "must've been" gay from an early age: "Even as a little boy, before I had orgasms, I used to look at men, and I was always attracted to men. So I mean, nobody seduced me, nobody came up to me. I just had the attraction looking at other men." In her early teens, Marge (81) said her response to seeing girls was strongly physical, but not recognizably sexual–she would "get a feeling and I would start perspiring. My sweat glands used to overact."

When talking about their early desires, some described key moments during which they became aware of their same-sex attractions or during which vague feelings suddenly became clear as sexual desires. Often, these accounts hinged on *how they looked at* what they saw: on an emergent, reflexive awareness of their distinctive interest in and focus on members of their own sex. Marilyn (66) recalled an instance in the early 1960s in which, while having a drink at the home of a co-worker to whom she was "very attracted," she found herself looking at the woman "with such a desire, such a *wanting* feeling, and she caught my expression and I was very ashamed." This shame affected how she interpreted and acted upon her same-sex desires; while "there were times along the way where I wondered about being gay because I felt more comfortable with women," she "never fully faced it." In the late 1930s, when Rodney (75) was "maybe seventeen or eighteen," he "really began to notice guys." He recalled attending a state fair with his uncle and realizing "all day long, literally, that I was just ogling every attractive male that I saw, every guy that I saw. And it stood out in my mind how interested I am in them." He remembers "that one day in particular" because "it seemed to be a demarcation for me." For Kate (76), this demarcation came at age "six or seven" in the context of childhood play, during which "somehow or other somebody got the idea . . . of putting" a local four-year-old boy, undressed, into "a great big piano case on one of the vacant lots near us . . . and then charging people a penny to come in and look at him." Kate remembers "being very much aware of the fact" that she was uninterested in looking at the captive, naked boy, but "wanted to look at the girls."

Others described making similar comparisons, realizing that their feelings for members of their own sex were stronger than their feelings for those of the opposite one. George (75) recalled being grabbed and held down by his ten-year-old female cousins, one of whom "would yell at everybody, 'We're married!' " His response, he recalls, was "We're *not*!", adding "Things like that," which "a heterosexual boy . . . would've *loved*," he "hated." This made him realize that he didn't "want [to be] attacked by these girls. I knew that I didn't object to the boys doing the same thing. I accepted that, but I wouldn't accept the girls." When, at three or four years old, she spent time with her next-door neighbor, Barbie (67) "recognized that there was just something about it, that gee, I enjoyed little girls' company better than boys, and I just had a stronger feeling toward girls that way."

A small minority cited gender differences as the source of their eventual identification as homosexual—indeed, as one of the sources (if not the sole source) of their same-sex attractions. Tony (70), for example, spoke of an early attraction to "feminine attitudes," which he only connected to his homosexuality in later years. Although he did not identify as a "sissy," he now feels that he "had to be sort of sissy in some of my actions, but I mean, I didn't recognize 'em. I didn't recognize the sissy in *me*. But it had to be there." He cited his having "almost cried" when, at age five, he was given "an Indian suit" instead of the tea set he had requested, and his desire for "an old black doll" belonging to one of his family's upstairs boarders, as examples of these early affinities. These "feminine attitudes" that existed "basically in the beginning"–before the emergence of his sexual desires for men–"grew into, basically, the desire, the physical attraction and the physical desire."

Indeed, for Val (74), gender differences continue to be the central factor in her identification as lesbian. She described herself as having always been "male-identified," and told me that her sense of self as essentially male, which began "before ten," led her to become attracted to women after she decided that she was not going to follow the social prescriptions associated with being female. Her lesbianism is, in her words, "a gender thing."

> I didn't say "homosexual," I certainly didn't say "lesbian," I just said "I don't feel like a girl, I'm not a girl, and I'm not going to live in the framework of a girl. I am going to live in the framework of me, and I have to live in a certain element of that framework, but I am going to read and learn, and understand about homosexuality."

Val emphasized that she "didn't say I was attracted to girls, at that time." When I asked her how she was thinking about herself at the time, she explained that she "knew I had a girl's body, and I just knew that I wasn't happy in it, and that somebody made a mistake, that's all. I identified with males, I always did, and I still do." Her attraction to women was, in her words, "the next natural step."

Some cited others' responses to their own gender nonconformity–real or ascribed–or to their suspicious same-sex interactions as critical to their ultimate sense of self and sexual identity. As a child in the 1920s, Rodney was taunted for being effeminate: because he was "a sissy," he "went through all this trauma a lot of gay fellows go through. Believe me, I got my share of it. I couldn't play ball–I hate sports, I hated baseball." This caused "an incredible amount of unhappiness" which, in turn, created a "sickly" and "very, very unhappy childhood." As Rodney put it, "In retrospect, I would say that I was a semi-invalid." As a result, he "had a nervous breakdown [at] twenty-one" and "really never refurbished." Jan (68) provided a contrasting account; when I asked her how she had interpreted having always known she was attracted to women, she described her mother supporting–indeed, even enjoying–her identity as a tomboy and her athletic activities and focus. As a result, Jan took her identity as a tomboy for granted, not questioning its consequences for self, and was secure in her athleticism and her eventual relationships.

> I was a quote tomboy, and she aided and abetted that. I think she kind of enjoyed the fact that I was quite an athlete, which was kind of unusual back in those days, when girls were supposed to be nice little girls and never get dirty and all that kind of stuff. I think she really rather aided and abetted in my relationships–the way I grew up and the fact that I was very athletic.

Three subjects spoke of being made aware of their nascent homosexuality by others' reactions to their same-sex interactions, although the subjects had not yet ascribed any significance to them themselves. Jeannine (66) "had my first relationship when I was sixteen," in the late 1940s, but "did not know anything about homosexuality, what it was, or anything else. I was walking around school with my girlfriend holding hands and people made remarks. I think somebody called us fairies." Although Val had been "getting flack" for being a "tomboy" throughout her childhood, she only began to connect her attraction to–and sexual encounters with–women with homosexuality when she "began to get flack for the way I felt or responded to women." This occurred only after she had left high school in the late 1930s, when the mother of her lover of several years "came and said, 'If you continue to see my daughter I will have her arrested and thrown into juvenile hall, I will see that your name is mud, that you will never work again. Don't call my daughter, don't come by the house.'"

As a freshman in a Catholic women's college in the late 1930s, Deborah (74) "had this big crush on this senior," whom she would meet and accompany to church every morning. Deborah characterized the friendship as "kind of this mutual thing" with no explicitly sexual overtones, explaining that "we didn't do anything about it, and I never thought to do anything about it, but I liked being with her." This was the first time that Deborah had had a crush on a girl, and when I asked her what she had thought that crush meant, she replied that she "just liked her a lot" and thought "great, gee, how wonderful." This benign understanding was corrected by one of the nuns in the college:

> I wasn't aware that we had done anything wrong and all of a sudden one morning I was going to meet her, this nun came out and said, "She's not coming, you go on ahead." And I said, "What's the matter, is she sick?" "No, she's not sick, you just go right on. You are not to meet her anymore." Just like that. You know, I've always thought of it because gee, she wasn't allowed to talk to me after that. No communication whatsoever, it was just (hand clap).

Deborah agreed with my suggestion that "it's almost as though [the sister] had a particular understanding" that she didn't have. When I asked her if she would have joined the nun in condemning her actions had she shared that understanding, she replied, "If I had thought I was doing something wrong, I wouldn't have done it. You know, it was just weird." When I asked how she had interpreted the situation, she replied that she "didn't know how to interpret it. I didn't know and I was really hurt, you know, I was really hurt." Deborah's inability to understand why her friendship with the senior was so quickly and summarily forbidden was exacerbated by that very ruling. Because "the girl was forbidden to talk to me, and she didn't talk to me.... I've never had any more contact with her. We wrote a couple of letters but they didn't explain anything and it just kind of dropped off." Thus the very person best capable of giving Deborah an unofficial version of what had happened was prevented from doing so by those who had organized the segregation and who refused to explain their actions or specify what, exactly, had inspired them to take them. Indeed, the fact that Deborah "knew that sister was angry, but didn't know why" was not only immediately upsetting, but was also, in retrospect, a missed opportunity to be educated in the norms of interaction and the nature and implications of breaking them. Deborah explained that "it was such a good opportunity for them to have talked to me because I didn't know what was happening and I didn't know–this felt so normal–that there was anything wrong with it." As it was, she lost both the opportunity to learn how to avoid such punishments in the future and the friendship that had meant so much to her.

Interestingly, few subjects provided accounts in which awareness of difference emerged from sexual experiences.[1] More often, first same-sex encounters clarified previously vague feelings of difference. Mark's (72) growing awareness, for example, was sharpened by a sexual experience he had in 1940, at age sixteen, with another teenage boy during which they "masturbated together. And that was the first time. We didn't *touch* each other, but I knew at that time that there was something different about me." With no available sexual taxonomy, no discourse through which to understand his difference, "the only thing I could think of was I enjoyed it. It was different than boys and girls touching each other. I had that experience when I was five . . . playing doctor underneath the front porch." Similarly, Tex's (72) first sexual encounter with a man in 1958, at age thirty-four, neutralized his sense that there was something wrong with him: "before, I always felt something was wrong, but I couldn't figure out what it was. And after that first experience, it wasn't wrong anymore." This statement is more complex than it appears to be. Through the encounter, Tex figured out two things: that the source of what was wrong about *himself* was his sexual desire for men, and that the source of what was wrong about *his life* was that he had not been pursuing these desires; and that what he had thought was wrong was, in fact, not wrong at all–again, the wrongness of his failure to pursue these desires could, and should, be corrected by having sex with men.

"Nothing to Latch Onto": Gender and Desire in a Symbolic Void

All the boys around ten, eleven, twelve years old, at puberty time, they know, I don't want the girl. I am different. They might not know the word for it, but they know they are different. –George

Hindsight is much greater than foresight. Now I detect, and even then there were a few incidents, but nothing was ever discussed. We didn't have school psychologists, we didn't have any gay [images]. I would develop a crush on one of my classmates or something, but I never did anything about it. –Abby

Virtually all subjects whose same-sex attractions had emerged in their early years spoke of being unable to interpret– or name–these feelings. Indeed, as we have seen, for some, these early desires, while palpable, were not yet clearly sexual. When I asked Jeannine if she had had feelings toward other girls around the time of her first affair with a woman at age sixteen, she explained that "I had, certainly"–indeed, had "had some *major* crushes"–but "wasn't aware of the feelings I had," or even "that my feelings were sexual." During her early teens, in the early 1930s, Kate "was very much aware within myself that my crushes were more than just crushes, that there was something else involved," but she "didn't know what" that something else was. Constance (74) echoed this thought: "I liked [girls] a lot, but I didn't know, well you don't, you know, *you don't know what's what*." Similarly, when he "was a little kid," Dan "used to look at men relatives," sometimes seeing "a relative nude," but "didn't know why." Indeed, he was even aware of his ignorance about homosexual sex in his dreams "about men chasing me, falling down on top of me"; although he would wake up "with a wet dream, nothing ever happened" in the dream because he "wasn't aware of what men did."

Not knowing the word for it reflects both the censorship of gay discourse of the 1940s and 1950s and the treatment of homosexuality as unspeakable except by the state and medical enterprises. Several informants explicitly likened the vagueness of their early same-sex desires to a lack of available terminology.[2] George, who "did homosexual things before" he identified as homosexual, "never put it into words" because "you don't know it exists." Phoebe (79) explained that, because "we didn't know gay in those days," she "didn't know what to think about it," adding that she "didn't really know what gay was 'til I got to [college]" in the early 1930s.

Knowing that something was wrong but being unable to define it deprived my informants of an identity with which to capture their feelings and desires, and their accounts clearly bore out Troiden's (1988, p. 269) statement that "people are unlikely to identify themselves in terms of a social category as long as they are unaware that the category exists, lack accurate information about the kinds of people who occupy the category, or believe they have nothing in common with category members (Lofland 1969)." Ricardo (66), for example, "didn't have identity, I didn't identify myself being gay." When I asked Barbie, who recognized her same-sex desires in high school but did not pursue them sexually until she was in her twenties, how she was thinking of herself–and her sexuality–at the time, she described having thought, "Oh, I'm having fun anyway, without doing, you know." This was also the case for Dan, who, while becoming aware of the existence of homosexual men when he was in the army in 1945, and, while having "the awareness and the desire," understood himself as "active neuter. Nothing, no sex, nothing." He added that his self-concept as neuter was also informed by the fact that he had "never dated a woman." Dan was explicit about the connection between his own ignorance and the lack of a discourse to explain same-sex desire, linking his private lack of awareness to a public lack of the same.

> I wasn't aware but what I'm saying is, there was no public *awareness*, there was nothing for me to latch onto. . . . Well, there was no gay identity in those days, I mean you couldn't have an identity when you have nothing to–there was no, what do you call it . . .
>
> DR: Vocabulary.
>
> No, no, there was no, what do you call it, there was no person, object.
>
> DR: Category.
>
> No, no, I don't mean category. There was no, not hero, but what's the word I'm looking for? There was nothing to *represent* anything gay, you know.[3]

Given the lack of representations of homosexuality, several subjects described simply not thinking about it. After Rodney described his experience at the state fair, I asked what he had thought the significance of the demarcation point had been at the time. He answered that he hadn't known, and didn't think that he had "thought in those terms." When they did begin to interpret their desires, though, some saw them as *personally idiosyncratic*, seeing themselves as "the only one in the world" and their desires as different, fleeting, strange, and even, in Sharon's (66) case, as evidence of mental illness. Barbie (67), for example, "would wonder if there's other people who feel the same way as I do." While she "accepted that feeling," it made her feel lonely at times—in her words, "I didn't feel *complete* when I was out there."

Others saw their desires as *relationally idiosyncratic*, emerging from the relationship they were having at the time rather than from any innate desire. George, for example, and a fourteen-year-old male neighbor were lovers between 1939 and 1940, when George was in his late teens. When I asked him how he had understood this relationship at the time, he explained that he "understood what [the other boy] was. He was the aggressive one. He was more aggressive than me." While these subjects knew that these desires were best enacted in certain contexts and not in others, pursuing them while ignorant of—and protected from—their severely stigmatizing "nature" allowed them to experience these connections as "natural." Jan (68), for example, said that she had seen her affair with her twenty-something high school teacher in 1941, when she was sixteen, as "the most natural thing in the world," explaining that she "didn't label it because I didn't know there was such a thing as a lesbian. . . . I don't suppose I knew what a homosexual was. If someone had asked me, [I would have said] 'I don't have a clue.'" When their "relationship was going full tilt," she "didn't consider herself anything." As a result, she "did not feel that [she] was different." When I asked her how she was thinking about the relationship at the time, she answered, "I *loved* her and I had such a terrible crush on her." Indeed, the relationship did not challenge her assumption that she was heterosexual: she dated men, and "always assumed that I would marry and do all this stuff because that was what people *did* where I grew up."

The expectation of heterosexual marriage as an essential feature of heterosexuality emerged in other accounts as well. Kate explained that when, in 1944, she and Jan had been "together for a year and a half," neither of them "admitted that we were lesbian or even homosexual, or–inverts, perverts, Uranians, any of the terms that were being used then. We didn't admit anything, we just loved each other." When I asked Kate if she had identified herself as "I am in love with Jan," she replied, "Yes. That was it. . . . I simply loved Jan! Both of us had expectations of getting married to a man." Similarly, Susan (75), who had been "aware of certain girls" in high school, "*always* thought of myself as a typical young woman who always wanted to have a family. I've *always* wanted to have children." In her early twenties, this self-concept was challenged by her first "actual experience with someone"–specifically, a nurse whom she had met at work at a World War II defense job and who, Susan emphasized, "was about to be married very shortly thereafter," a fact she felt "was fine." While the nurse "was reluctant," sensing that this was Susan's "first experience" and not wanting "to push me into it," Susan "probably *encouraged* it. I wanted it to happen, so it *happened*." When I asked her how she had defined the encounter, she answered, "I don't know that I defined it." When I asked her to compare how she had been thinking of herself before and after the encounter, she described a contradiction that she resolved by defining the encounter as a happy yet isolated experience of going with her feelings:

> I guess I couldn't cover up my feelings that I had, when perhaps she made some moves toward me, and I wasn't about to,

I wasn't *horrified* by it, let's put it that way. That was a long time ago. I don't know that it did affect me. I think I accepted it. I don't know why or how I can say that, but I mean, it was just *something* that I was feeling, I went with my feelings at that time. I don't know what I felt, to tell you the truth. I felt it was a happy experience, it was something I *enjoyed*, something we both enjoyed.

Asked if the experience made her feel less straight or more gay, she replied, "No, I didn't think of myself in that category at that particular moment, because I went ahead and pursued it," suggesting that, had she felt that the encounter would have threatened her status as a "typical young woman," she would not have engaged in it. Knowing that "that was the end of that experience," Susan simply "went on with my life after that," marrying and having three children.

"What I Learned Was That I Was a Mess": Discursive Encounters

Given the paucity of information about homosexuality, subjects' recollections of encounters with a discourse explaining their feelings–however imprecisely and disapprovingly– are compellingly clear.[4] Informants described learning of the existence of sexual deviants in two ways: by reading and responding to texts, and by hearing about and/or seeing sexual deviants–notably, obvious gender inverts.

Textual Representations

Without exception, the textual accounts informants encountered formulated same-sex desires as constituting homosexuality and (with the exception of Jeannine, who turned to the dictionary) constructed it in stigmatizing terms (e.g., as a pathological yet curable condition). Reading the early sexologists Krafft-Ebing and Ellis in the late 1940s, for example, showed Kate that "I was abnormal, that I was a menace to children, that there was no hope for me, or that there was hope for me but that it would mean turning myself inside out on the therapist's couch or twenty years of psychoanalysis or God knows what. But basically what I *learned* was that I was a *mess.*" In the early 1940s, during her early teens, fearing that her interest in other girls was a symptom of a "brain disorder," Sharon searched medical texts for a possible "cure," and emerged with an understanding of her desires as an expression of homosexuality, a mental disorder:

> Probably by the age of ten or twelve I was getting books at the library on Havelock Ellis and Krafft-Ebing because I would look up the term *homosexual*–don't ask me how I found that word–but I would look up the term *homosexual* and would refer to notes. And it told about all the horrible things that the insane people did, so I thought that's what gay people did.

Clearly, these texts depicted homosexuality as having severe consequences and thus as something to be avoided. Indeed, having "never heard the word *homosexuality* even though it existed," Rodney was cautioned against pursuing his same-sex desires when, in the late 1930s, at the age of eighteen, he wrote the editor of *Strength and Health Magazine* to determine "where I stood in life."[5] Concerned with anonymity, he "wrote it General Delivery . . . under an assumed name," and remembers "saying in the letter that I didn't understand, and I'm attracted to my own male sex." The response was "a very nice letter which was not realistic," depicting male body building, and its restrained appreciation, as "a beautiful thing and a lovely thing and a lot of bullshit that doesn't define being gay at all," and suggesting that if he "were to keep going" in the direction that his desires indicated, he would become a homosexual.

The editor said they considered themselves the epitome of masculinity, you can get all kinds of narcissism and people are [attracted] to their body, how close it is to homosexuality. He used the word *homosexual*, this was the first time in my life that I'd ever heard of this. And this is where I learned that I was homosexual.

Interestingly, some of those I interviewed engaged in a more creative reading of the texts they found. Aware of the negative implications of homosexuality to which the texts laid claim, they critically appraised these claims, focused on the information they provided, and declined to adopt the devaluing, pathologizing stance they took toward homosexuals. Upon reading Ellis in 1940, at age fourteen, Tony learned that, in order "to find myself, to really go out and *be* myself and perform what I wanted to," he would "have to be secretive about" his tendencies and activities: "I would not be able to expose it to the family or friends or anybody." However, he "didn't find it wrong, 'cause I sort of enjoyed it." Although he "*was* scared," he "never thought about being sick. I thought it was being different." Val also learned from sexological texts the nature of her desires and the need to keep them secret. After being threatened by her lover's mother, Val "began to think OK, this apparently is not acceptable behavior," and, "because obviously people seemed to think that something was wrong with me because I was not like everybody else," she set out to find "what everybody else was like" to understand the comparative standards they were using. The texts she read in the late 1930s led her to discover two things: first, that "this is homosexuality," and second, that "nobody approves of this, everybody thinks you are nutty and sick, and they lock you up for this sort of thing, so you [have to] be very careful and you live your own life, and be yourself, but you're not out, so to speak." Despite the strong condemnation of her sexual practices and orientations, however, Val "felt perfectly normal" because, as she put it, "you look at it, and say do I fit or do I not fit? Some of it I fit, and some of it I didn't."

Similarly, in 1943, while in high school, Abby (70) "read about Radclyffe Hall in *The New York Times'* obituary" and sent away for Radclyffe Hall's infamous book *The Well of Loneliness* when, months later, "*The Times* had a discreet advertisement that the book was available." While she "didn't like the ending," she found its pathologizing, negative depiction of lesbianism ("how horrible the ending [was] . . . how we're doomed from the moment we're born, and so on")[6] less significant than the identity category it provided. She emphasized that "everybody's negativity about *The Well of Loneliness*" needed to be balanced by the benefits the book provided to readers who were confused about–and isolated by–their sexual desires. As she put it, "What everyone fails to realize is that for someone at that age–I was, I think, seventeen–that here was the first time that I ever read in print that [the] feelings that I had about other women" were not idiosyncratic, but were criteria for membership in a social group.

> And it was funny because even though the book itself was, I guess, basically an unhappy book, I didn't feel like that. I picked out only the parts that were not negative. And, I felt like, well, like everybody, I think, feels the same thing: I'm not the only one. There are other people.

Pansies and Dykes

The discourse of difference available at the time was not only found in texts. On the contrary, it could be found, in however vague a form, in everyday interactions and encounters that made the dominant equation between homosexuality and gender inversion unavoidably clear. Several subjects spoke of having overheard people discussing gender inverts, usually "pansies." Rhoda (89), for example, "heard about boys first, because their being feminine was so obvious," and remembers people using the word *sissy* to describe them. Kate (76) also recalled having overheard a friend's mother talk about pansies in 1932, when she was twelve.

> Somehow or other the conversation with her mother got going on the subject of men who were called "pansies." And that's how I first learned that there was such a thing as a homosexual *male*. And I remember thinking: women—question mark.

Subjects didn't only hear about these gender inverts; they saw them as well, although they didn't necessarily connect them with homosexuality or see their personas as reflecting their own feelings. That the dominant taxonomy of the time emphasized gender inversion as an essential component of homosexuality allowed subjects who did not consider themselves gender inverts to place themselves outside of the homosexual category, although not necessarily without causing a certain amount of confusion about the nature of their same-sex desires. In the 1940s, when Dan was in his twenties, he "knew [that] in Greenwich Village there were like drag queens and things," but, ignorant of the homosexual subculture, he "didn't connect that with men loving men or anything." Julius (89) had had sexual encounters with trade,[7] but "when I saw gay people"—specifically, "these flaming types" who "acted real gay and swishy"—had thought, "Well, if that is gay people, then I am not gay." Leonard (72), who had felt that he "was probably the only one around anyway," amended his thinking to "there may be half a dozen of us around someplace or other" when he "heard about queers and things, that ran around with lipstick and painted fingernails and screaming 'Faggot!'" Although he "didn't know any of those words then, that's what I expected."

And I went through the beach crowd and the Greenwich Village group, looking and looking and looking at this. "God! Is that what I am?" And remember, that was the era of, "Get you, Mary!" I mean, the dishing queen, that was the public style. Of course, there were plenty of closet queens that were around that were not that way, but in the public places it was that exaggerated, limp-wristed kind of a [thing]. The fifties were like that, with all the jargon and stuff they were using at that time. And I was horrified.

Others were taunted themselves, although the vagueness of the insults didn't help them clarify their feelings or desires. Rodney (75) knew he was attracted to men, but his ignorance of sexuality had prevented him from verbalizing or understanding that attraction. When I asked him if he had thought that that attraction made him "different from other people," he said that "in the earlier years I didn't" because, although he was taunted for being "sickly" and unathletic, the terms with which he was taunted, while hurtful, did not clarify his feelings. "When I was called a sissy," he explained, "I wasn't called a faggot. They didn't use that much in those days, they called you a sissy or pansy or maybe a fruit." When I asked him if *sissy* meant "the same thing" as *faggot*, he answered, "Not to me, no. Although I didn't understand, there must be some relationship. It was all very, very vague, it was very, very unclear."

Subjects also described having observed the harassment and ridicule of "obvious homosexuals" discernible by their transgression of gender norms. While painful to witness, these incidents showed subjects the stigmatization of gender deviance and its strong, presumed association with homosexuality, and provided identity categories for their own emergent differences. Marge (81) recalled that she came to understand her sexual attraction to other women as evidence of (a stigmatized) homosexuality in the mid-1920s, when she was in her early teens, "because there was a female that everybody called 'old dyke' because she was out and she had a girlfriend." Marge described the fact "that she was called 'dyke'" by people who claimed that "she liked women [and] did not get along with men" as "a terrible thing," explaining that the woman "was almost like an outcast." She also heard about "people like this, not only women, but men too that were feminine" from "the kids that I would associate with."

Here, Marge describes her first encounter with a stigmatizing discourse of homosexuality, one that equated homosexuality with social deficits (an inability to get along with men) and with gender inversions (tagging men as homosexual only if they were "feminine"). Encountering this formulation while actively seeking an explanation for her own feelings provided Marge with an identity peg–a category of person which, should she claim membership in it, would make her difference intelligible and accountable. But this identity peg was clearly a stigmatizing one, and, in associating herself with those being ridiculed and condemned, Marge would be producing herself as a stigmatized person and opening herself to the same treatment.

Encounters with the stigmatizing discourse thus provoked the seemingly insoluble problem of making the self intelligible while preserving its value through the properties of a devaluing discourse. Subjects described feeling caught between a need to understand and pursue their desires and the negative implications of a stigmatized homosexuality–specifically, a devalued self, and associations which, while fulfilling sexual desires, might serve to discredit them and thus make them subject to ridicule. Many subjects found the implications of a stigmatized identity so severe that they worked to avoid interpreting their desires in its terms, managing the tension between their desires and the consequences of enacting them by distancing themselves from one, the other, or both of these.

Distancing

Distancing is a gloss for a variety of ways in which subjects modified, weakened, or rejected the applicability of the term *homosexual* to themselves; these consisted of "putting it on the back burner," pursuing heterosexual relations, and formulating a heterosexual identity, which included reshaping the discourse itself. *Putting it on the back burner* is, of course, another gloss for the work of making same-sex desire a background concern of significantly less importance than are other interests, needs, obligations, and the like, which provide their own rewards. After witnessing the harassment and ridicule of the "old dyke," for example, Marge "knew I was connected with it, but I wanted to stay away from it because I did not want to be ridiculed." When I asked how she was defining herself at the time, she answered, "You mean as a person who had feelings toward females? I rejected it. I just put this out of my mind." Rodney "would see men that I thought I *liked*, you know, at a distance, and I would like to get better acquainted with them, but I didn't dare go any further than that, and I just let it go at that." Similarly, during the Second World War, after other members of his air force squadron learned that he had had a sexual encounter with another squadron member, Leonard found his relations with his colleagues "pretty uncomfortable." His response was to begin "avoiding it and being aware that sure, I'd like to do something with this one or that one, [but] just avoiding it" because of the negative implications of homosexual associations and reputation. Marilyn (66) was even more explicit, explaining the logic behind avoiding it by citing "the stigma against gays" and the "trauma" that accompanied recognition as homosexual and that, she explained, was typical of the 1950s and 1960s.

> I did think about being more interested in women, because I had already decided at that point against ever trying to have a relationship with a man, but at the same time I was very much aware of the stigma against gays and how unacceptable gays were in the society. One of my co-workers had a boyfriend and it came out that he was gay and the *trauma* of how that was handled in the office, I can remember that. I didn't really face up to it the same way I did when I got to California. It was something I [wanted to] avoid. I didn't want to face it.

For many, putting it on the back burner included pursuing heterosexual relations. Marge "didn't do anything about" her same-sex feelings, and "went out with guys" instead. Leonard, who avoided it "until I was thirty . . . would date women and go out. With Penny we had a heavy romance for a while there." Patricia (77) "had boyfriends," Kate "occasionally would accept a date, usually fixed up by anxious family or anxious friends," and Ryan (81) saw heterosexual relations as "the lesser of two evils."

Subjects said they had thought to preclude or offset the frustration of unmet needs and desires by replacing them with others that were more easily met and that had no negative implications for self. After psychoanalysis failed to cure her of her lesbianism, Kate sought to fulfill herself through her job throughout the 1940s and early 1950s. "I was deeply involved in my school and my teaching which was very satisfactory, very all-consuming. And the other stuff I put on the back burner." But, while protecting the self from a stigmatized homosexual identity, distancing techniques also caused subjects to see themselves as without value or definition. Dan defined himself as "active neuter," Deborah "wasn't defining myself at all," and Kate considered herself "a mess, sexually, practically without identity." This distress led some to actively *pursue a heterosexual identity*, which they saw as providing both a fulfilling family life and protection from the harassment and ridicule homosexuals faced. Subjects did this in two ways.

Some engaged in conventional heterosexual marriages, not to hide their homosexuality (a practice we'll consider later) but to achieve a heterosexual identity that provided positive rewards.[8] Similarly, Mark (72) left his lover, Jack, for a woman after he discovered that Jack did not love him and decided that there was "no future in being gay," marrying June in 1952, at the age of "twenty-eight or twenty-nine."

> I decided that I was going to give up being gay. I figured that [there] just wasn't any future in it for me. So June came along. We went to a dance, came home. I took her underneath the porch. I had sex with her, and then four months later, she says, "I'm pregnant." And you could see that she was pregnant. So I says, "Well, better get married." We got married and I gave up Jack.

Others constructed a liminal heterosexuality, negotiating discursive parameters by foregrounding certain features of self and society and disattending others to produce themselves as falling just on the heterosexual side of the homo/heterosexual divide. While their desires could be interpreted as homosexual, an elaboration of certain aspects of self and/or society demonstrated that they were, in fact, heterosexual. When Kate heard her friend's mother discuss "pansies," for example, and saw that "it was laughable, everybody was giggling over it," she "was only too happy to go with the assumption that this was something that happened only to men." Manny (77) described a form of achieving a liminal heterosexuality in which he saw "white boys" engage during his two-year stay in Atlanta in the 1950s. He told me that "a lot of the football players from Georgia Tech," who identified as heterosexual, "wouldn't go with white boys, but they would go with these colored boys. You see, to have sex with a white guy, they didn't think that was right. But to go with a black guy, it didn't matter." In other words, in the context of the entrenched racism–and segregation–of that time and place, limiting one's same-sex partners to African-American men allowed these white men to maintain their heterosexual identities. Leonard described having engaged in the same practice in New York in the 1950 and early 1960s. Even though he had identified as homosexual at the time (see Chapter 3), he said, choosing African-American men as his sexual partners allowed him to distance himself from his homosexuality, a goal his friend Walter also pursued. When I asked him if this was a question of managing his identity, he said, "that was part of it."

> Walter, the guy I was closest to, his specialty was black teenage boys, youngsters. He was always bringing home a fourteen-year-old, but black. He was southern. In Mississippi, you know. This is a way of avoiding something. This is not–you know, this is another side of the world. You're not exposed in this way. Because the world at that time was, like it is today, pretty separate.

Tony (70) achieved a liminal heterosexuality by "playing trade" in the early 1940s, during his mid-teens. "After a date, I'd go to the Village [and] just let them do me. 'Cause my doing him, in the church bit, was the sin." Tony recounted falling in love with a neighbor, who was attracted to Tony as well; one night, "he stayed over at my house, we went up to the upstairs room, and he asked me to do him." To avoid identifying as homosexual, Tony "wouldn't allow myself to be the giver"; he fulfilled his friend's request, but only in the "sixty-nine position . . . in other words, to both receive at the same point":

DR: Okay, why? Because if you had just given, that would have meant you were gay?

Yeah, that would have made me—if he was gonna receive, I wanted it to be the same feeling as I did. I wanted to give and receive. Because it was an ego thing, definitely an ego thing. If he's gonna do me at the same time, it at least puts him in the same category as I am. And so everything kind of comes in.

DR: In categories. Being a homosexual rather than trade.

Right. It didn't, right. OK, you—that's it.

There were, of course, two competing medicalized discourses that respondents could have negotiated to produce themselves as liminally heterosexual. The Freudian one depicted homosexuality as a deviation from normal heterosexual development caused by the individual's failure to proceed from one normal stage of sexual development to the next, thus delaying the final goal of normal heterosexuality. The sexological one posited homosexuality as a function of an innate gender inversion. Informants' accounts uncovered the differential use of these discourses based on the likelihood of each discourse's producing them as liminally heterosexual. Because the gender inversion model would have placed him squarely in the homosexual category, for example, Rodney applied Freudian logic to interpret his interest in trade—again, in the pre-Stonewall era, a heterosexual identity—as evidence of a latent heterosexuality.

> Freud said that the male cannot get at the female without a torturous detour through another male. The fact that they would cohabit with women, that made him totally much more exciting, but I didn't want to touch the women, I was totally interested in him. 'Cause the way I defined it is that makes him heterosexual, and yet was I really after women?

> Was there some latent–[for] some period of my life I thought
> I was a latent straight, and instead of being latent gay and
> having problems, I may have been latent straight.

Tony, whose gender inversion was not evident to others, however, used the gender inversion model to produce himself as different but essentially heterosexual. Although he felt that his desires meant he was different, he "didn't think I was a fag, and that's what I heard my brothers say, or people at school. A faggot was a sissy, a person [who] acted feminine. *Acted* feminine." His emphatic linking of the embodiment of gender inversion to membership in the faggot category is key here: although he felt that his "feminine attitudes" had led him to the "physical attraction and the physical desire," the fact that he did not *enact* these attitudes made the term *faggot* seem inapplicable to him. Tony thus distinguished between the "warm feeling" he had always had toward "feminine men and feminine attitudes" (which he saw as necessary but insufficient for membership in the faggot category) and the public enactment of these feelings (both necessary and sufficient for such membership).

The medicalized discourse also provided its own liminal heterosexuality, to be achieved by adopting its formulation of homosexuality as a manageable, even curable, deficit. Some informants pursued this goal, becoming compliant patients. Rather than see themselves as permanently diseased, they embraced the medicalized discourse's most positive version of "pervert," specifically, one who is committed to a cure. This constructed them as, although homosexual and thus stigmatized, adequately oriented to the medical establishment's norms and goals and committed to achieving a normal life. Rodney, for example, "had so much therapy it's coming out of my ears and so there *was* dealing with sexuality but to no avail, it didn't do any good." After reading

"Krafft-Ebing, Freud, who was the other bastard? Havelock Ellis" in the late 1940s, Kate also adopted the role of compliant patient and spent nine years consulting various doctors in search of a cure. Her first stop was an endocrinologist's office to "find out if there's something physically wrong with my *glands*." When the doctor found that "if there was anything wrong with my hormones it was that I had too many *female* hormones, which I was not supposed to have at all!" he was "bewildered"; Kate, however, was "relieved" to find that she was

> not a *male* in disguise kind of thing. You know, the doctrine was that female homosexuals were somehow or other *men* in disguise, there was something the matter with you in terms of your *basic* sexuality in the sense that you really were supposed to be a male but you turned out to be a female.

Subjects, then, distanced themselves from homosexuality in a number of ways. Some declined to identify as either homosexual or heterosexual, becoming "active neuters" and/or pursuing heterosexual relations while aware that their "true" desires were for those of their own sex. Others worked to identify as heterosexual, marrying or pursuing a liminal heterosexuality. It is, of course, possible to balance same-sex desires and encounters with a heterosexual identity indefinitely. After all, subjects were strongly committed to these distancing techniques, just as they were committed to the heterosexual, normative identities they provided. How invested subjects were in these techniques can be seen in the two instances that arose in which subjects were "shocked out of distancing," and then resumed distancing by adopting other distancing techniques–specifically, therapy designed to produce a liminal heterosexuality.

Kate had been lovers with Jan for several years while thinking of herself as heterosexual ("we both intended to get married to a man"), an identity achieved by viewing her sexuality as relationally idiosyncratic. This logic, however, was challenged in 1946, when, at the age of twenty-six, she encountered self-identified (and identifiably)[9] gay women at a camp at which she was working as a counselor. Because these women engaged in same-sex relations while identifying as lesbian, she realized that her own desires and relations placed her in the same category.

> I went as a counselor to a Campfire Girls' camp. And discovered that I was not alone. Half, probably two-thirds, seven-eighths, nine-tenths of the counselors were lesbians. So this I think probably was what triggered, you know I suddenly realized, hey, this is not just some little minor thing you're doing with Jan. You are involved in something that is very big and very important and you're lying to yourself or whatever.

Although what had happened was "hard for me to pin down," Kate gave a particularly insightful description of the process of recognizing that certain characteristics or practices are not idiosyncratic, but are, instead, criteria for membership in a social category. "It was the recognition—I guess it's if you think you're the only red-headed person in the world and you go to a party and everybody there has got red hair, you suddenly think to yourself: Hey, I'm not unique! This is not just something to *do*." Although she could have responded to the realization that she was not unique by accepting, even embracing, membership in this newly found group (a response several others had) she "hit the panic button, threw Jan out, broke up with her [and] threw her out." When I noted that this recognition that she was not unique could have been a relief, Kate responded that "it wasn't, though, because I was by that time also aware that it was abnormal." It was at this point that she began to read the sexological and psychological literature on homosexuality, and soon thereafter that she devoted herself to seeking a cure for her sexual desires in the psychiatric and biomedical enterprises.

In 1954, at the age of thirty, during the McCarthy era's "*big attack* on gay people in the government," Leonard "got fired from the State Department," where he had been an intelligence officer in the China Division, "for being gay." The firing came when Leonard, although he "knew myself that I was gay, was attempting" to achieve a heterosexual identity by living a heterosexual life—was, in fact, "about to get married and all that stuff." The distancing technique he used centered on reshaping the discourse on sexuality by distinguishing between *having* same-sex desires and *pursuing* same-sex encounters, and characterizing the latter as the sine qua non of homosexual identity, a formula that (he was surprised to find) was rejected by federal investigators.

> I was fired because I knew I was gay and when they asked me, "Who do you, what do you think about?" I had thought, "Well, hell, I don't do any of these things, but I can say what my feelings are." And they said, "No, you can't do that, that makes you a *faggot*. Out, out you must go!" And they told me, "Go to New York . . . and get cured!"

Despite their deep commitment to distancing, however, my informants *did* eventually identify as homosexual; those who did not do so could not be included in my sample. How subjects came to make this shift is, of course, a key feature of their identity careers, and one I will outline in the following chapter.

2

"I Picked Up That I Was Gay"

ACCORDING to Ken Plummer (1995), the coming out story is a clear example of the modern sexual narrative. It centers on a journey to end suffering and discover the self by surviving contests and conflicts and by vanquishing those who caused the suffering to begin with.[1] Most of my informants produced narratives that followed the parameters of the typical coming out story almost perfectly, but several did not. Some, in fact, resisted these themes when I raised them, even raised them themselves only to deny ever having experienced them. Displaying a familiarity with the prototypical coming out story line, they actively renounced what they perceived to be an expectation that coming to identify as homosexual was any one of the following: lengthy, complicated, difficult, frightening, isolating, or life-altering. There were no epiphanies, no exceptional realizations or startlingly clear moments. While sociologically interesting, the fact that, for these subjects, there "isn't much to tell" makes their accounts barely stories at all. In fact, most of them are rather dull (Rhoda's "I just knew that I was gay, and that was it" comes immediately to mind), especially when compared to the dramatic, sometimes-lurid stories told by others.

42

These informants identified as homosexual as soon as (or soon after) they encountered a stigmatizing discourse of difference, despite its implications. Patricia (77) "always knew I was gay," not only because she was always aware of her desire for women, but also because she encountered the discourse of difference, in the form of talk about homosexuals (or *manfloras*),[2] at an early age, and identified with its terms. As she explained, "There are things that you don't ever need to ask anybody. You just pick them up. You know it, you know what they're talking about." As a result, by the time she had sex with a woman for the first time, she "knew what it was, what gay meant. I knew that I was a lesbian, I knew that I was gay. I knew that I was a *manflora*." After Jeannine (66) and her girlfriend were called "fairies" in high school, they "talked about it, and we thought we'd heard the term *homosexual* at some point, so we looked it up in the dictionary," where they found a relatively "neutral" construction defining "a homosexual [as] a person who has a sexual relationship with a person of the same sex." While the definition "made a lot of sense," Jeannine was "annoyed, because it appeared that I would never be able to follow the major mode of what women were expected to do: get married and have kids. It put me out of the norm. . . . I was annoyed because it put me beyond the pale, basically." Despite this insight, however, Jeannine "never had a negative reaction to it at all." This statement was echoed by several others. Indeed, without being asked whether they had found their sexual desires, or their need to interpret them, to be traumatic, members of this group told me that they had not, in fact, gone through any distress on their path to a homosexual identity. Indeed, they contrasted the ease of their identification as homosexual with the difficulties they had heard others had suffered. Phoebe (79) did this when recounting having been spotted in an unusually intense interaction with Joanne, with whom she had "had a little brief flurry":

> One time I remember Joanne and I were leaning over the drinking fountain at school and the schoolteacher came by and said, "What are you girls talking about?" Oh gosh, we had been standing there for about fifteen minutes, gazing into each other's eyes. I am sure she knew something was going on.

When I asked her how she had been thinking of herself at the time, she answered, "I don't think I was suffering a lot of trauma, I don't remember. I just thought of myself as a damn good musician and that I liked women, I guess." Brian (74) began to realize his attraction to men at "the age of seven or so." When I asked him what those feelings had meant to him, he answered, "Nothing, really. It just was *there*. No nothing, there weren't [any] heavy experiences or anything." When I asked Michael (78) about coming out, he answered,

> Did I ever sit down one day and say, "Yes, I'm gay"? No, I knew it. I never doubted it. It meant as little to me in matter of choice as whether I choose to have brown or blue eyes. I was gay.
>
> DR: And this was something that you knew, from day one?
>
> Sure. I'm not one of those people that I hear kids sometimes argue *I was gay when I was three years old*. Well, I don't know how in the hell you can be gay at three, or what you do for that matter. So I didn't do that.

Michael went on to explain that he "never went through these things you read about in books of great struggles, 'Who am I, and shall I commit suicide?' I decided I am gay and I loved it and I couldn't get enough of it."

Here, informants raised four distinct themes they associated with the classic coming out story: trauma (or, in Brian's words, "heavy experiences"), a conscious admission to self (sitting down and saying, "I'm gay"), a struggle with an emergent identification so intense that it leads to suicidal thoughts, and identification at an extremely young (even presexual) age. Indeed, regarding the latter theme, Julius (89) explicitly charged those who raised it with retrospectively reconstructing their pasts to reflect a culturally sanctioned, but practically impossible, invention.

> When people say to me, "Oh well, I knew I was gay since I was three, or five or seven or ten," I always wonder what they are talking about. I think what they are doing is going back and reconstructing. I don't think that when they were seven years old they said, "You know, come to think of it, I am gay," but when they talk about it they act as though that is what happened.

In raising these themes and then denying their presence in their own lives, these subjects invalidate others' claims that identification as homosexual is anything other than a reasonable recognition of the nature of one's own desires, and is either processually or substantively distressing.

This was, of course, in strict contrast to the trauma that subjects who had distanced themselves from homosexual identification described having undergone. Tex (72), for example, spoke of struggling with his same-sex desire for years: "I knew there's something different about me, and all: I was attracted to men! Much as I *fought it*, the more I fought it, the more I dreamed about it." Ricardo (66) also described undergoing an internal struggle throughout the 1950s, when he was in his twenties. Being "the oldest of the family," he explained, he "was supposed to get married, and I was not getting married because I had my directions to *men*. And I was fighting myself continuously, of course." For these informants, identification as homosexual occurred as the result of new emotions or new contacts and contexts which, for a smaller group, consisted of–or led them to–the accrediting discourse of homosexuality.

"This Wave of Emotion"

Informants who had engaged in distancing described internal changes inspiring a reformulation of their same-sex desires and of that relation to self. Many spoke of the emergence of emotional needs that could be fulfilled only through erotic or romantic relationships with same-sex partners. While they had initially limited their same-sex connections to sexual ones that did not, to their minds, implicate a homosexual identity, these new desires caused them to reevaluate their sexual identities. While George (75), for example, "did homosexual things before," he didn't "realize" he was gay until

> that night that I told James. We were sitting in my car, I drove him home. We were holding hands. This is when I had this wave of emotion, and I turned and looked out the window and I said, "I want to tell you something." And he said, "Don't worry about it, so am I." He was also at the same point where I was. In coming out we were discovering ourselves. I knew that I wanted him, he knew that he wanted me.

When I asked him why, when he had previously declined to apply the term *homosexual* to his same-sex encounters, he began to identify as gay that night, he told me it was because "perhaps before James, I was thinking of it as sexual contact. 'Let's have fun. Let's smoke a cigarette.' You know, led by people to that. 'Let's do something different.' With James, well then, we were really in love." This, he said, made him "realize the urging toward [men]." Similarly, by the time Julius's ex-fiancée left her husband and offered to get back together with him, he had begun "to raise more and more I'm gay" when he fell in love with a young man and realized that he "had loved people before, but not this same way." Ryan (81) stated that he did not "admit" his homosexuality until he was forty and began to seek companionship rather than exclusively sexual relations with men; before that point, he had been going "in and out, back and forth, and bisexual or whatever you want to call it."

> The things I did after forty were things that I wouldn't have done before forty. Maybe it was a quickie like in the army, just a fast blowjob or something like that. After forty then if I'd meet somebody I'd stay all night or they'd stay at my place all night. Before forty I had some excuse why I had to get home: I was afraid to stay overnight anyplace, I had to get home. [After forty I was] spending the night and trying to find out if that's what I wanted. And I admitted it.

Mark (72) also spoke of recognizing a growing commitment to men, one sparked by the sacrifices he made to save a Marine in battle during the Second World War. Not only had he "disobeyed the first order by trying to save his life," he had also disobeyed a second one (to refrain from using his gun under fire) by killing a sniper who had shot him as he tried to patch up the Marine. Later, he "realized I was gay when I associated what I had done, disobeying a direct order to save a Marine that probably would have died anyway." Such disobedience could, of course, led to a court-martial, and almost did. While Mark eventually got away with a Purple Heart, a Silver Star, and the docking of six months' overseas pay, the fact that he had risked stronger sanctions made him realize the strength of his desires and reevaluate their significance.

For Gabrielle (77), the increasing importance of fulfilling her emotional needs tipped the scale in favor of women. Although, from as far back as Gabrielle can remember, she "was gay without knowing what gay was," she was also, in her own words, "fucking everything." Classifying herself as a "true bisexual," she described a lifetime of "compulsive" sex with men and women that began in her childhood and continued throughout her two marriages. As long as the men

were "very subservient to me," they provided sexual pleasure, but not the emotional satisfaction she enjoyed with
women. "Emotionally," she explained, "I have *never* been
able to really love a man." This created "such a conflict" that
she "had eighteen years of deep therapy . . . about straight or
gay, because I could not fall in love with a man." Gabrielle
resolved the conflict by committing herself to Betty, whom
she met in 1963, when she was forty-five years old. Giving
up men was "very difficult," but when I asked her if she was
sorry she had done so, she answered, "No, probably because
I had her, but I have missed it." When I asked why she remained with Betty when she missed being with men, she
cited making

> compromises in life. And it was not easy. . . . But I tell you, for
> thirty-three years I've never been unfaithful. And not many
> people can say that. And neither has she. So we have our sex,
> [which] is very unimportant.
>
> DR: What is important?
>
> *Caring.* We have different values but there are lots of things—
> for instance we *love* a lot of the same things. We love to play,
> we love people, we love parties, we love jokes.

While Susan (75) had had a lesbian encounter at age nineteen, before her marriage, she had continued to think of
herself as a "typical" (read: heterosexual) "young woman."
This changed in 1958 when, in her late thirties, she fell in
love with another army wife, with whom she had an intense
three- to four-year affair. Susan spoke of the growing conflict
she felt between the affair and her marriage in the strongest
possible terms: "We *tried*," she said, "to keep it a secret from
my husband. I *tried*, but it reached the point where I *could
not* lead a dual life. I couldn't. I felt that I can't. This is not
fair to him, this is not fair to me, it's not fair to anybody, and
I had to tell him. I had to tell him."

Susan explained that while her marriage "was good for a long time," she "never found it super thrilling." She loved her three daughters, who "fulfilled my life as children can, but when I met this gal, it was a very electric thing, something that neither one of us could avoid. . . . We were neighbors and one thing led to another, and we started an affair. It was very powerful, we found it very difficult to stay away from each other." Shortly thereafter, both husbands were sent overseas, and since "you can't stay in army quarters if your husband is not with you," both women had to vacate those quarters "and find another place to live." Susan did not want to return to New York to live with her mother, and when her lover suggested that they and their assorted children move to the lover's hometown so that they could be together, she agreed. They lived in separate apartments in the same duplex and "floated back and forth," an "arrangement" Susan described as "wonderful." In 1962, her husband returned, "and that was the point . . . [that] I had to tell him what the situation was. And so I told him who and what I was, and what my feelings were, and I didn't think it was fair to him, and that I think we should separate." His response was to ask for "one more chance," and they spent a year together overseas, after which she left him. They divorced a short time later.

When I asked Susan how she was thinking of herself at the time, she answered, "I think I probably just thought, 'This is the way I'm supposed to be, and I can't fight it anymore.'" Asked if she had any words for it, she told me that she had not, and when she explained her decision to separate from her husband, she spoke in relational terms, not in categorical ones:

I just said, "I know what I feel when I'm with Jane, and it's just more–I don't feel it, with you. I love you dearly, as the father of our children, and I care about you. But I can't be a wife to you and I don't think that's fair. I know you want more from me than I can give you." He didn't have to be punished.

When I asked Susan if she was thinking of herself as gay at the time, she said, "I didn't put a label on it. I just know what I was feeling. I suppose if I sat down and thought about it, yes, I would have to say what it was." She did, however, use the term *gay* when she explained the breakup to two of her daughters: indeed, Susan thought that was "the first time that I probably put words to it. Then I declared my–I used that expression."

Sexual and Romantic Encounters

> I wanted to get rid of my glasses, so I went for eye exercises, and the guy giving it was gay. So, he started massaging my eyes and things and I was very attracted to him, and then finally he kissed me. I was in heaven. . . . And that's when I became aware, when he kissed me in New York. –Dan

As we saw in Chapter 1, several subjects who had had same-sex desires but who did not know how to interpret them described their first sexual or erotic contacts as clarifying, but not defining, these desires. Others told of having identified their desires after their first sexual encounter, but of then distancing themselves from those desires and/or associations once their nature had become clear. For some, however, first sexual encounters served not only to clarify, but actually to solidify their desires into a concrete identity. Some described these contacts as the first same-sex contacts.

Dan had been aware of his same-sex desires since childhood, and had encountered homosexual persons and situations which, "completely oblivious" to their significance, he had failed to appreciate or to use to clarify, let alone define, his own feelings. In his twenties, for example, a young man commented on Dan's tie in a public restroom, and, while he "felt a vibration," he "didn't know why or anything. And he lived with his mother. You know, looking back you note things, but I didn't know." In 1951, when Dan was twenty-five, however, a gay man giving Dan a massage treatment kissed him, and a number of critical things happened. Dan connected his long-standing desires with erotic encounters with men, and both confirmed and understood these desires upon reading a book on homosexuality that the man recommended. Moreover, Dan, his new contact, and his new contact's lover corresponded when they moved to San Francisco, and, although "for one year in New York, I didn't do anything in gay life, *nothing*, I didn't know anyone or anything," his new friends inspired him to move to Los Angeles in 1952, where he reconnected with an old friend from fashion school, who was gay. While "we had nothing to do with each other, we came out to each other, we told each other we were gay. And so we went out. He took me to gay bars and things." Dan had his first sexual experience that year, at the age of twenty-six, and immersed himself in the gay subculture of Los Angeles and, when he moved to San Francisco in the late 1960s, in the gay underground of that city as well.

William (76) "had had heterosexual relationships all my life," but only recognized as he looked back that he "was attracted to guys and just didn't realize what it was." This changed in 1954 when, in his mid-thirties, two things happened: the woman he had been going with for two years became engaged to another man, and he met Bobby (with whom he would become lovers a year later) at a party given by a mutual (gay) friend.

> And the first people who came in [were] a beautiful guy and a lovely girl. And he was a magnificent dancer and I, who

can't dance, always admired dancers. And I guess we were playing charades and I had a long low bench. I was sitting on the bench, the girl was in the middle of us, the guy was on the other side of her, and you know I had my hand around her like *this*, and suddenly he squeezed my hand. And I had to go to the bathroom and he found me and kissed me.

Bobby was an aspiring actor whom the "beautiful girl"–a "would-be singer from a wealthy family in Philadelphia"– was planning to take on a family-funded trip designed to launch her singing career. "At the last minute," however, the family decided not to bring Bobby. Having "told everybody he was going," Bobby moved to Chicago, but, since "he was getting no modeling jobs there . . . he ran out of money and he called me and I wired money and he came back and he moved in." They lived together for "a couple of years," during which time William "came out to myself."

Deborah (74) had her first same-sex erotic encounter in 1949, at the age of twenty-eight, with an ex-co-worker from the East Coast. When this woman moved to California, where Deborah had settled after she left the army, she invited her to share living quarters. Although she "wasn't sure about living with her because I knew she was gay," she consented because the woman "didn't seem to indicate that she wanted anything other than a roommate." When the woman propositioned her, Deborah "thought, 'Well, I'm not getting anywhere, my whole life has just been so out of it,' so I did." Although the encounter itself was only "OK," it "probably convinced me of what I already knew, because emotionally I was always more attracted to women than men." As it had done with others, identifying as homosexual led her retrospectively to recast her previous actions as leading up to, and/or as making sense in the light of, that identification. "I guess," she said, "that was one reason I didn't have any problem with dating men in the army, because I knew it was temporary."

"I Found My Own": Homosexual Associations

Meeting and associating with other homosexuals was also key to subjects' interpreting their desires in a new light. At the very least, these contacts showed them that they were not, in fact, "the only ones in the world," and that there were venues for associating with others like themselves. Chapter 1 pointed out that subjects often saw gender inverts in public, and that their stigmatized identities drove them to distance themselves from both the inversion and the homosexual category that was virtually interchangeable with it. Not surprisingly, however, these gender inverts also provided an opportunity to connect with the gay world, and some subjects spoke of doing so by befriending these sexual and gender outlaws. While Patricia had been attracted to a young woman whom she saw at a college basketball game, for example, she did not approach her until "all of a sudden one day I see her with this girlfriend, [who] was butchy as hell." Realizing that "they were living together," she pursued the woman and they became lovers soon thereafter. As a young man in Israel in the 1930s, Franz (86) met gay men in private homes because "at that time it was a *sin* to be gay and it was considered people who are gay as an *outcast*. So I didn't tell people that I'm gay. And I met one guy on the street and he was swishy and so on and so on." Franz "got closer to him," and the new contact introduced him to other gay men. After Mary's (66) first lesbian affair ended in the early 1970s, she approached "a man who worked at the Y that I had gotten very friendly with who was very obvious, well, most people would look at him and think he was gay" and asked him "if he knew any ladies [so I could] try this again.

So he eventually introduced me to a person that I hit it off with, and we started an affair."

These connections were often very powerful, especially for those who, although already identified as homosexual, had been very isolated and saw their futures as isolated as well. In the late 1950s, Rodney (75), who had "learned that I was a homosexual" from the letter he received from the editor, found a secretive but thriving gay community through contacts he made with other gay men at the Salt Lake City public library, the main local cruising spot:

> Then I started to socialize, started talking to people and meeting people maybe years younger than I was who knew the ways of the world and started to inform me. I learned there was this whole subterranean world of gay life and that there was a gay bar, and I met this one person and I fell head over heels for this person.

This person, with whom Rodney was lovers for "maybe two or three months" was, in his words, "my mother, so to speak," teaching him about a gay world with which Rodney was "rather intrigued because I was so intensely lonely. I thought 'Now I'm coming into my own, I'm finding my own niche in life.' " Rodney told me that he didn't "know that my view of myself changed, but my view of *life* changed and I began to realize that there I was, in my own element."[3]

Similarly, upon immigrating to the United States from Argentina in 1959, at the age of twenty-nine, Ricardo found a thriving gay culture in Chicago and Seattle in the late 1950s and early 1960s–a period of extreme repression of homosexual (indeed, all sexual) life, but an open and welcoming one compared to the paucity of gay life he had experienced in Argentina. "One of the reasons I left," he said, "is because I thought I was the only gay person in Argentina." Admittedly, much of the "liberation" Ricardo described had to do with his separation and independence from his family, which remained at home. Indeed, his desire for "a release of that responsibility of getting married and be able to free myself of any responsibilities or expectations from my family" was another compelling reason for the emigration. But much of this liberation was due to what he saw as the positive celebration of homosexuality in North American cities. As he explained, "Obviously, since we are part of this society, society tells us that what we are doing is wrong, so my way of thinking about myself was despicable in many ways." Once in Chicago, however, he found the freedom to "pursue whatever I want to pursue in my life," including homosexual associations and liaisons. Immersion in this relatively open gay world led him to

> start feeling, little by little, through the [example] of many people that I saw around, and how all the peoples was acting freely without any remorse or anything, I learned by example I would say that gay society was a society in itself. We are part of a *society*, a commonality, whatever you are. And so I identified myself with this society.

This new sense of belonging to a group of homosexuals who felt no remorse about their sexuality was a radically new one. While in Argentina in the 1940s and 1950s, Ricardo had been subject to "the norms in society . . . of my religion and my upbringing" that "tell us that what we are doing is wrong," and, as a result, his self-concept had been "despicable in many ways." Once he encountered this gay subculture, he began to question both the societal norms condemning homosexuality and his previous self-concept: "Then I said, 'Well, I'm comfortable, why should I be despicable in any way? I am what I am,' you know." In fact, he embraced the homosexual subculture so strongly that he "dropped anything that was heterosexual, just to go exclusively to *gay* people." To this day, he said, "I don't have any heterosexual relationships or friends or anything."

Sharon (66) described a similar widening of horizons upon immersing herself in the gay cultures of Tampa, Los Angeles, and San Francisco, although she found the first of the three vastly more stigmatizing–and limiting–than the latter two. The unequivocal association of gender inversion and homosexuality that Sharon found in the medical texts she read as a child led her to believe that she "had to go with straight women. I didn't know that I was supposed to go with another lesbian because of reading the books I read." This belief was borne out by the fact that, in the Tampa of the 1940s and 1950s, "there were very few women that came out"; instead, Sharon found herself socializing with "queens" and sleeping with heterosexual women, which she found frustrating. While she

> got a lot of straight women, I didn't want it, I didn't want that. They had husbands. And I remember one guy he came up one night [and] said "Sharon"–I knew him from the bar–he said, "Here's fifty dollars, take my wife out, she wants to sleep with you!" I said, "No, no, I don't want that!"

It was only in 1954 that she "started realizing that there were other lesbians," and only when she "came to California [in 1956] that I realized that there were other people like me. That I wasn't *alone*." She also saw that, in California, "everything was open, at least as open as I thought it could be, that I could wear pants and be myself."

For those not yet "in the life," however, these connections could be extraordinarily difficult to make, because places in which homosexuals could present themselves as such were, although not always few and far between, necessarily secret and secretive. As with all underground subcultures, gaining access depended upon the help of insiders who were themselves difficult to find. Indeed, two subjects spoke of discovering gay bars only through the guidance of heterosexuals who, presumably, thought the subjects were heterosexual as well. While they entered these bars under the guise of heterosexual "tourists," both Abby and Leonard quickly identified with the lesbian and gay patrons.

In 1951, when she was twenty-five years old and working for a newspaper in New Jersey, Abby (70) overheard a young female co-worker (who, as Abby later found out, was gay herself) describe a recent foray into a gay bar in New York's notorious Greenwich Village. Abby knew the woman, and asked if she could accompany her "next time you go over there." The woman agreed, and on a Friday night, they and some other co-workers went to a gay bar on Bleecker Street named The Swing Rendezvous.

> It was primarily women. As soon as I walked in there, I don't think it took me very long to realize that this is *exactly* where I belong. And that was my first introduction.

After he was fired from the State Department in 1954, Leonard (72) moved to New York, where he got odd jobs, including a Christmas stint at Macys. When one of his co-workers suggested that they go to a gay bar after work, he found himself in "a very nice bar that I'd been going to for a long time in Greenwich Village" and which he had thought was a heterosexual establishment because it was devoid of the stereotypical "fairies" that he had seen in the area. Indeed, his sense that homosexual men were all "dishing queens" was so strong that "of course I tried to keep a straight face, you know, I was just certain that they were mistaken about that being a gay bar." Realizing that he had, in fact, been comfortably associating with gay men in a safe place had a strong impact on him, since it offered a homosexual identity in direct contradistinction to that of the public fairy. Although he had, as we have seen, engaged in same-sex erotic encounters, and had seen clear instances of "queers and things . . . running around," Leonard considers this event to be "more like my first introduction to anything that was gay," and it affected him so strongly that

> it was shortly thereafter that I picked somebody up or some-body picked me up. And so I came out at that point. That was coming out. [Because I] had sex with somebody and I com-mitted myself basically that I was gay.
>
> You know, I had been trying to make it with Penny. And we did all right! We did all right. I'm not saying that we didn't have a good time, we *did* have a good time. And it was not that I was incapable of handling the situation. We were doing all right. And that was before I got into this other [thing]. But I found that I liked the gay stuff much, much better.

Decisions, Decisions

Several subjects described their identification as lesbian or gay as a decision, explaining that they had never had same-sex desires in childhood and that these desires arose as the result of contexts and contacts that emerged in adulthood. Thus it was the same-sex feelings that were new, not the category that explained them. Lillian (69), for example, "was never gay" before she decided to "get involved in gay life" in the early 1950s, having "never had any particular interest in women." Raising the theme of the sexual versus nonsexual gaze that we visited in Chapter 1, Lillian described a way of looking at women that is distinctive to heterosexuality and in which she would routinely engage before she made her decision. "I mean, if I saw a woman that was pretty and dressed nicely, I would say, 'Oh, isn't she attractive, I love what she's wearing, I'm gonna ask her where she got it,' you know that sort of thing." Her interest in women developed as the result of a chance meeting with an old schoolmate, who provided her with knowledge about and access to "new

interests." After Lillian drove her home, "she invited me in
and I went in and she was living with this other woman. And
that's how I got introduced to lesbians."

Lillian explained that she met this woman after she had
been dumped by her fiancé when she was "twenty-two or
twenty-three," a "devastating" rejection that "shattered" and
"overwhelmed" her. This rejection was so hurtful because
of a long-standing suspicion of men, begun when her father
deserted her and her mother: "I was," she explained, "leery
of men to begin with because of that." As a result, Lillian
"wanted to get away from the rhetoric of having my friends
question me on why did you break up with Al or blah blah
blah and I just didn't want to deal with that. So I was looking for another area, to open another vista to myself, new
friends." When her friend "informed me she was gay," Lillian became "curious" and asked her to take her to a gay bar
in the Village. Once there, she became "very intrigued with
the whole thing" and "got involved with a woman." When I
asked her what had intrigued her, she told me that, as someone who was "not what you would call promiscuous" but
who "enjoyed sex," she was curious: "How would a woman
make love to me differently than a man would? And I kind of
enjoyed it." Not only did she "not have to be concerned about
becoming pregnant," but

> a woman making love is much more gentle and tender than
> a man, and I enjoyed that aspect of it. And that's how I got
> involved in gay life. And I decided when I was doing all that
> [that] it was a matter of my choice. Not that I was born with
> this feeling, I chose this sort of lifestyle.

Similarly, Mary "made a conscious choice to my way of
thinking to *become* a lesbian," having identified as heterosexual throughout her childhood, early adulthood, and middle age. In the early 1970s, when she was in her early forties,

her husband requested "an open marriage"–an idea she didn't particularly welcome, but to which she agreed because, as she remembered explaining to him, "I've been through lots of other things with you, so why not?" After "going around with a girlfriend of mine who had always played around," she found the attention of the men in her friend's circle unsavory. "All the men that we ran into," she said, "everybody was telling me how good-looking I was and what they could do for me, and I thought 'oh no.'" Having "always had gay and lesbian friends," she suddenly "realized I was looking at women differently than I had before." Her first lesbian affair "didn't last very long, and I thought, 'Well, maybe I was wrong.'" Her next affair, however, lasted three years and forced her to reconsider her marriage. In addition to "other problems in the marriage that had nothing to do with the sexual part of it," Mary cited strong emotions that emerged during her first long-term lesbian relationship to explain her decision to separate from (and eventually divorce) her husband in the early to mid-1970s.

> I think once I got involved with the relationship with the woman, the one that I had for three years, there were some things about that that I found more satisfying emotionally. And so yeah, I guess it was at that point I had probably made the decision that this is what I am going to do.

Finally, when Henri (67) joined a dance troupe in 1947, at age nineteen, he considered himself heterosexual–indeed, "had had girlfriends before I was in the show, from the age [of] fourteen." Pursued by a gay man he met through the troupe, Henri had his first same-sex encounter at age twenty-one, "and it worked out. I mean I went from considering myself pretty much heterosexual, to being gay, mostly because I didn't know much about gay life, or what gay love was all about." Henri described deciding "to go that route," citing his discomfort with the gender order of the times rather than previous same-sex desires or attractions:

> I decided that the homosexual sex was something that I wanted to invest in, find out more about. I seemed to feel more comfortable with it, because with women I was never that comfortable. Well, I was comfortable enough, but when it came down to playing the dominant role that the male had to play, I was not very good at that.

Ten years later, however, Henri "went back to the other side," marrying a woman because he had not found a long-term relationship with a man and because he felt he was "getting too old for gay life," with which he had become "thoroughly disgusted." They remained married until 1968, when they divorced because his wife did not want to have children, whereas he did.

The Gender Order

Positing discomfort with the gender order as a key factor in the decision to adopt a gay identity appeared in other accounts as well, although not in very many. Mary echoed Henri's unease with the gender-based "role-playing" typical of heterosexual relationships. Although she and her husband had not played these roles, she assumed that they would shape subsequent heterosexual relationships and, because she lacked what it took to engage in the roles, she decided to explore lesbian relationships. In her words,

> I didn't think that I had what I needed to have to have the kind of relationship I wanted to have with a man. Not as I saw our society and the relationship. 'Cause I had never had that typical kind of relationship, 'cause even with my husband, whoever did something best did it, there was no role-playing.

Another critique of the gender order was its expectation that heterosexuals have and raise children—a constituent feature of heterosexuality which, as we saw in Chapter 1, subjects used to construct a sense of self as essentially heterosexual. When Marilyn (66) "was growing up, I could *never really* imagine myself being married and having children. I knew it was the norm and the expectation, but I didn't see myself in that role." Jan (68), who had had affairs with both men and women throughout her teens and twenties without identifying as either heterosexual or gay, decided to limit her sexual encounters to women, not because of the quality of the sex she had been having with men,[4] but because she wanted to escape the traditional female/family role, which included child rearing. "The crowning thing" that tipped the scales in favor of women was a particularly traumatic illegal abortion she had in the late 1940s, when she was in her twenties, after which she knew "with relief" that she "never had to play this role again." Jan characterized the time when she realized that she "didn't have to do this anymore" as "the happiest period of my life. I wanted never to continue this."

When I asked Jan if it had been the abortion that forced the decision, she answered that it was not, but that after the procedure had been done, she "*knew* that I was never going to have to play this game again." She stressed that heterosexual life "was a kind of game because one was expected to marry," one she was never interested in playing because "having a family was never that big a concern. I never have felt like having children. I just didn't want to be married, I didn't want to be saddled with the responsibility. I certainly didn't want kids." Jan described her decision as "a very *deliberate* thing, and that was it: I don't have to play that game anymore."[5]

The Accrediting Discourse

So far, we have seen a wide range of factors that inspired informants to cease distancing and adopt a homosexual identity. Tex, Dan, Kate, and Abby encountered self-identified homosexuals and thus reassessed the "nature" of their own actions, desires, and selves as homosexual, while George and Ryan experienced romantic feelings that challenged their previous understandings of their same-sex associations as "just fooling around." Clearly, these subjects abandoned their nonhomosexual identities for stigmatized homosexual ones because the contacts and contexts through which *these* identifications were made were embedded within the stigmatized homosexual subculture. None of those who adopted stigmatized identities did so in the context of an accrediting discourse that emerged in their later years. Needless to say, because images of gay men and women that challenged their stigmatized "nature" were, for all intents and purposes, nonexistent before the mid- to late 1960s, accredited identities were simply unavailable before then. Indeed, in the accounts of homosexual identification that figure above, no mention was made of meeting gay men and/or women in the context of open, public gay and lesbian groups, for the simple reason that these did not yet exist. Instead, they mentioned meeting homosexuals at work (a problematic place in which to do so), in the armed forces (even more so), in gay bars and cruising spots (less problematic), and "on the street." Although these contacts often introduced informants to a gay life that was, if not always celebrated, at least collectively engaged, it was a life organized around stigma and its appropriate enactment. As a result, no subjects have yet mentioned encountering a discourse of difference that was explicitly gay-positive in the gay liberationist or lesbian-feminist sense. As we've seen in the previous chapter, the only gay-positive messages available in texts, for example, were gay-positive only because of the interpretive work in which the readers engaged, and consisted of the availability of an identity category—a useful tool through which to construct a homosexual identity, no doubt, but one with severely stigmatizing implications.

But, beginning in the late 1960s, the discursive landscape began to change—radically. Kate (76) made the change explicit when I asked her if she had been getting any positive imagery of homosexuality when she was trying to determine the nature of her desires: "I was getting no positive anything. I don't think there *were* any positive anythings out there, when I look back at it." When I asked her to identify the first positive image of lesbianism or homosexuality she ever encountered, she said, "I'd have to stop and think, I can't come up with anything until gay liberation started. Isn't that funny? I'm drawing a real blank." For those who were still engaged in distancing practices when gay and lesbian liberation emerged, these movements provided both a new social context in and through which to contact gay men and lesbians on the one hand (i.e., feminist organizations) and a new symbolic one through which to assess their desires and actions (i.e., the liberationist discourse outlined in this book's introduction) on the other. For those who had declined to identify as homosexual through the stigmatizing discourse, these contexts inspired reformulation—not from a nonhomosexual self to a stigmatized homosexual one, but from a nonhomosexual self to an accredited one.

These social and symbolic contexts often overlapped. Kate encountered both the ideology of lesbian-feminism and the lesbians who embraced it at a meeting of the National Organization for Women (NOW), which she attended in the early 1970s at the encouragement of her therapist. After she and

Jan broke up in 1964, Kate began to question her lesbianism once again, and went into therapy "for years and years" to take care "of the flailing doubts that I had" about her sexual identity "because Jan left me." While "there were things wrong with the relationship," she explained, "I was putting them under the rug, too" (the word *too* implying that she had been putting her lesbianism under the rug as well), and remembers "saying to [my therapist] 'Maybe I'm not really a lesbian, maybe I should try again with a man.'" In contrast to the therapists and other medical agents who had worked with her to achieve a heterosexual identity in the past, however, "this time I got a good one" who responded to her suggestion that she do so again by saying "'No way!' And it was he who not only reinforced and helped me with my lesbian identity, but who shoved me into feminism."

At her first NOW meeting, Kate "sat on the sidelines" while some "interesting-looking, bright-looking, normal-looking women" finished up a membership meeting. Kate recognized a friend whom she knew was a lesbian among them, and, after the meeting ended, she asked her friend, "'Rosie, are there any lesbians around here?' And she started to giggle and she said, 'Uh huh.' And I said, 'Well like at that table, how many would you say?' She said (whispering), 'Almost all of them.' Whee!!!! I was home, I was home free." Through NOW, Kate discovered that she was an important member of both the lesbian-feminist and the larger feminist movements, not the "freak" that the stigmatizing discourse portrayed lesbians to be. This, in turn, led her to abandon her distancing practices and undergo a lesbian-feminist "rebirth," emerging as both an identified lesbian and a strong radical feminist.[6]

I have a certain amount of sympathy for a born-again Christian. It was like I was a born-again lesbian. Not only I wasn't a freak but I was a part of what was a really big important group *and* my lesbianism *fit in*, there was no problem with it . . . I was not an outsider anymore. I belonged. I had full validation. . . . it was acceptance, it was validation, it was belonging. It was really remarkable. It was a wonderful feeling.

The lesbian-feminist movement of the early 1970s also offered Marilyn the opportunity to associate—and identify—with accredited lesbians. "Very soon after" she moved to Los Angeles from New York in 1969, Marilyn identified as a lesbian in the 1970s, an era she described as "a *fantastic* time for feminism and gays and lesbians." This identification "came through a gradual process." She joined the National Organization for Women at the suggestion of a feminist woman who attended "a workshop about career women, assisting women to become better in their jobs." She began receiving NOW's literature, and identified strongly with one particular piece:

> What really kicked it off for me was reading an article by a woman in the National Organization for Women, and I just came to it, I said, "Hey, that's me!" And it was just a revelation. . . . What she was describing was what I felt and thought and had experienced.

She also cited her growing interest in women's music, which provided a venue for meeting other gay women, as instrumental in speeding up the "gradual process" of adopting a lesbian identity. Attending a women's music concert "at the old Women's Center . . . was the first time that I had lesbians around me. It was an experience that I hadn't had before, is identifiable lesbians." She also "met other women who identified themselves as lesbian" at NOW meetings, becoming "very fond" of one.

Marilyn's new lesbian identity both informed and was informed by her own increasing political radicalization, which began, she said, "with the Nixon acknowledgment and resignation." She also pointed to the right-wing attacks on women's liberation by Phyllis Schlafly, who "made me a NOW member," and to Ronald Reagan, who "made me a Democrat," as key players in the personal and political changes she made at the time. As she put it, "I was so annoyed [and] upset about what those people said, it forced me into changing my affiliations." She was also "disturbed greatly by some of the questions and values in the Vietnam War, and Nixon." These were, she explained, "questioning times," and these "times," and "then the coming out, too, were all changes for me in my personal life." These personal changes radiated outward, changing her social circle. By her own estimation, they led her "into meeting some people that were very much my social support system and my belief support system and I very much appreciated that." She immersed herself in lesbian-separatism "for several years,"[7] joining the

> Califia Collective, which you may not have heard about. We were a group of women who put on summer camps, some would like to show them as lesbian summer camps, but they were for all women. And we looked at some of the issues that divide us and unite us, sexism, classism. We were also vegetarian, and that's when I became a vegetarian, that was another change.

These new personal and political associations and identifications were, clearly, a far cry from those Marilyn had made when she lived in New York, when she "didn't want to face" the implications of her same-sex desires. In stark contrast to her previous policy of distancing, once in the context of lesbian-feminism and the radical politics of the early 1970s, Marilyn "was comfortable in making those changes."

Not all informants who fashioned a gay liberationist identity did so through contacts with explicitly–or exclusively– gay activist organizations. This is especially true for the two male accredited subjects that figured in my sample. After all, while women could find emergent lesbian-feminist thinking and contacts through the women's movement, no similar stepping stone existed for men. Leonard discovered the accrediting discourse through his involvement with civil rights work, and Tex found it in an early gay liberationist book. But it also is true for women: Sharon encountered gay liberation through her involvement with the hippie counterculture in California and, later, through a gay church.

Unlike Kate and Marilyn, Sharon (66) had been involved in gay causes before lesbian-feminism or gay liberation emerged. She spoke of having developed a feminist sensibility early in life, when she saw her mother die of a brain tumor after the family doctor diagnosed her seizures as symptoms of menopause. Her frustration with the gender order continued into college, where she "was fighting with my individuality as a woman. I was realizing I can't do all these things the men do 'cause I'm a woman." By her own assessment, this early feminism "was the most important thing before the lesbianism."

In 1956, at the age of twenty-seven, she moved to California, where she "started the Daughters of Bilitis in Manhattan Beach." Her focus shifted when she became involved in a series of Eastern religions, then embraced astrology, which led her to become "like the flower children" in the 1960s, when she "was always in San Francisco with my friends." Her spiritual search ended when she attended Troy Hunter's fledgling, but quickly growing, openly gay Metropolitan Community Church (MCC),[8] which she discovered when she went to the Women's Center that housed it. Sharon's entrance into the church was a momentous one which shaped her subsequent priorities and commitments. Although she "wasn't impressed" the first time she attended, by 1971 she "realized that I had to have something, a religion to hold *onto.*" Attracted by the fact that, in MCC, "you could be a

Christian and *gay* and *women* would be accepted" (a claim to feminism she now sees as having been false), she joined the church. At an MCC "spiritual renewal weekend," Sharon decided to become a minister. She pursued a BA in theology, and received it in 1979, becoming a "candidate pastor," a status she felt she did not receive because she was a feminist and ministered to the poor, who did not provide enough tithes to satisfy the MCC leadership. She left MCC and founded her own "gay and lesbian church" in 1984, but had to close it because of poor attendance.

Leonard admitted that he was "not really sure" why he stopped thinking of homosexuality in stigmatizing terms and became committed to gay liberation's call for public disclosure, but suggested two overlapping explanations. First, he "eventually got this relatively decent job where it wouldn't matter whether you were gay or not. Part of the central organization of it was gay, and I became its vice-president." Second, just as he had used same-sex encounters with African-American men as a way of achieving a liminal heterosexuality in the late 1950s and early 1960s, he began to question the stigmatization of homosexuality by reconsidering the racial arrangements of the time. For him, the agent of social change that inspired this reformulation was the civil rights movement, which he and his friend Walter, both of whom had been having sex with African-American men for years, joined by virtue of their sexual and social contacts.[9] His almost complete immersion in Harlem, where he made his sexual and social connections, where he lived, and where he engaged in political activism, sensitized him to issues of passing. When he saw that a co-worker's passing as white was hindering their organization's goals in the early 1960s, he realized that passing was both unsettlingly possible and ultimately unreasonable:

I was supposed to be doing research on Richmond, Virginia, proving that they did not have a race problem. I just could not do it. We had done Greenville, Mississippi, and my boss wouldn't let me go there, because he said my attitude was just sort of hopeless, that I would get arrested and he would be in hot water. We went to Atlanta and I said, "We should hire some black guys to help us." He said (stage whisper), "No, this is the south, we can't do that sort of thing." I found it *really* wouldn't have been any problem at all. I didn't realize until we went to Atlanta that he was passing.

Indeed, when assessing the consequences of homosexuality for self, he equated homosexuality with race (specifically, being African-American), both stigmatizing statuses whose treatment by heterosexuals and whites, respectively, tempts members of both groups to pass—even to live—as members of their oppressor's group. Leonard argued that homosexuality, like race, is an essential aspect of self, which no amount of repression can mask, and which attempts at masking only frustrate:

Gayness is like being black. There isn't any way to *escape* it! You've got to deal with it, you've got to come to terms somewhere along the line, some *kind* of terms. There's no *escape* from it! Even if you do what people did fifty years ago, they got married and they lived a straight life and they'd go through lives all frustrated, never having touched any other person of the same sex and all that, but *thinking* about it from time to time. There's an *enormous* amount of effort that *buries* that person in that married life. And that would be as close as I can figure to not being affected by being gay, is by denying it and just living a straight life. Which is, until, say, 1920, *basically* what gay people did.

Clearly, then, Leonard's case complicates matters. On the one hand, he had identified as gay well before the advent of gay liberation—in 1954, when, inspired by his recognition of "normal" homosexual men, he "had sex with somebody and committed myself basically that I was gay." On the other hand, he came to see his exclusive choice of African-American male sexual partners as another form of distancing, and reassessed the validity of the stigmatized homosexual discourse's mandate to pass as heterosexual when, while conducting civil rights work in the south in the early 1960s, he recognized the absurdity and political liability of passing as white. Leonard's generalization of his critique of passing as white to a critique of passing as heterosexual prefigured the gay liberationist argument that passing was both personally and politically damaging, as gay liberation (and, indeed, all radical identity politics of the late 1960s and early 1970s) would adopt both the ethnic and racial models of identity and the insistence upon the authentic enactment of identity that emerged from the civil rights movement (see Epstein 1990, especially pp. 139–141).

Here, in direct contrast to other informants' identity careers, Leonard's identity cohort membership does not strictly follow the historical parameters I have laid out. Instead of embracing a fully formed gay liberationist discourse, he created and then adopted what can only be seen as its embryonic version, one that preexisted (and prefigured) its formal and public emergence. Those who did not engage in this creative reinvention of homosexuality encountered its fully formed and doctrinaire version in the late 1960s and early 1970s, when the reinvisioning in which Leonard and others had engaged had been concretized into a more or less standardized political agenda and a more or less standardized discourse of homosexuality. Again, those who were engaged in distancing when they encountered the accrediting discourse embraced that discourse whereas those who were not thus engaged rejected it (and, indeed, continue to do so). Leonard is thus the only member of the accredited identity cohort who did not embrace a fully formed accrediting discourse of homosexuality. But Leonard, who created and adopted this discourse before it became a significant challenge to the stigmatized discourse of homosexuality, is no less a member of the accredited identity cohort for having been one of its *first* members. As I discussed at the book's outset, the central fault line dividing my informants' identities and identity work is the historical era in which they identified as homosexual: that in which homosexuality was constructed as a stigma, and that in which it was constructed as a source of status. The fact that, for Leonard, this "era" emerged–to a great extent because of the political work in which he and his colleagues engaged–sooner than it did for others does not erode the significance of the late 1960s and early 1970s for other members of this identity cohort, since this is when they first encountered the accrediting discourse.

Identifying through the properties of the gay liberationist discourse had implications for past as well as present selves. Again, the accrediting discourse constructed the stigmatization of homosexuality as an invalid system of oppression that could and should be politically overthrown through personal transcendence, and the self-stigmatizing as colluding in their own destruction due to cowardice, ignorance, or self-hatred. These reformulations called on actors to interpret their same-sex erotic and romantic desires as homosexual in nature, and to reassess and condemn their past homosexual identity work–work which, as we have seen, included distancing and formulating a heterosexual identity and even, in the cases of Kate, Abby, and Leonard, adopting a stigmatized homosexual identity.

In 1967, when he was forty-three, Tex (72), who had declined to interpret his actions and his self as homosexual, read an early gay liberationist book that depicted the public or private "denial" of homosexuality as an assault on authenticity. Tex described having seen that the only legitimate solution to the stressful "double life" he was leading (having sexual encounters with men in parks while living with his wife) was to "be himself"—in other words, to see his homosexuality as an essential self that could be authentically enacted only outside the confines of heterosexual life. The book

> straightened me out a lot better than any priest. It showed me not what I was, but what I wasn't. I wasn't what I was pretending to be. And that the only way I would get myself in order is to be myself. I don't think I was feeling anything until after I got through it and digested it. And it's really a great book! That's all I felt. You know, this is the answer to what my questions are.

In speaking of getting himself in order, Tex displays his understanding of his previous pursuit of a heterosexual identity through marriage as an essentially disorderly state of being. Having the new option to interpret his desires and actions in accrediting terms, however, Tex "felt more comfortable" and told his wife he was gay.

Relatedly, some subjects understood their past pursuit of a heterosexual identity as an exercise in self-deception or ignorance and their identification as homosexual through the accrediting discourse as a discovery of their "true" self. Indeed, Kate recast her painful, decades-long efforts to negotiate a sexual identity, an identity career that included identification as a stigmatized homosexual, as invalid attempts that did not really count as coming out. In her words, "I can't say I truly came out until feminism with NOW—in the early seventies. . . . But anyway [in 1973] coming out and getting to the point where I felt real comfortable saying, 'I am a lesbian.' That's, I guess, the real coming out." Kate contrasted the visceral, authentic romantic and sexual experience she had with Jan with their "denial" of its "real" nature as lesbian "or even homosexual"—categories that resonated in the medicalized discourse of the 1940s as "inverts and perverts."

She characterized their pursuit of a heterosexual identity–
designed to avoid the designation mentally ill–as itself being
"out of touch with reality."

> Neither of us–we were together for a year and a half at that
> stage–and neither of us admitted that we were lesbian or even
> homosexual or inverts, perverts, Uranians, any of the terms
> that were being used then, we didn't admit anything, we just
> loved each other. Total, total, *total* denial of what was really
> happening. . . . It was total insanity, if you really want to look
> at it that that way, I mean we were totally out of touch with
> reality.

Identification as gay through the properties of the accrediting discourse was not limited to the 1970s. Abby (70)–who,
as we have seen, adopted a stigmatized lesbian identity in
the 1950s–subsequently moved to California, where, she explained, she underwent treatment for alcoholism. Because
she associated her alcoholism with her lesbianism, she distanced herself from both after her treatment. Having given
up her lesbian contacts, she

> plunged into work, and it was only later on that I realized that
> I was equating my coming out in 1952 with–that is exactly
> when I started drinking. So for all of that period of time [1981–
> 1992] I was working very long hours, and had no time for
> any social life. I was completely unaware of all the changes
> that had occurred in gay life, I guess, since the seventies, that
> the centers were evolving and everything. Before, my only
> acquaintances with gay life had been socializing in bars. I
> didn't realize the whole world had changed.

Abby only reengaged her lesbianism when, in the early
1990s, she saw an announcement for the West Hollywood
annual gay pride festival, which she attended. There, she
searched for and eventually found information about groups
for gay seniors and began attending them, becoming friends
with women from other lesbian groups.

And that's how I started going. Then, I started getting the *Lesbian News,* because of going up to the Metropolitan Community Church. I hate to use that phrase "born again," but my God, it was like seeing a whole new picture on everything. And I went "Holy Moses! All this has happened?" And I couldn't believe the publications, and everything else. It was remarkable.

3

Biography and History

From Identity Careers to Identity Cohorts

Social theorists have suggested that individuals may seldom be aware of the intricate connection between the course of their own lives and the course of national or world history. But in order to fully understand human development, it is important for us to better grasp history, biography, and the relations between the two, and changes in these over time. . . . These connections are so important that Riley, Kahn, and Foner (1994) recently described them as the "new challenge" for developmental scientists: the challenge of understanding how individual life paths, and the collective life trajectories of birth cohorts, are shaped by changing social structures and the course of history. This new challenge serves as a reminder that history, and the imprint it leaves on human lives, lies at the heart of one of the most central concepts with which developmental scientists must wrestle: cohort.
—Settersten 1999, p. 13

The Situational Contingency of Homosexual Identity

Certain themes and patterns are apparent across informants' careers. Although not all subjects described having experienced their sexual and gender differences in a conceptual void, virtually all spoke of having initially interpreted these differences through the properties of a stigmatizing discourse of homosexuality. Of these, approximately half (19) responded to the negative implications of their same-sex desires as posited by this discourse by distancing themselves from their desires, a practice they eventually replaced with identification as one of two types of homosexual as new contacts and contexts led to a paradigm shift. New *contacts* included sexual encounters that clarified, validated, and structured their desires, providing a means of satisfying them; chance encounters with identifiable homosexuals in public, or with self-identified homosexuals in subcultural spaces such as bars and parks; and encounters with people involved in the gay liberation or lesbian-feminist movements. New *contexts* included the emergence of emotions and needs that subjects used to elaborate their desires from the purely sexual to the romantic; the breakup of marriages and engagements; and an emergent accrediting discourse through which subjects could assess their desires in non-stigmatized terms. The latter, of course, also provided a new set of associations through which paradigm shifts could be made. Obviously, these triggers often overlapped, with new emotions leading some informants to new contacts and/or contexts, and vice versa.

Clearly, though, respondents' identity careers varied in a number of ways. Some subjects underwent more than one paradigm shift, the second potentiated by the emergence of the new symbolic contexts described above. This underscores their identity careers as consisting of a shifting range of options and actions whose enactment, while significant, by no means precluded subsequent changes or condemned them to a particular homosexual identity. Figure 1 shows the various paths subjects took on their way to identifying as homosexual.

To explicate the flow chart, subjects fall into four separate paths:

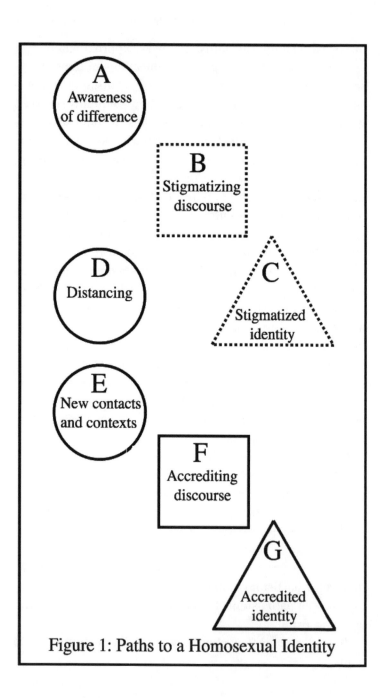

Figure 1: Paths to a Homosexual Identity

Group 1 (A → B → C) ($n = 14$): Rhoda, Franz, Jeannine, Patricia, Phoebe, Brian, Michael, William, Manny, Constance, Maria, Dan, Val, and Barbie all began their identity careers with an awareness of difference; encountered the discourse of difference that stigmatized homosexuality; and adopted a homosexual identity through its discursive parameters. None of these informants described having engaged in distancing practices. As we saw in the beginning of the previous chapter, many of these subjects explicitly denied having undergone any trauma or difficulty in adopting a homosexual identity.

Group 2 (A → B → D → E → C) ($n = 12$): Once they encountered the discourse of difference that stigmatized homosexuality, Marge, Julius, Gabrielle, Jan, George, Tony, Deborah, Mark, Ricardo, Ryan, Rodney, and Susan engaged in distancing practices, then encountered new contacts and/or contexts, at which point they adopted a stigmatized homosexual identity.

Group 3 (A → B → D → E → F → G) ($n = 2$): Tex and Marilyn circumvented a stigmatized identity completely, moving from an awareness of difference to the stigmatizing discourse to distancing, at which point new contacts led them to the accrediting discourse, through whose parameters they identified.

Group 4 (A → B → C → D → E → F → G) ($n = 4$): Leonard, Sharon, Abby, and Kate ran the entire course, following the same path as did group 1, then engaging in distancing practices, at which point they, like members of group 3, formed new contacts that led them to the accrediting discourse, through whose parameters they identified as lesbian or gay.

Group 5 (E → B → C) ($n = 2$): Henri and Lillian, who decided to become gay upon making new contacts, embraced a stigmatized identity.

Group 6: (E → F → G) (*n* = 1): Having decided to become gay upon making new contacts, Mary encountered gay liberation, and identified through its properties.

Thus, the specific paths that informants followed on their way to identifying as homosexual varied widely. Indeed, one of the most striking aspects of these identity careers is their *situational contingency*. While some (but not all) informants cited strong, sometimes overwhelming same-sex desires as driving their search for homosexual identities, others pointed to specific circumstances, some of which occurred by chance, as having clarified and/or solidified these desires, leading them to distance themselves from or embrace homosexual identities, and/or potentiated certain courses of action over others. We can only imagine what would have happened if some of these circumstances had not arisen–if Gabrielle, for example, had never met Betty. Consider that Leonard, Brian, Jan, William, Julius, and Lillian were all on the verge of marriage when circumstances led them away from that particular commitment. Clearly, these circumstances varied–from being "dumped" (in the cases of William, Julius, and Lillian), to realizing their discomfort at the thought of having children (in the cases of Jan and Brian), to discovering a "different type of gay male" (in the case of Leonard)–but were similar in their consequences, and speak to the fact that, in the absence of these sometimes fleeting interventions, subjects' futures would have been very different, perhaps even abidingly heterosexual. Furthermore, three subjects would have stayed heterosexually married had the dynamics of their marriages not changed. Mark would probably not have left his wife had he not found her in bed with his brother; Mary may very well have remained married had her husband not suggested that they enter the world of "swingers" that emerged in the late 1960s and early 1970s; and Henri would not have divorced his wife had she not declined to have children, an expectation he had brought to the marriage.

Certain narratives bring these contingencies to the fore more clearly than do others. Henri (67) had "decided" to become gay when he considered his disaffection for the "gender roles" of the time; when these expectations changed, however, he reentered heterosexual life, marrying a "career woman" who did not fit the strict gender roles with which he had grown up. "What happened at that point," he explained, was that "the women's movement changed a lot of that, where males no longer had to be the head of the family and the boss, and run the show, and support the family, and all that." When his wife declined to have children, they divorced, and he continued to date women, but compared his dates to his ex-wife, finding that they did not measure up. At that point, he "ran into Leroy," and they became lovers, despite the fact that he was "missing my other life."

> But somehow I couldn't, you know if a woman had come up instead of him, that would have been all right, or as right as it could be for the time. I might have gone the other way, but it happened to be him.

Another example is Kate, who met Jan in 1944, when they were both working in San Pedro as shipbuilders:

> I met [Jan] because she missed her bus. She was scheduled to be on a different crew. She missed her bus so they put her on my crew. Otherwise, if she hadn't missed her bus, God knows what my life would have been, I don't know what would have brought me out.[1]

As we have seen, Kate broke up with Jan when she recognized the implications of the relationship for her identity after seeing "recognizably gay women" while a counselor at a summer camp, and began a long period of distancing, during which she worked to formulate a liminal heterosexual identity. While on the waiting list for "The Los Angeles Psychiatric Association or something," she "started dating again" and met a man she "rather liked." When he "pressed" her to "spend the night together," she said,

> "All right–gonna do it!" And so we arranged to spend the night together. And turns out he's impotent! I think back now and I guess yeah, poor guy, because he really was under a certain amount of pressure. And I've wondered what would have happened if *that* had worked.

These careers, then, are situationally contingent. They are also, of course, *historically contingent* on several levels, most notably access to information about homosexuality and to homosexuals who were not gender inverts (as well as to spaces where they could be safely met), and the nature and structure of the gender order both within and outside of heterosexual life. In other words, the social, cultural, and political terrain in which same-sex desires are interpreted, and homosexual identities negotiated, all underwent radical changes as the stigmatized discursive and practical treatment of homosexuality and homosexuals was challenged and ultimately overridden by the new gay activism of the 1970s. Although informants' identity careers are compellingly complex, they become clearer when we consider that the homosexual identities they eventually adopted ultimately hinged on the historical era *in* which–and thus the discourse *through* which–they did so.

The Historical Contingency of Homosexual Identity

While the historical contingency of identity as an empirical matter has not been widely examined, the effect of historical and life-course location on a range of attitudes, beliefs, and behaviors has (see Sherkat 2001; Robinson and Jackson 2001; Bergstrom and Nussbaum 1996; Wilson 1996). This work emanates from sociological analyses of aging, which link life patterns to changing historical contexts and to people's location in them (see Hardy and Waite 1997). These analyses are theoretically informed by Mannheim's (1952 [1928]) work on generations and by later research into birth (and other) cohorts (a problematic category, as we will see).

Generations

Extending Pinder's argument that each generation creates its own "entelechy"–an expression of that generation's phenomenological approach–Mannheim proposed that members of the same age group share a common location in the sociohistorical process, and are thus capable of sharing a common, generational *Weltanschauung*. Should these members engage in "the characteristic social and intellectual currents of their society and period," the resulting commonality of experience will give birth to distinct generational perspectives, which forever shape that generation's experience. As Mannheim theorized them, then, age groups require more than a common historical location to be a generation; rather, they require a conscious awareness of common experiences, beliefs, and life chances linked to their shared location in history. Mannheim thus posits conscious reflection as an essential feature of generations and their relations and tensions, and emphasizes the tendency of outlooks to vary along generational lines.

The generation is both dynamic and complex. The pace of social change is essential to Mannheim's framework, since a distinctive entelechy develops in response to the obsolescence of "traditional modes of experience, thought, and expression" (Settersten 1999, p. 112) brought about by rapid social change.[2] Thus, while each generation has the capacity to develop its own entelechy, not all have the opportunity–or, indeed, the inclination–to do so. Moreover, generations are riven by conflict, with groups of actors looking to opposing ends of the generation's culture for guidance on how to interpret and react to specific events. These groups constitute "generation units" that share interpretive "formative principles" (Mannheim 1928, p. 306) that provide distinct, competing patterns of response to events. But generation units neither exist nor function in isolation: because members of all generation units are members of the same generation responding to the same events, they "always interpret their world in terms of"–and thus monitor and interact with–"one another" (ibid., p. 314). This dialogue between generation units potentiates intragenerational change.

The concept of the succession of generations producing social, political, and ideological conflict is powerful, as is the idea of a historically specific yet complex interpretive system upon which all people of a certain age group rely. Yet Mannheim's work implies that the generation unit is the smallest unit that (1) is shaped by sociohistorical circumstances, and (2) shapes specific responses to events. If considered concretely, this would mean that the ideologies and perspectives of stigmatized groups would be virtually identical to those of the generation unit to which they belong. This would preclude the very existence of these groups, which, by definition, always differ ideologically from the dominant culture–and, as we know, every generation unit has such distinct, often ideologically opposed, groups. Mannheim thus provides us with an extremely useful generational and historical framework that is nonetheless too undifferentiated to apply to homosexual elders.[3]

Cohorts

A more fruitful concept is that of the cohort, a catch-all term for a group of people who experience the same thing, or adopt the same role, at approximately the same historical moment. This concept was introduced by Norman Ryder in 1965 as an alternative to the consciousness-driven generation of Mannheim which, Ryder felt, obscured the fact that successive age groups replenished and changed the social structure without always being aware that they were doing so. As Hardy and Waite (1997, p. 5) note, in Ryder's formulation, cohorts "could be implicated in the process of social change without presuming the self-conscious development of a shared sense of purpose."

According to the "life-course principle" (Elder 1995), birth cohorts–comprised of people born at more or less the same time–experience historical events and situations in similar ways,[4] because these events occur at the same point in their lives (i.e., youth or middle age) and thus at times when they tend to be married or unmarried, working or retired, healthy or sick, financially secure or not. This leads them to patterns of action and interpretation different from those of other cohorts, for example, supporting certain policies over others. For instance, people born in 1925 and those born in 1945 experienced the Vietnam War and women's liberation in their forties and twenties, respectively, with significant consequences, since these events resonate differently for the married middle-aged than for college students and those beginning their careers. Thus, while all actors encounter the same political, ideological, and cultural conflicts, economic crises, and the like, these are filtered through the circumstances, commitments, and concerns typical of a certain location in the life course.

Ryder (1997 [1965], p. 72) explicitly cautioned against equating the cohort with the birth cohort; although the latter is clearly the most obvious way to conceptualize the introduction of new groups into the social fabric, he suggested that the concept would be best served by "emphasiz[ing] *the context prevailing at the time members of a cohort experience critical transitions,*" and that the underlying "approach can be generalized beyond the birth cohort to cohorts identified by *common time of occurrence of any significant and enduring event in life history*." Cohorts could, he wrote (pp. 72–73, emphases added), be based upon time of entry into or exit from a number of institutions, activities, and contexts (e.g., schooling, the workforce, and city life), since "each of these events is important in *identifying the kinds of situations to which persons respond differently,* and *establishing a status to which future experiences are oriented.* . . . The strategic focus for research in social change is *the context under which each cohort is launched on its own path*."

While a less limiting measurement than the generation, the cohort poses its own problems. In 1978, Rosow raised the difficulty of establishing meaningful cohort boundaries. While the definitional boundaries of a specific generation are provided by the members of that generation, since it is the very consciousness of those boundaries that constitutes the generation in the first place, cohorts are purely exogenous, analytic constructs (in Braungart and Braungart's words, categories "in themselves," not "for themselves") rather than endogenous, reflective achievements. As a result, the application of the term *cohort* to a group of actors using arbitrary temporal criteria may be ultimately meaningful only to the analyst herself. Settersten (1999, p. 116) notes that this exogenous tendency is compounded by the fact that most researchers usually "first define cohorts and then search for empirical clusters of behaviors and attitudes" rather than use "empirical clusters of behaviors and attitudes as a means for defining cohorts." The trick, then, is to "show that each cohort, relative to those adjacent to it, responds in its own way to a phenomenon of interest," since it "is this unique response that constitutes a 'cohort effect' " (p. 116). Moreover, citing Uhlenberg and Riley (1996), Settersten (ibid.) reminds us that cohort analysis must be mindful of variation within cohorts due to the classic race/class/gender triumvirate, or to distinctive engagements or contacts with historical events, and that cohorts may thus contain subcohorts "with shared life-course patterns and experience."

While these critiques would apply to any type of cohort analysis, in the context of this book, birth cohort analysis resonates as problematic on other fronts as well. This analysis assumes a typical life course, an assumption made easier by the institutionalization of the life course itself over the nineteenth and twentieth centuries and its standardization of life transitions according to age and life-course location.[5] Cohort analysis becomes more challenging, however, when we consider that certain statuses, while neither adopted nor ascribed at predetermined points, may nonetheless have great significance for the lives of those holding those statuses— indeed, may even become master statuses. Clearly, sexual identity comes most readily to mind, since, as we have seen, the ages at which one experiences, becomes aware of, or identifies sexual desires are not fixed in advance. But other identities come to mind as well, such as those inhering in medical conditions or in class, professional, spiritual, citizenship, or marital statuses. Thus, just as historical conditions may affect the experience of a predictable, "on-time" life transition, so may the perceived temporal idiosyncrasy of the life transition—or adoption of an identity—affect the experience of the person undergoing it, particularly in relation to the experiences of members of that person's generation who underwent it at different, perhaps more collectively patterned, times.

Clearly, then, reliance on the birth cohort—and on the institutionalized life course that undergirds it—shifts the analyst's focus from identity, which is, as we have seen, historically grounded and subject to rapid reformulation. As I noted at the outset of this book, identities are *interpretations made with an awareness of (and, often, in conflict with) competing discourses and categories of the self.* That key interpretive moments may occur at different points in the actor's life and at different points in history—may, in fact, be inspired by the emergence of sociohistorical changes that take place within the actor's own lifetime—suggests that older homosexuals' identities may vary according to the historical-discursive contexts in which these key moments occurred. Because this phenomenon has less to do with age than with historical period, capturing and theorizing it requires a new vocabulary.

This need remains despite the fact that recent work in lesbian and gay studies has noted that generational and other life-course rifts may have significant consequences for homosexual identity. Citing Mannheim's work on generational outlooks, for example, Escoffier (1992, p. 8) notes that "generations in lesbian and gay life are more often characterized by the historical context of the time at which one comes out publicly than by closeness in chronological age,"[6] yet does not pursue this concept as an organizing feature of ordinary homosexual identity work. Rather, he goes on to examine the existence of gay generations of scholars within lesbian and gay studies, connecting the era in which lesbian and gay scholars entered lesbian and gay life with the intellectual perspectives they bring to their academic and political work. Vera Whisman (1996, p. 19) points to, but does not theorize, a distinct type of cohort composed of those who came out as gay or lesbian "at the same time," and links different life-course patterns on the one hand and different accounts of the nature of homosexuality on the other to cohort member-ship.[7] Despite the theoretical potential of this insight, Arlene Stein (1997, p. 7), citing "the wide range of ages at which people come out" and the fact that "coming out is often a life-long process,"[8] rejects Whisman's categorization of peo-ple based on when they identified as homosexual. Yet the fact that people do indeed identify as homosexual at differ-ent times via distinct, historically specific ideologies is less a problem to be accommodated than a phenomenon to be explored, and my concept of the identity cohort–comprised, again, of actors who identified as members of a particular category of person (in this case, a homosexual one) in dif-ferent historical periods with distinctive, historically specific ideologies of self and other–provides a way to do so.

Identity Cohorts

An identity cohort can–and most assuredly will–include members of different birth cohorts, even of different gen-erations. As it happens, my subjects were members of the same generation, but, obviously, younger people also iden-tified as homosexual in the late 1960s and early 1970s. While I am looking at variations within a single generation, iden-tity cohorts can–and do–span generations and birth cohorts. For an identity cohort, however, the age and generation of its members are far less relevant than the historical period in which the actor came to identity herself or himself as a member of a sometimes-stigmatized category. This is due to the distinctive influence of historically specific identity dis-courses, through which actors produce their new identities, on the shape of those identities. An individual who identified herself as an alcoholic in the 1940s, for example, certainly conducted her crucial identity work using premises adhered to by the alcoholic subculture that were dominant or exclusive at the time. For someone who identified as an alcoholic in the 1990s, however, those premises would be very different and would produce different outcomes.

Distinguishing an identity cohort from a generation on the one hand and a birth cohort on the other raises the issue of consciousness. Again, while consciousness of membership in generations and generation units is essential to their existence, the cohort is a purely analytic category that exists whether or not members of that cohort are aware of it at all. But given the fact that actors are members of an identity cohort because of conscious, reflective identification, they would be aware of the historicity of their own and others' identification as members of a particular group, and would be responsive to competing ideologies of self and other with which they and others align themselves. The ideological suppositions of these other groups may invoke an identity cohort's responses to them, these responses often becoming part of its cultural and discursive tradition. Indeed, the conflict between newly adopted and other outlooks may be invoked and used as a resource through which personal and group identities are achieved, elaborated, and assessed.[9]

To return to my data, most subjects' identifications were made through the properties of the stigmatizing discourse. For them, the accrediting discourse was not available at the time they made their commitment to homosexuality. At a certain historical moment, however, an alternative–even competing–set of options did become available, and those who were engaged in distancing techniques *when this new discourse emerged* found a new horizon of meanings through which a new paradigm shift could be made. These subjects, having declined to identify as homosexual through the stigmatizing discourse, embraced the liberationist one once it emerged, and constructed a homosexual identity through its accrediting properties. Thus, despite important similarities, subjects came to understand their own and others' homosexuality in distinct, even competing terms. This is because they responded to the stigmatizing discourse in different ways, and embraced different discursive representations of homosexuality that prevailed in different historical periods. Their homosexual selves are not infinitely various, but they do differ: a discreditable self called up by a stigmatizing discourse of homosexuality, versus an accredited self mandated by the formulation of homosexuality as a source of status. The identity careers of homosexual elders thus clearly vary according to the historically situated discourses through which they identified as homosexual. Specifically, while I have focused on ideal–indeed, even extreme–types of experience and thus have not documented every subtlety, all my respondents' careers can be fit into the following categories: those who identified as homosexual through the properties of the stigmatizing discourse, and those who did so via the accrediting one.

Table 1 shows the subjects' ages, the historical period in which they identified as homosexual (broken down into the first and second half of each decade), the age at which they did so (broken down into the first and second half of each decade of life), and the identity cohort into which they fall by virtue of having identified as homosexual either before or after the emergence of gay liberation in the late 1960s. Twenty-eight subjects identified as homosexual between the early 1920s and the early 1960s and are thus considered members of the discreditable identity cohort. The accredited identity cohort is composed of six informants who identified as homosexual after the emergence of the accrediting discourse of homosexuality (between the late 1960s and the early 1990s), and of Leonard, who, as explained in Chapter 2, identified as gay in this discourse's formative years, in the early 1960s.

Table 1 also depicts the vast time span during which members of each of these identity cohorts identified as homosexual: for the discreditable cohort, forty years (from, say, 1924 to 1964) and for the accredited cohort, twenty-nine years (from, say, 1965 to 1994). Within these spans of time, however, are particular periods around which these identifying moments are clustered (Table 2). For the discreditable cohort, this period was the Second World War and the immediate postwar era; fourteen informants–a full 40 percent of the total sample and a full 50 percent of the discreditable cohort–identified as homosexual during this period. For the accredited cohort, this period was the late 1960s and early 1970s, when gay liberation and lesbian-feminism had emerged and was becoming dominant: 14.5 percent of the total sample, and 71 percent of the accredited cohort, identified as homosexual during these years. The impact of the social upheavals taking place in American society during these periods on subjects' homosexual identities and identity careers is clear. For the discreditable identity cohort, the social upheaval of the Second World War inspired a thriving homosexual subculture that emerged during and after the war, providing new and important contacts and contexts; for the accredited, the relevant social upheaval was the identity politics of the Vietnam War era.

Despite the strong correlation between these periods of social upheaval and identification as homosexual, this book's claim that the historical era during which–and the relevant discourses through which–informants identified as homosexual is more important to identity cohort membership than is age needs to be examined in the context of their identity careers. Table 3, depicting the ages at which informants

Table 1: Historical Era in Which Subjects ($n = 35$)
Identified as Homosexual

F = 19   M = 16

Name	Sex	Age	Period Identified as Homosexual	Age Identified as Homosexual	Identity Cohort
Rhoda	F	89	early 1920s	early teens	discreditable
Franz	M	86	late 1920s	late teens	discreditable
Marge	F	81	early 1930s	late teens	discreditable
Michael	M	78	early 1930s	early teens	discreditable
Val	F	74	early 1930s	early teens	discreditable
Phoebe	F	79	late 1930s	late teens	discreditable
Patricia	F	77	late 1930s	late teens	discreditable
Barbie	F	67	early 1940s	early teens	discreditable
George	M	75	early 1940s	early twenties	discreditable
Manny	M	77	early 1940s	early twenties	discreditable
Constance	F	74	early 1940s	late teens	discreditable
Julius	M	89	early 1940s	mid thirties	discreditable
Jan	F	68	late 1940s	early twenties	discreditable
Lillian	F	69	late 1940s	late teens	discreditable
Tony	M	70	late 1940s	late teens	discreditable
Maria	F	64	late 1940s	early teens	discreditable
Deborah	F	74	late 1940s	early twenties	discreditable
Henri	M	67	late 1940s	early twenties	discreditable
Mark	M	72	late 1940s	late twenties	discreditable
Brian	M	74	late 1940s	late teens	discreditable
Jeannine	F	66	late 1940s	late teens	discreditable
Ricardo	M	66	early 1950s	early twenties	discreditable
William	M	76	early 1950s	early thirties	discreditable
Ryan	M	81	early 1950s	early forties	discreditable
Dan	M	70	early 1950s	late twenties	discreditable
Rodney	M	75	late 1950s	late thirties	discreditable
Susan	F	75	early 1960s	early forties	discreditable
Gabrielle	F	77	early 1960s	early forties	discreditable
Leonard	M	72	early 1960s	early forties	accredited
Tex	M	72	late 1960s	early forties	accredited
Sharon	F	66	late 1960s	late thirties	accredited
Mary	F	66	early 1970s	early forties	accredited
Kate	F	76	early 1970s	early fifties	accredited
Marilyn	F	66	early 1970s	early forties	accredited
Abby	F	70	early 1990s	early sixties	accredited

Table 2:   Historical Period of Identification
by Identity Cohort Status

Discreditable Identity Cohort ($n = 28$)

Historical Era	Number of Subjects	Percentage of Total Sample (35)	Percentage of Identity Cohort
Early 1920s	1	3	3.5
Late 1920s	1	3	3.5
Early 1930s	3	8.5	11
Late 1930s	2	6	7
Early 1940s	5	14	18
Late 1940s	9	26	32
Early 1950s	4	11	14
Late 1950s	1	3	3.5
Early 1960s	2	6	7

Accredited Identity Cohort ($n = 7$)

Historical Era	Number of Subjects	Percentage of Total Sample	Percentage of Identity Cohort
Early 1960s	1	3	14
Late 1960s	2	6	28
Early 1970s	3	8.5	43
Early 1990s	1	3	14

identified as homosexual, shows that twenty-five discreditable subjects (or 89 percent of that identity cohort) identified as homosexual between their early teens and late thirties, while all accredited ones did so between their late thirties and early sixties. Twenty (almost 60 percent of the sample)–*none of them accredited*–identified as homosexual by their early twenties, and of the ten subjects (or 29 percent of the sample) who identified as homosexual during or after their late thirties, seven (or 20 percent of the sample) are members of the accredited identity cohort.

Age thus appears to have some relationship to identity cohort membership–not the average age of the members of the

Table 3:   Age of Homosexual Identification
by Identity Cohort Status

Identity Cohort	< 20	20–40	40–60	60+	N
Discreditable	14	11	3	0	28
Accredited	0	1	5	1	7

Table 4:   Average Age of Subjects by Identity Cohort Status

	Discreditable	Accredited
Male	75.5	72
Female	74	69
All	74.5	70

identity cohorts themselves, which, as Table 4 shows, differs
by a maximum of five years, but the age at which members
of each identity cohort identified as lesbian or gay. Having
distanced themselves from their same-sex desires for longer
periods of time, accredited subjects identified as homosexual later in life than did members of the discreditable identity cohort. This would appear to undermine the integrity
of the identity cohort as I have defined it: as a group composed of people who identified as a member of a particular category of person during a particular historical era, but
who are not necessarily the same age. But these patterns
in age are to be expected among people who *are* the same
age. In order to identify as a liberated homosexual, a person
born before 1930 had to do so after the age of thirty-nine,
because the liberated discourse was simply not available before then. Nonetheless, we cannot avoid the following question: can the same circumstances that led the accredited to
decline a stigmatized homosexual identity for these lengths
of time also account for their distinctive understandings, actions, and orientations?

I did not find any distinct reason for accredited members having spent such a relatively long time distancing themselves from homosexuality while the discredited spent much less time doing so,[10] and so cannot fully consider the question. I am, however, less concerned with *why* subjects identified as homosexual during particular eras with distinctive discourses of homosexuality than I am with (1) the fact *that* they did so (established here), and (2) the resonance (if any) of current identities and understandings with the discursive properties through which subjects came to identify as a particular type of homosexual (examined in the following three chapters). Before this resonance is examined, however, we need to remind ourselves of the horizons of meaning through which subjects conduct/ed their homosexual identity work. Table 5 shows that the parameters through which my subjects construct their homosexual identities are narrower than those outlined in the introduction.

Table 5:   Operative Discourses of Homosexuality

	Homosexuality as Stigma	Homosexuality as Status
Relation to self	Aspect	Essential
Implications for self	Discreditable	Accrediting
Appropriately enacted in	Private	Private and public

What practices and orientations does identity cohort membership inform? If, as I have suggested, identities are shaped by discourses, and if people use homosexual identity discourses to produce selves and others as particular types of homosexuals, then we can speak of the production of the self as a particular type of homosexual, one consonant with the discourse with which one affiliates. We should, in short, be able to speak of distinctive types of homosexual selves that correlate with homosexual identity cohort membership.

Moreover, identity discourses should suffuse formulations of the world as well as those of the self. Subjects should therefore differentially use, invoke, and elaborate those formulations of homosexuality that inhere in the discourses of homosexuality as stigma and of homosexuality as status in the process of constructing intelligible homosexual selves within intelligible homosexual worlds. In the following chapter, I examine how those I interviewed see their standing in the world given their homosexuality, and consider whether the worlds they construct vary according to identity cohort membership. Having demonstrated the identity cohort membership of each subject, I will begin identifying each subject by that membership, as well as by name and age, with the letter "D" after a subject's age signifying membership in the discreditable identity cohort, and the letter "A" signifying membership in the accredited one.

4

"Dangerous Territory"

The Heterosexual World

You can't go outside the stream of things and for things not to be–you know, society functions in a certain way. We don't function that way, gay people and lesbians, and so you have to expect that we're going to face a lot of challenges because we're not in that social movement that everybody else is in. We're a minority. –Maria

Oh, back then, honey, it was hard. It was hard. I mean, they didn't care that much for gays. Believe me, they didn't. –Constance

SUBJECTS' homosexual identities and identifications affected how they envisioned the world and their place in it. The very distinction between the two is, of course, an analytic and exogenous one, and suggests that the construction of identity and the construction of the world are separate projects that occur at different times. As I noted in the introduction, however, this is not the case. While actors experience "the" world as having been organized before their birth and continuing after their death, and take for granted its existence independent of their production and experience of it (see Schutz 1962, p. 7), in the course of assuming or describing a common world, they are constructing and elaborating it as well.[1] Informants' accounts of how the world is organized, and the implications of this organization for self, provide an opportunity to explore their reconstruction of the world and of their perceived place in it as expressions and features of their homosexual identity work.

My informants' perceived worlds are distinctive re/constructions grounded in the discourses through which they identified as homosexual. While all subjects saw their worlds as constrained by, and structured around, conflict with heterosexuals, the *nature* of the conflict differed on the basis of the identity discourse through which subjects identified as homosexual. For members of the discreditable identity cohort, heterosexuals posed a threat to homosexual *persons* through the denial of essential resources such as physical safety, privacy and other civil liberties, and social inclusion.[2] For members of the accredited identity cohort, however, heterosexuals constituted a threat to person *and* to the homosexual self. They did so by demanding that homosexuals suppress that self in the course of protecting themselves from threats to person by passing as heterosexual, and this, clearly, is in keeping with gay liberation's rejection of passing as an inauthentic practice.

Fear and Loathing: Heterosexual Constructions

In their accounts of past and present circumstances, respondents described a range of prejudices and incivilities homosexuals could expect from heterosexuals, from physical attacks and public identification and harassment by strangers to the withdrawal of emotional support by friends and family—assuming, of course, that these heterosexuals knew of homosexuals' sexual preferences. Some subjects had experienced these discriminations, while others had witnessed or heard about them, but all understood these dangers to be both real and ubiquitous, and all heterosexuals to be prone to them, although to varying degrees. Underlying these tendencies was a perceived belief on the part of heterosexuals that homosexuals were committed to seducing them, particularly children, into homosexuality, a belief that resonated with the construction of the homosexual as a predatory pervert that had become dominant in the 1950s. Tony (70, D), for example, recalled his mother asking him if he had made his lover homosexual, a question he felt was absurd, but which he recognized as having been inspired by the stereotype of the homosexual as capable of seducing "normal" men into an "abnormal" life. Other informants also spoke with disdain of heterosexuals' reliance on this image of the homosexual as, on the one hand, "an untouchable, almost like a disease" (in Rhoda's words) and, on the other, as seducers of heterosexuals. Leonard (72, A), who oversees a local gay senior group's outreach to old gay men and women in a downtown senior housing complex, found residents' suspicion of him ridiculous: "I've been denounced as a devil's advocate or something of the sort, I'm 'recruiting innocent senior citizens.' Can you imagine?" Similarly, Constance (74, D) portrayed heterosexual parents as overcome by fears of their children being recruited into a homosexual life:

> The straight people, they worry a lot, when they're married, about kids getting involved in gay life, and you'd think that the gay people would go there and say, "Hey! Come on, you're going to be gay." That's what's wrong with the straight people. They're fearful of gays.[3]

While all heterosexuals were portrayed as fearful of homosexuals' influence over heterosexuals, those who were insecure about their own heterosexuality were depicted as most committed to condemning homosexuals, because they were most concerned with maintaining an intact heterosexual public persona. Ryan (81, D) described having recently explained this connection to his older sister Emma, who had told him that the women in her social group were "forever criticizing gays," a statement to which he responded by saying,

> "Emma, when you hear someone blabbing about gays, you can be sure they're either gay themselves or they have a child who is gay and they're trying to act so strong against them to make it appear that they're not gay or have no gay connections." So I said, "Keep your mouth shut," and she does.

Some male subjects described a subgroup of heterosexuals whose concern for their own sexual identities made them especially dangerous. This group is comprised of those who abhor and/or deny their own same-sex attractions and acts and who are thus particularly prone to attacking homosexuals as a means of eradicating that aspect of self and/or precluding others' identification of them as homosexual. According to the discourse associating homosexuality with gender inversion, masculine men who had insertive sex with feminine men were seen as trade–an essentially heterosexual male category. Rodney (75, D) described the dangers inherent in picking up these men, who, he says, tend to turn their confusion over their own same-sex activities to violence against their male sexual partners:

> You are dealing with a dangerous territory here, because these people–there's gonna be guilt on their part and they can be very vicious. Trade could be dangerous 'cause you're dealing with some people that are probably mixed up sexually and you've got to be very careful. A lot of gay guys have been killed by trade.

Murder is accounted for here by the intense guilt trade feel in having engaged in homosexual behavior and in having thus momentarily undermined the legitimacy of their claims to heterosexuality. The "source" of the homosexual encounter is, according to Rodney, deflected from the heterosexual self and toward the homosexual. This deflection preserves the "essential" heterosexuality of the attacker by documenting and punishing the allegedly predatory nature of the attacked. Here and elsewhere, attacks on homosexuals were interpreted as an essential feature of heterosexual identity work. Mark (72, D), for example, explained that when he was a child, two neighborhood boys "beat me up because they were blatantly gay themselves and didn't want to admit it." He also explained that they were now gay and that "they beat me up all that time for nothing." Indeed, when he was in his twenties, Tony had been publicly beaten up by his lover, Hank, in New York during an argument that escalated when Tony implicated him in the category *fairy*.

> He made a comment to me about, "You half-assed fairy" and I made a comment back to him about "Well, you weren't too good either" or something like that. And he raged, we got on the sidewalk and I stood there and he beat the shit out of me.

As Mark noted, even those who may be heterosexually secure are prone to attacking those who suggest a homosexual encounter, seeing that suggestion as so repulsive that it merits a violent reaction. After he saved the Marine's life during combat, Mark saw him in the shower "playing with himself." Although he was excited, Mark felt that he "had to leave because I knew that if I stayed there I was gonna do something I'd be regretting the rest of my life." By leaving, Mark felt that he saved his own life, since the Marine would undoubtedly have killed him had he made a sexual move. According to Rodney, even an appreciative gaze, which, as we have seen, caused many informants to recognize their same-sex desires, can elicit an attack; as a result, he feels fortunate that, although "I ogle and look too much, I haven't gotten my teeth bashed in yet." Clearly, then, respondents suggested that heterosexuals' condemnation of homosexuality and homosexuals carried with it the self-declared mandate to attack, even kill, them. But this threat, while significant, was mentioned much less often than were other dangers. In explaining actual or foreseen mistreatment by heterosexuals, subjects most often described a complex set of ritual avoidance practices that centered on denying known homosexuals a range of resources essential to practical, emotional, and psychic health—specifically, the right to safety and privacy to which all citizens are, presumably, entitled, and the right to inclusion in social networks, including the family. Underlying the physical and social threats posed by heterosexuals is the real possibility of being tagged by the "scarlet letter," a designation with far-reaching consequences, as we will see later. Henning Bech's (1992, p. 138) description of modern homosexuals' sense of "existential uneasiness . . . injury and of feeling watched" is borne out in subjects' accounts of the actual or immanent denial of these basic needs and in their construction of the heterosexual other as a threatening agent.

Harassment in Public Places

In *Passing By: Gender and Public Harassment* (1995, p. 16), Carol Brooks Gardner recommends thinking of certain groups as "situationally disadvantaged in public places." Regardless of their status in other contexts, public places render members of these groups subject to a range of insults and invasions.

> Public places are . . . sites for mockery and downright humiliation, the threat or the reality of interpersonal violence, verbal insults and injuries, avoidances and shunnings, and the

> mere withholding of the rituals of civility, an act that commu-
> nicates to the individual that she or he is not entitled to the
> small courtesies of everyday life due every stranger. At the
> same time, the accessibility of public places offers the victim
> of public harassment clear evidence that others receive better
> treatment. (p. 44)

The implications of this are severe. "Routine pleasures" associated with public places, while often enjoyed, are done
so "with the knowledge of what can occur" (p. 2), and actors
find that certain taken-for-granted rights are denied them—
indeed, are "still in the process of being morally earned."
Exclusion denies them the right to legitimate access to public places and questions their very citizenship by suggesting
that they do not deserve to inhabit the same places as do others, *exploitative practices* (i.e., open inspection) deny them
the rights that others enjoy while inhabiting public places,
and *evaluative practices* that "critically appraise, character-
ize, and rate the category member" (p. 82) make public
places an open forum for insult and humiliation.[4]

As we saw in Chapter 1, subjects spoke of having witnessed the ridiculing and condemnation of homosexuals as
a group. Indeed, as we saw in Chapter 2, many had distanced
themselves from homosexuals and homosexuality to avoid
just such treatment. Several informants feared being publicly identified and denounced by heterosexuals as a prelimi-
nary step to communal or relational exile. In explaining why
he did not want his neighbors to know he was gay, George
(75, D), described the manager of his trailer park having recently publicly identified and attacked another homosexual
tenant, whom he tried to eject from the park. This manager,
who "hated homosexuals," verbally attacked the man "on
the street, called him all kinds of things, a fag, and he told
him to get out of the park."

"An Unknown Quantity": Intimate Ties and the Threat of Rejection

Mistreatment was also seen as immanent in the more personal realms of friendship and family ties–social arenas constructed, in the dominant discourse, as a neutral, safe haven from the hostilities of the working world. Heterosexuals with whom respondents had intimate and enduring relationships were seen as equally capable of, and predisposed to, terminating the relationship abruptly should they learn of their homosexuality, and of depriving them of the emotional and/or instrumental support which they valued and on which they had grown to depend. This is not to say that subjects did not enjoy relationships with friends and family–on the contrary, as I have shown elsewhere (Rosenfeld 2002), many described rich friendship and family networks, and often cited family members who did not know of their homosexuality as the people to whom they were the closest. But the threat of exclusion by friends and family, or of a weakening of the strength of those ties, remained a palpable one.

A large number of these subjects named heterosexual friends to whom they were close and with whom they had never discussed their homosexuality. For many, the endangered resources were essential to their physical and emotional well-being. George (75, D), for example, explained that he remained close to his best friend, a vocally homophobic neighbor, because the relationship, providing a basis of physical safety, was "necessary." He also explained that the essential practical support he derived from his friend was contingent upon his keeping his homosexuality secret from him. Similarly, Barbie (67, D) expressed concern that her "church family"–her central support system–might reject her if its members knew she was a lesbian, depriving her of social and psychological support. "When I'm not healthy and need help, they're the ones that come forward and help. [But] if they knew what I was, I don't know how they would feel toward me."

In contrast to the harm posed by strangers described above, the heterosexual friends discussed here share direct, intimate relations. These friends, however, are understood to be just as prone to denying homosexuals important resources as are those with whom subjects interact superficially, if at all. As a result, Barbie and others suggested, subjects can lose social worlds in which they are deeply, even primarily, invested, a risk posed even by relationships that are unusually close. A strong example is Rhoda's (89, D) account of her betrayal by a very close friend, who told members of a club to which she and Rhoda belonged that Rhoda was gay and had "made advances" toward her. Rhoda emphasized both the closeness of the relationship and her own innocence in the matter, explaining that she had neither introduced her friend to homosexuality (they had never talked about homosexuality, and she had only exposed her to homosexuals because her friend associated with homosexuals on her own), nor made the advances toward her of which she had been accused. The story resonates as a cautionary tale: because the accusation was false and was made in the knowledge that it would cost her emotional and instrumental support, even extremely close friends can harm gay men and women by invoking the image of the sexually unrestrained homosexual.

Informants also feared being rejected or banished by family members, even those to whom they feel emotionally close. Citing an inability to really know the inner feelings of family members regarding homosexuality in general and their own as-yet-unknown or unacknowledged homosexuality in particular, respondents spoke of assuming rejection by family members should the latter learn of their homosexuality. Assumptions about the tenacity of family ties, the commitment of family members to maintain relations despite internal conflicts or problems, were reflexively modified to apply only to heterosexuals: homosexuality was seen as constructed by heterosexuals as an exception to the rule of unequivocal family acceptance. As Abby (70, A) explained:

> There's a chance it's unacknowledged and if I said anything there might be rejection. You can read everything you can lay your hands on and it'll say, "Your family loves you," but you really don't know. It's an unknown quantity. 'Cause you always keep in the back of your mind that blood is thicker than water, but sometimes it's not.

Tony also pointed to the uncertain standing homosexuals have within the family. Given the family members that are openly homophobic and those whose feelings toward homosexuals are unknown, and the tendency of heterosexuals to reserve their love for heterosexual family members, he explained, the known homosexuality of relatives becomes a master (and degrading) status, overriding previously significant family ties.

> You have the homophobic too within the family. A straight person doesn't have that problem. You have more people concerned about you straight than you would being gay. You multiply that and the people that you don't know that are homophobic, you really have nothing [but] "Goddamn faggot." Or "She's a lesbian." It's like you're marked with the scarlet letter. You're homosexual.

Subjects gave concrete examples of being rejected by family members after their homosexuality was discovered. The strongest was Manny's (77, D) account of his family's response to discovering he was gay after someone saw him at a gay bar in 1937, when he was only nineteen. "When I tell you that my mother and father sat *shiva* for three days," he said, "you can imagine how it made me feel. Well, I was too young to really [grasp the significance], but I was very upset about it. It means that they considered me dead."[5] In 1949, Jan's (68, D) sister moved out of the apartment they shared when "someone felt it was her duty to inform her" that Jan was a lesbian, and "just absolutely refused to have anything to do with me. She would never allow me to discuss it and it was shortly after that she went into the military to get away from home and get away from me. She could not handle it." Similarly, Tex (72, D) describes the hostile reception he and his lover received from his sister, with whom he had been very close while growing up, and her husband, who left the house when they arrived. The interaction was so hurtful and the rejection so strong that Tex did not know whether the sister was still alive: the close sibling relationship was thus effectively destroyed.

> There might be one sister left, but I'm not sure of that. She met Jim and I and that was a real row. My brother-in-law was even worse, he wouldn't even come home to his own place while we were there. We only spent about an hour there and left. That was the last I seen of her. And it's sad too, because she was the sister I was the closest to when I was growing up. I used to practically live at her house. Sometimes I did.

Finally, those I interviewed described the refusal of family members to recognize the relationships in which homosexual relatives engaged. Marilyn (66, A) explained that "for some of the older gays who are in long-term relationships, one of their concerns is if one of them passes on, how that person's family will treat the [survivor]." She cited "some horrendous stories" she had heard "where they come in and completely take all the possessions and they will not even allow the gay person to be recognized at all."[6] George (75, D), whose lover died of AIDS in the early 1990s, told of having been mistreated by the man's family. Although the lover had made his own funeral arrangements, he had never made a will. Because the deceased left approximately half a million dollars in assets, the lack of a will "ripped the family apart. They even accused me of hiding the will," something George emphasized he "wouldn't do." When I asked George if the family knew that the two had been in love, he said he thought that "they suspected" it.

For many, these threats to person had been a stable feature of their everyday lives, and remained an envisioned consequence of identification as homosexual in public places. Several did not see the sociohistorical changes reformulating homosexuality as having made either public harassment or rejection by intimates less likely. Marge (81, D), for example, told me that it was "still the case" that gay people had to pass as heterosexual to avoid being taunted in public. "You know," she said, "my ex-lover told me last year about someplace she lived, and somebody called her a bull dyke." Maria (64, D) was more direct about the continuing danger to gay men and women: while her generation's vulnerability to attack had waned, it had been passed on to a younger generation of "obvious" homosexuals.

> I don't think it affects us [older gays and lesbians] as much as the younger people. Because at my age, I thought that by now, I should think that by now, after all we went through, things would be a lot better, but they're not. I still read in the paper where they're beating the hell [out] of young people. They don't beat the hell out of us anymore, 'cause we're too old, they figure we'll drop dead anyway. It's the young people that are getting picked on now. I mean, the obvious ones.

Subjects did, however, describe a form of civic denial that had been a dominant feature of their own and others' lives in the pre-Stonewall years but which had since waned: police harassment.

Police Harassment

While some had been protected from this persecution by Mafia ownership of the bars they frequented in the past (as Jeannine [66, D] explained, "Any bars I went to, the Mafia owned and paid off the cops, so we didn't get raided"), others had suffered it almost routinely. Maria spoke of the constant police harassment she suffered throughout her young adulthood; officers would arrest her "almost every weekend" for masquerading, "a law that they had that if you had men's clothes you could get booked for that, that was a misdemeanor," or on the "trumped-up charge" of public drunkenness. She emphasized that the goal of the police was not to maintain public order, but to cause her emotional distress, noting that she was verbally harassed even though she "wasn't bothering anybody." In citing the familiarity with which the police addressed her, Maria invoked their harassment of her as an enduring, long-term relationship of hostility based on the former's commitment to deny Maria her right "to live." Her account echoes aspects of harassment outlined above: being treated as an "open person" and being denied privacy, courtesy, and basic civil rights. When I asked Maria how many times she had been arrested, she said she had "lost count," but figured she had been arrested "almost every weekend, because that was when I was out on the street more, during the week, I was working."

> I was pissed off because I wasn't bothering anybody. I was working my ass off, trying to be productive, and they wouldn't let me live. A lot of times the cops would just tease the hell out of me and harass me and say, "Well, are you a bachelor now, Maria? You're alone tonight," and all that crap. I would just ignore them and keep walking until they told me, "All right. Put her in the back seat."

Being picked up for masquerading was a humiliating experience. Maria described the police making her relinquish her clothes at the jail and change into used women's clothes "that were all in really bad shape, plus nothing fit, everything was either too small or too big."

For many, there had been few, if any, safe spaces in which gay men and women could congregate. Places subject to police raids included private parties: Dan (70, D) was arrested, not by the vice squad, but by policemen who raided a gay party and "arrested everybody for making noise," an overreaction that Dan felt was inspired by the officers seeing "drag queens in the party." Although Dan himself was not in drag, "they threw me in jail overnight. It was like a drunk tank, I slept on the floor. It was horrible. You know, they didn't treat gays too well then." Gay bars were also raided. Brian (74, D), for example, knew of several gay bars, but explained that, until the early 1960s, he and his friends were "kind of fearful" of patronizing them.[7]

Given the presence of undercover vice squad officers who would entrap gay men and women in bars, this was a reasonable fear. In the early 1950s, Sharon (66, A) "was in lots of raids" organized by the vice squad, an experience she described as "horrible." She told of having incited one such raid by tapping the waitress on the shoulder and asking if she had seen a friend of hers. Since Sharon had touched another woman in a gay bar, an undercover vice officer said, " 'Come on, lesbian, let's go,' and arrested me for lewd and lascivious conduct and drunk and disorderly," as well as a dozen other women for the latter charge, and took the arrested women to jail. Once there, but before they were booked, the precinct captain took the women into a separate room and distributed "dirty books" to the women. These books had "pictures of men in the nude having sex, pictures of men and women doing it all kinds of ways, just dirty things." According to Sharon, he then offered to release those women who agreed to perform oral sex on him and the rest of the officers. Sharon convinced the police to release her and an-

other woman by threatening legal action, but a friend of
hers had to pay $125.00 to avoid spending the night. "The
others," she explained, were "held overnight in jail because
they wouldn't go with the guys." When I asked Sharon if the
cops used to rape any of the women, she said, "Oh, I'm sure
they did, I don't remember. That stuff was so prevalent, you
didn't pay attention to it."

Entrapment occurred outside of bars as well, primarily in
public parks. Franz (86, D) described "an unpleasant experience" he had had in 1952 in a park near downtown Los
Angeles. "Somebody was sitting on the bench" and, having
been "warned not to talk to strangers," Franz attempted to
leave, touching the man on the knee and saying, "I have to
go now." The man, who was an undercover vice squad officer, arrested him, and Franz spent two or three weeks in
jail–an experience he described as "horrible"–and suffered
the humiliation of knowing his sister and boss had been "informed." Although found not guilty by a jury, Franz was still
concerned that the charge could "be retroactive after forty
years." Indeed, Val (74, D) described the Los Angeles Police
Department, in which she was one of the first female officers
and from which she retired in 1967, entrapping its own officers. "One of my best friends was kicked off the department,"
after she was found in a motel room with another woman,
even though they had not engaged in sexual relations. Police
officers, staked out in the motel parking lot, had seen the
second woman–an undercover police officer–signal them
through the open drapes.

With the exception of Sharon threatening legal action,
only one other informant spoke of having even considered
approaching the judicial system for protection from the police.[8] The others knew that, as sexual deviants, they were not
only unprotected by the state, but were its central target. As
Val explained, "In those days they didn't ask you shit, they

just fired you. Actually, if anyone wanted to contest them they really could, if they ever had an attorney, but they had you so riled and upset, and you believed what you heard, you didn't know. You didn't have any ACLU, or any of this stuff. Life was very different." Rodney described the liabilities of being identified as homosexual during his youth as too severe for "the younger gays" to even understand; as he put it, "When I was young . . . your livelihood was at stake . . . and they have no idea what it was like in those years because of stigma." He gave the poignant example of his friend Philip, a gay man whose "class ring had been stolen by some semi-hustler types."

I guess he was screaming at them to give him back his ring. Some of them came out of the house and he said, "He's got my ring, he won't [give it back]," and [the man who had stolen the ring] said he was a faggot or something like that and threw the ring at him. And then Philip says to me, "We don't have any civil rights." We had none. This was years ago. He said, "We have no recourse if anything goes wrong, we have no place to turn." And he was essentially right, we didn't have.

Subjects described the momentous impact on their lives of changes in the state's treatment of homosexuals, noting that police harassment of homosexuals had abated, primarily because of legal changes such as the dissolution of masquerading laws and changes in police policy. After telling me the story about Philip, Rodney noted that "things have changed in some measure now [since] Stonewall." Jeannine thought it was "wonderful" that "society's gotten to a point where they don't just clap you in irons if you come out and say that you're gay." Maria, who had, in fact, been clapped in irons over the course of many years, felt that she had "it better now because it's so open, at least they're not throwing me in jail every time they see me," adding that she'd "hate to be going to jail at this age." Constance (74, D) remarked,

> Honey, being so damned old now, I've seen it. I've seen it all, when they didn't like us, and then they started accepting us. It's going to be acceptable more and more as time goes by. Everything has changed for me now that you don't have to worry about the law. I can take care of myself. I mean if you want to talk to me or you want to put me in jail—"Hey, wait a minute!" I can go to the gay community, a gay place, and say, "Hey, I need a lawyer. This and this and this happened." And I know they'll come to my defense. Big change there.

The Scarlet Letter

These incivilities, assaults, denials, and banishments can, of course, overlap, and/or result from a single instance. In the late 1940s, after Tony was beaten by his lover, Hank, his privacy—and his world—began to unravel once the public fight, which was broken up by the police, "got around to the neighborhood"—including, of course, his family. The result was embarrassment for both families, and a downward spiral of gossip, spurious interaction, and open taunting that continued even after Hank "went off upstate."

> He was embarrassed, his family was embarrassed, I guess they figured this was sort of a gay [thing, but] nobody ever came out and said it. My family, I didn't want to embarrass them . . . by being a homosexual. You know, people are very narrow-minded, it was a very narrow-minded group, and at that point the word got around in regard to me. I didn't hear much of it. Every once in a while I'd hear some comment that would be indicative of it. Like this gal, sort of a buddy of mine, was horsing around with everybody [and said,] "Oh, that's Tony, everybody thinks [his parents] had two girls but they had three." I could have kicked ass. These kinds of people were really, really very deep and very hurting. But it was the kind of mind-set you had in those days. And your best

bet was to leave. They offered me [a position] in Philly and I
said, "Yeah, I'll take it." 'Cause I thought that it's about time to
get out.

That being discovered as a homosexual, or tagged with
the scarlet letter, has such far-reaching consequences makes
it resonate in subjects' accounts as the most damaging thing
that can happen and, clearly, as something to be avoided
at any cost. Subjects treated as axiomatic that biographies–
and reputations–unravel as discreditable information is distributed in ever-widening circles. Patricia (77, D), for example, described becoming aware that members of her community were suspicious of her heterosexual claims when
she had still not married in her late twenties: "A lot of people
began to talk about me," she said, "because [they thought]
'She has not married, there must be something wrong.' And
you know how that goes and goes and goes." Rhoda (89, D)
broke up with Betty to protect Betty's "reputation," which
was threatened by Rhoda's ex-lover, who, in the hopes of
breaking the new couple up, had told a mutual heterosexual
acquaintance of the love affair.

> It scared Betty, so she said she couldn't live her life like that–
> people will talk about her reputation and everything. I said,
> "Betty, it's not worth it, I love you and you love me but it's not
> worth it, us going on together and having our home together
> and everything." I didn't want to hurt her reputation. She had
> a marvelous reputation built up.

When I asked Rhoda why she hadn't just denied the al-
legation, she explained that "You don't do that, once they
hear, there's the association and the feeling," adding that she
"was never gay in the community. Very few people know
that I'm gay, because most of the time they didn't understand gay people." In the language of labeling theory, labels
are "sticky," and (as we have seen in Marge's account of the

"old dyke" in her childhood neighborhood) in a heterosexual and heterosexist world, positing homosexuality as a danger designates sexual deviance as a master status–one that
subjects understandably want to avoid, given the dangers it
introduces.

Moreover, a lifetime of incivilities and rejections–immin-
ent and/or actual–can have long-term psychological and
practical consequences. One such consequence, of course,
is the decision to preempt such attacks or treatment by, for
example, passing as heterosexual, or avoiding certain situations or types of person. Some informants explicitly described or evoked the long-term consequences of being
homosexual in a world organized and run by and for heterosexuals. For Ricardo (66, D), "being gay in a heterosexual
world" negatively affected his professional life because his
discomfort with the heterosexual world, and his colleagues'
suspicion of childless men, constructed a "barrier" between
them. He explained that he

> would have been a better professional person if I would have
> been straight. Because my relationships, that feeling that I
> have that I don't belong in their world, has created some sort
> of a *barrier* in my life. I think I should have become a leader, I
> would say my leadership would have been different if I would
> have been openly heterosexual with a family perhaps, kids
> and everything else. Because there was a barrier there and
> that barrier created some sort of suspicion, some sort of a
> negative withdrawal into yourself, and that was possibly a
> negative approach to my life.

Brian described having felt the same distance between himself and his heterosexual co-workers, caused by his disincli-
nation to socialize with them after hours.

> I remember one place I worked, where the guys got together
> and played cards once a week. I didn't want to go to a place
> with a bunch of straight guys. I'd have been bored, I don't care

for the cards, I didn't care about being around them. I mean it was all right at work. So what in the world would I do? I don't know how I got out of it. I had to make [something] up, just said I didn't want to or something. But there was an effect there, I felt. It made me distant from them or something, at work. I know other occasions where they had family things at work. Perhaps a holiday Christmas party, bring the family. That disturbed me. I didn't want to go, so I didn't go. So I'm thinking of things like that.

As Rhoda's story has shown, it is not only strangers, but long-term intimates—even homosexual ones—who can embrace negative stereotypes of homosexuals. Jan's (68, D) account of a particularly painful series of events surrounding her rejection by her long-term lover, Rachel—a rejection brought on by Rachel's conversion to a homophobic religion—shows that homosexuals themselves can adopt antigay attitudes and impose them on homosexual acquaintances, and that heterosexuals' condemnation of homosexuality can reach into the most intimate realms, at the most intimate moment: the death of a long-term lover. Although Rachel "had not been religious at all," she became so religious while staying in the Seventh Day Adventist Hospital after discovering that she had inoperable lung cancer that she told Jan "that she wanted no more of our relationship. Our relationship was finished."

> I guess it was about six months before she died, they let me know that it was over, that at any rate that she had her religion. Now this was a woman that all her life thought of herself as being gay, there was never any question. . . . She was gay through and through, there's just no question about it. But she now felt that it was evil, you know, the whole spiel.

Moreover, because Rachel refused to allow Jan to visit her, Jan only learned about her death through a former colleague. Another painful element was the fact that "there was absolutely no closure with Rachel because when she died and they had a memorial service, her brother-in-law finally called me and invited me to the memorial service and I didn't go to it. I just couldn't handle it, it was at White Memorial Chapel [the same chapel that turned Rachel against her]. That was one of the most painful things." Even more painful was the fact that their mutual friends assumed that Jan had abandoned Rachel because of Rachel's terminal cancer–a rumor that was circulated by a woman who had always been jealous of Jan's relationship with Rachel. As a result, Jan lost not only her lover of many years, but her entire lesbian social circle, and it took her years to build another one.

Of all my informants, Maria was the most vocal about the consequences of her lesbianism on her life–specifically, the long-term financial and psychological effects of the harassment she suffered from the police, from passersby, and from co-workers. The fact that she had a long history of arrests, for instance, meant that when she bought a bar in 1953, at the age of twenty-one, she could not get a liquor license in her own name. After her lover, who co-owned the bar, got a liquor license in her name, the relationship soured, and the lover stole all the money from the sale of the bar, leaving Maria penniless and homeless. Employment was almost impossible to secure, and when she managed to do so,

> I had to work extra hard, harder than the next guy, harder than anybody else, just to keep my job. Why? Because I was a lesbian. I worked a long time for a factory, it was a glue factory. I knew how to do everything in that place, and I learned it purposely because every now and then there were layoffs and if you know how to do everything, you don't get laid off. And they were always threatening me, like, "This will be your last chance." I wouldn't ask any [questions], I knew why.

Maria was also harassed and physically threatened on the job–indeed, was even accused of molesting a female co-worker because, she said, the co-worker's fiancé was threatened by her lesbianism. Although she knew that "stuff like that" was designed "to keep me off balance," she admitted not knowing "what their kick was. I really don't understand why people would pick on another person like that, when all you want to do is work." While her response to this chronic harassment was "just get in there to work my ass off, just out of anger," she was hampered by the long-term effects of "those two things, that general harassment and the fact that I could never get ahead no place because I was such an obvious lesbian, no matter where I went the other guy had the better deal, whether they were smarter or not." Maria links her currently precarious financial state, and the depression that partially results from it, to her limited career opportunities. In her words, "I began to lose my self-esteem, I didn't think I deserved any better."

"You Can't Have It Both Ways": Threats to Self

While respondents were unanimous in their characterization of heterosexuals as prone to the type of treatment outlined above, only members of the discreditable identity cohort saw this as the sole threat they faced. In keeping with gay liberation's emphasis on homosexuality as an essential, political identity that should be proclaimed rather than hidden, accredited subjects saw a more insidious moral threat to self lurking beneath this more "obvious" one. Although they appreciated the potentially dangerous and painful consequences of disclosure or recognition, these subjects strongly condemned passing–a practice that, while ensuring continuous relations with heterosexuals, constituted a suppression of the authentic self. Specifically, for these subjects, heterosexuals threatened to seduce the homosexual into a life of duplicity in exchange for protection from heterosexual punishment. By treating one's homosexuality as an aspect of self to be enacted in secret, homosexuals were cooperating with the self-styled enemy in an ultimately self-destructive process of denying the authentic self, and the threat to person paled in comparison to the moral threat posed by coercion into an inauthentic life.

When talking about managing their homosexuality, accredited subjects stressed that revealing the "self" was essential to respecting and embodying it authentically. As we saw in Chapter 3, some likened homosexuality to race, an essentialist artifact of both 1960s identity politics in general and early gay liberationist constructions in particular (see Chapter 1), variously underscoring both its vast implications for the actor's life and the futility of denying them. When I asked Abby (70, A) how being gay had affected her life, she explained that, just as race cannot be seen as an independent variable affecting one's life, neither can homosexuality, since both constitute "who you are."

> That's almost like asking an African-American, "How has being black affected your life?" It's part of their life. They think it's a separate entity, that it is, quote, a lifestyle, unquote, and it is not. It's who you are.

In this context, passing becomes both a denial of the essential, authentic self–rather than a management of an aspect of self–and damaging to relationships. Accredited subjects equated the failure to present the authentic (homosexual) self to others with presenting an inauthentic one; relationships based on passing are thus based on a "lie" and are both weakened and insulted. As Tex explained,

> It just irks me because these people aren't being honest with themselves. I think if you are or believe in one way, and you project a belief or an idea of what you are contrary to that, then you're not being honest with yourself or them, because

you do have to interact with other people. I mean, you can't have it both ways.

Similarly, Mary (66, A) posited coming out to others as contingent upon "acceptance of self" and as essential to being "the best people they can be"–clearly a critical step in the achievement of homosexual and personal authenticity. In her words, "most people need to accept themselves and come out of the closet and be the best people that they can be and get away from so much of the self-destructive stuff." Finally, for Marilyn (66, A), while passing is understandable, the cost is a diminution of self-hood–an inability to "be completely" self. As she explained, "If I have a straight friend I can enjoy their presence in going out and being social but I wouldn't be completely *me* if I'm not out to that person." In fact, Marilyn gauges how close she is to others by whether she has come out to them; her cousin, to whom she came out, is "almost like a sister to me," while her relationship with her biological sister is not as strong:

> I enjoy my sister and we talk at least once a month. She lives in Louisville, Kentucky, and we see each other about every three or four years. But if you're asking me *close*, I'm not out to her, I don't tell her my personal problems. I tell her about problems with the apartment and other things. But she's not somebody I would go to with relationship problems.

* * *

For all subjects, regardless of identity cohort membership, the threat they faced was both ubiquitous (embedded in the deep structure of society) and situated and idiosyncratic (embodied by individual people with distinctive relationships to self and others). Whatever the nature of the conflict, then, subjects' accounts depict homosexuals as needing to maintain a constant vigilance against "the" threat, and needing survival strategies that succeed in both the public and the private realms. Moreover, despite differences in identity career, the basic understanding of the world–specifically, that it is organized around the condemnation and punishment of homosexuality–endures. Attempts by heterosexuals, including intimates, to repress and punish homosexuality and those who engage in it, while ultimately futile, are nonetheless both real and immediate. Heterosexuals, driven by a misunderstanding of homosexuals as predatory and/or by their own sexual insecurity, attack homosexuals as a constituent feature of their own work to construct themselves as morally (and heterosexually) competent. However, this perceived threat to person is elaborated and reframed by members of the accredited identity cohort, who envision a more insidious and dangerous threat to self lurking beneath and potentiated by the threats to person described above. This is the threat of accepting heterosexual society's offer of protection from threats to person in exchange for passing–and passing, according to gay liberationist tenets, entails accepting and treating one's homosexuality as a stigma and failing to disclose and thus to honor the essential self.

Clearly, the worlds my respondents construct vary according to identity cohort membership. While members of the discreditable identity cohort see themselves as inhabiting a world poised to punish them for failing or refusing to pass, members of the accredited identity cohort see themselves as inhabiting a world eager to encourage the denial of an essential homosexual self. Moreover, in the course of assessing the implications of homosexuality for self, subjects produce different orders of person whose basic parameters are potentiated by distinctive discourses of homosexuality. For example, while discreditable subjects see heterosexuals as oppressors, the accredited see them as both oppressors and moral seducers offering a Faustian bargain: a suppression of the authentic self in exchange for protection from

Table 6:   Expanded Discourses of Homosexuality

	Homosexuality as Stigma	Homosexuality as Status
Relation to self	aspect	essential
Implications for self	discreditable	accrediting
Appropriately enacted in	private	public and private
Heterosexual threat	to person	to person and to self
Relation of heterosexuals to self	oppressor	oppressor and moral seducer

physical and social harm. This new category of heterosexual–that of moral seducer–was potentiated by gay liberation. These findings complicate our previous understanding of the discourses of homosexuality through which subjects identify as homosexual; Table 6 summarizes the discursive properties we have seen subjects use and invoke thus far.

5

Homosexual Competence and Relations with Heterosexuals

I'm not out because I am a very conservative person and I would prefer to carry on in life as a quote normal person. I've never been out. So far as being out, it's not just specific to [the nursing home]. I just would like to carry on the persona of–I don't like that word exactly, but normal person in terms of the eyes of the way society defines normal. –Rodney, 75, D

I've always hid it. But you know, we can't go up and apply for a job and say, "I'm homosexual." So it's affected my life I suppose in that way. I do try to hide it for that purpose. –George, 75, D

I was constantly in jeopardy most of my life, and this is one reason why I am not out, and I am not about to even come out today to a lot of people. –Val, 74, D

The Technicalities of Passing

To state what we can now treat as a given, members of the discreditable identity cohort held the commitment to passing among heterosexuals while enjoying homosexual relations as the most central project of their identity careers. This is significantly different from distancing the self from one's homosexuality, which we saw in Chapter 2. Here, the goal is not to avoid enacting homosexuality, but to enact it in particular ways–that is, to pass with heterosexuals and to associate with homosexuals as a homosexual.

This goal is seen as obvious and logical. In the accounts cited below, holding to basic orientations necessarily and logically leads to particular types of actions and evaluations, although these actions are situated and malleable. The homosexual who understands the way things are and does not want to incur any one of a range of damages can and will set passing as heterosexual as a lifelong goal and will develop passing techniques of his or her own. Thus, while passing is made easier through access to closely guarded secrets or even to cultural capital, it requires (and can be achieved through the use of) a basic, "correct" understanding of the world on the one hand and the instinct to survive in it on the other. Given this, however, subjects described four basic passing devices: concealing, covering, managing the movement between regions (all of which I outline below), and managing associations (which I deal with in Chapter 6).

Subjects spoke of *concealing* evidence of their homosexuality by achieving appearances consonant with prevailing gender norms. The particular norms they worked to manage, however, varied on the basis of their sex. Female subjects described a tension between their desire to wear pants and their awareness of this dress as a discreditable characteristic–a tension resolved by wearing pants only in homosexual contexts and not in heterosexual ones. In the 1950s and early 1960s, for example, Abby "would wear slacks down in the Village, but I would never wear slacks in mid-town Manhattan. It just wasn't the thing to do." In contrast, male subjects spoke of suppressing their tendency to use gestures or mannerisms associated with women. When George (75, D) was in his early teens, he "realized" that he had developed "the habit" of holding his hands in a stereotypically

feminine way, which he defined by turning his hands palm-
down and making his wrists limp. While this was a difficult
habit to break, he "started hiding it, and I got to be very good
at it: watching my hands. Not doing this." He later developed
a "butch attitude at work," presenting a masculine persona
by talking about sports, in which he had no real interest:
" 'How are the Tigers doing today? Who's pitching?' I didn't
have the slightest idea. I didn't even care. It's a butch thing I'd
be interested in." Julius (89, D) spoke of being made aware
of–and cautioned against–having "certain types of characteristics" by the young teens that would congregate around
him when he was in his twenties.

> Kids always liked me, and two or three of them would be
> walking down the street with me and they would say, "Julius,
> take longer steps," and these would be kids that were twelve,
> thirteen years old. And one of them would say, "Julius, be
> careful, you use your hands quite a bit, you should not do
> that." I think that they sensed that I was gay, but they didn't
> want me to show it. It made a lot of changes with me, be-
> cause I took it seriously when they would say these things. At
> the moment it wasn't serious, but later you think about it, you
> think about these things. So I learned to take longer steps.

Subjects also described *covering* their homosexuality,
using preemptive and/or restorative strategies. *Preemptive*
strategies involved constructing heterosexual biographies
that prevented others from interpreting their actions (or lack
thereof) as homosexual. This included discursively reformulating actual homosexual relations into heterosexual
ones. George spoke of changing the sex of friends or lovers
in order to give these relations a heterosexual cast.

> I'm always talking about women. Juan's always standing out
> there, looking for me. He says, "What are you waiting for?"
> "I got a girl I know coming to visit." I'm talking about some
> boys in my past: it's a girl. I cheat. Even over at the pool, I'll

tell them, "Oh, I had a girlfriend over this afternoon, that's why I didn't show up on Thursday."

Another preemptive strategy was to change the nature of their relations with members of the opposite sex. Male subjects turned female friends into "girlfriends." Brian (74, D) told me that he called his "little old lady friend" his girlfriend during conversation with heterosexuals, a device he explained "makes them reverse things around a bit." Similarly, Dan (70, A) noted the practice of reformulating romantic relations into those resonant with the heterosexual family: "If you're a lesbian, you're always living with your cousin. If you're a gay man, you're living with your nephew or cousin." Yet another was to engage actively in relations that were heterosexual in form, if not intent. This distinguished these practices from those designed to achieve a liminal heterosexuality that were described in Chapter 1. Here, subjects emphasized that they engaged in heterosexual relations not to distance themselves from their homosexuality, but to embrace it, pursuing homosexual relations in relative safety by passing as heterosexual. Barbie (67, D) described taking gay men to faculty parties as dates and attending business events with them to "put on a front." Rhoda (89, D) spoke of having double-dated to construct a heterosexual image in high school, then spending the night with her lover once the evening had ended.

Furthermore, family and other pressures caused some subjects (two male and two female) to pursue marriages of convenience,[1] marrying, with two exceptions, other homosexuals to, as George put it, "continue the deception of being straight, to please the family." In 1933, at the age of nineteen, Marge (81, D) married a heterosexual man who lived in New York to make it appear that it was the marriage that accounted for her move there, when in actuality it was her desire to be near her New York-based female lover. As Patricia did in Chapter 4, several informants described sensing that their "unmarried status" became increasingly damaging to their projected heterosexual image as they approached or entered their thirties. As Michael (78, D) put it, "The minute you turn over thirty and you aren't married, they have some suspicion, except for my idiot third cousins in Wisconsin, who at my age of seventy-eight have said you still haven't found the right girl." George emphasized that the pressure from his family was not explicit–they were not, he explained, "particularly riding me"–but more subtle, consisting of statements about other family members his age who had gotten married.

> I'd get, "Your cousin Danny is married already. Your cousin Alex is married already." They never said, "What's wrong with you?" They said, "They're married." So that was it. And two girls that lived upstairs, [one] wanted to get married to me for the same reason I wanted to get married. They were both lesbians.

Brian (74, D) used almost identical language in describing his marriage to a lesbian in the early 1950s, when he was twenty-nine. He stressed that "they weren't pressuring me," but that "the rest of the family was married, and all my friends back [home] were married. I just decided, here I was, twenty-nine, and never had been married. It wouldn't matter if I'd been married and divorced." The pressure he felt to marry came not from "any particular thing," but from "the whole thing in general"–expectations from family and work. "At work," Brian explained, "people were married, people had families, [and] there was that uneasiness." Given the goal–to pass as heterosexual at home and at work–the marriage was a success for both parties: "I must say that this did certainly work, I thought for me, in my mind, and for her too."

When I got married, then it got in the newspaper back home that I was married. It didn't matter what happened after that. If all my high school friends and everybody saw that, fine. And the same thing for her, out here. I think I would say this, it would look more normal to have been married to a woman. . . . So the whole thing worked out in that I was not going to go through life never having been married. I've been married and divorced. That was of use to me, like at work– "Oh, he's divorced," or in my hometown. Everything, I felt, it was very useful.

While they exhibited a strong allegiance to the need to pass as heterosexual to heterosexuals, however, these informants saw passing in the context of marriages of convenience as potentially problematic. On the one hand, passing was essential to social, even physical survival; on the other hand, passing was morally acceptable only if it deceived those who posed the threats outlined in Chapter 4 without harming those who did not. Consequently, subjects saw passing in front of a fiancée/fiancé or spouse–presenting a homosexual front while secretly engaging in homosexual associations–as (mis)using the genuine intimate affections of another to achieve purely personal ends, and damaging to the unknowing spouse as well. Ryan (81, D) spoke of his church social club as a meeting place for two sets of actors with distinctive yet complementary marital agendas. These were passing gay men, for whom the trappings of heterosexuality were essential for advancement, and "old maids that were left out and would marry anybody."

It was just one of those things, but it was better than nothing. I guess the girls knew they had to marry somebody. They'd marry the gay guys and the gay guys felt that if they got married nobody would know they were gay. A lot of them were in jobs that they weren't advancing [in], and once they got married then they started going up the ladder, they came out all right.

The wives in these sham marriages, however, did not come out all right—on the contrary, many suffered from the marriages, as did one "sweet girl" who married an obviously gay man. After "they had two children, she just got big, fat like that," the result of "obvious nerves. But—it worked out, but . . ." Thus, while the marriages worked out for the gay men, they did so at the expense of the women, and constituted unequal, even parasitic, and thus unethical relationships.

Those who had engaged in marriages of convenience contrasted these damaging because unequal relationships with marriages of convenience in which both parties accepted the homosexuality of one or both spouses and understood the marriage to be designed to fulfill practical, rather than sexual or romantic, needs. An example is Constance's (74, D) account of her marriage to a merchant seaman who accepted the fact that she was a lesbian, that the marriage was purely nominal, and that she would not provide him with conjugal rights. Constance emphasized that both parties benefited from the marriage: it provided her with a much-needed cover (she had just been arrested for sodomy), and her husband with "a place to come home to" whenever he returned from sea.

> When I was in San Francisco I got married to a merchant seaman. He was never home, he'd take off and maybe stay two years, three years out at sea. But we were married in name only. And the reason I got married was because I got caught with this woman. Threw the book at us. This was in the 1960s. So I says, "Oh, bullshit." So when he came in he asked me if I'd marry him. I says, "All right, but I'm gonna tell you something, we're gonna get married and I'll get married in name only." I said, "That's all."

Others emphasized that they had married homosexuals who benefited from the arrangement as well. Lillian (69, D) specified that, in the 1960s, she and "a gay boy" married out of a mutual need to pass (a claim made by George and Brian as well)–he in front of his business associates, she in front of her mother. The marriage was therefore conducted out of both self-interest and mutual concern.

By making these distinctions, informants displayed a concern with the moral consequences of passing, and constructed and invoked moral standards according to which homosexuals can and should pass. Marriages of convenience were considered acceptable only if they were consensual, honest, and useful from the perspective of the married couple, and helped the homosexual party or parties pass. The dishonesty of passing is seen as morally justifiable only if essential to protecting the self from the heterosexual threat.

Restorative covering practices were repair strategies designed to protect the self from the immediate threat of suspicion brought on by the "leaking" of homosexual indicators or by the emergence of situations that questioned the subjects' sexual identity–in Lillian's words, to get them "off the hook." These situations sometimes emerged when heterosexuals intruded into homosexual space. Val (74, D) recalled meeting a fellow police officer at a gay bar in her neighborhood in the 1960s and thinking, "How do I explain this?" When the man phoned her at home and asked what she had been "doing at a place like that," she asked him the same question, only to be told that he and his partner "were about to make a bust." Val provided the man with the following account:

> I said, "I live not far from here, and my friends that I worked with at North America were coming up to visit, and to see what goes on on the other side. I said I would join them." "Well, you were dancing with girls!" "Well, it's all the same group, and that's what you do in a place like that, what else do you do in a place like that?" So he said, "Forget it."

Some informants described having been put on the hook when, despite the care they had taken to pass, they had been questioned about their sexual identity. Because of the danger of these suspicions, they responded quickly to shore up their threatened image, providing vague responses to direct questions about their own sexuality or reframing the question as "ridiculous," as Lillian did when business associates asked if she was gay:

> Someone would say, "Oh, you're not married, you don't have children—are you gay?" I would laugh! I would say, "Oh, don't be ridiculous!" I wouldn't get defensive—"Oh, it's none of your business"—because I didn't want to really put myself in that position. So there was always a pat answer I had, I don't remember what, but it was enough to get me off the hook. And that's all I was interested in.[2]

Others responded to such questions by shifting the source of their apparent failing away from sexual terrain and onto more neutral ground.[3] When people asked why he had not married, Franz (86, D) would tell them it was because he was "too choosy"—situatedly depicting himself as not only a heterosexual, but as one with high standards.

> My family and everyone else, it's two and two is four: eighty-six and never got married. So people ask me, "How come you didn't get married?" I say, "Because when I came to this country I was forty, and then I was already too choosy."

Similarly, in the late 1950s, George (75, D) covered for his sexual interaction with a young man by presenting the time they spent together at George's home in a nonsexual light. At an after-work party, the young man had "a little bit too much to drink" and propositioned George. After they had sex at George's house, George dropped the man off at work. When the man's mother asked George why he had taken him to his own home, he explained that he wanted to shield her son's drunkenness from her. This replaced her nascent understanding of George as a (predatory) homosexual, and of her son as a victim, with an image of him as a concerned protector of a transgressing child.

> His mother called me up and she was, "You took my son home?" She was mad. She said, "Why did you do that?" I said, "Because he was too drunk to go home." That changed things. Instead of attacking me, she was going to attack *him.* So nothing was said about it.

But while these covering and concealing practices took place in direct interaction with heterosexuals, they did little to cover observed interactions with other homosexuals. Subjects described the need to engage in discreditable activity—specifically, to associate with other homosexuals—without in fact being discredited. This presented two problems: entering and exiting gay spaces without being seen, and passing as heterosexual while in the company of other homosexuals who can discredit each other by association. I deal with the latter problem later in the chapter. For now, I'll concentrate on the problem of managing *the movement between regions* in which subjects passed as heterosexual and those in which they could safely associate with other gay men or lesbians—areas Goffman (1963, p. 81) termed "back places, where persons of the actor's kind stand exposed and find that they need not try to conceal their stigma, nor be overly concerned with cooperatively trying to disattend it."

Before the advent of gay liberation, these places were limited: homosexuals could count on meeting each other in parks and other cruising areas, in bars, or at private parties. Parks were particularly dangerous, because, as we've seen in Franz's case in Chapter 4, undercover vice squad officers often entrapped gay men. Despite being subject to raids, bars offered one of the only meeting places for gay men and lesbians, and were patronized by a large number of subjects during their youth and middle age. But even in bars, homosexuals could be seen and discredited, not just by police and vice squad officers, but by heterosexual "tourists": many "gay bars" were merely sections of a larger bar or restaurant, providing heterosexuals with an open view of those on the "homosexual" side. Others had semi-transparent divisions, which, while somewhat obscuring the view of those on the "gay side," did little to obscure the sight of those entering it.[4] Abby (70, A) spoke of working to make sure that no heterosexual acquaintances saw her entering homosexual space in New York in the 1950s and early 1960s.

> It was an outlaw society in those days. You slunk around, you checked out before you walked into a place to see if there was anybody that you could *possibly* know, that would see you going into any of these places.

In response to these dangers, many respondents avoided gay bars completely, constructing safer back places in their own and others' homes. Barbie (67, D), a retired teacher, describes socializing with homosexuals at private houses and parties rather than bars "in case you got caught, somebody from the school board might have their policeman out or something, trailing you." Informants noted, however, that the relative safety of these private homes was deceptive, since being seen moving from "civil" to "back" places was itself discrediting. While Val "could"–and did–"dress the way I wanted" (in men's clothes) at a friend's house, "nowhere else could I dress that way, nor could I travel back and forth that way."

While these techniques (concealing, covering, and managing the movement between regions) required distinctive skills, they also required a *sensitivity to context*–specifically, an ability to distinguish between contexts in which it is safe to exhibit one's homosexuality and those in which it is not. George explained that "if I was living in an area in San Francisco, or over in West Hollywood," rather than in a trailer park away from the city, he would not have to change the sex of people in conversation as "protection." Marge (81, D) distinguished between her life in New York, where homosexuality was relatively accepted, and her life in Los Angeles. In New York, where "nobody cared" if people were homosexual, she "didn't hide it." When she moved to Los Angeles, however, she kept her homosexuality hidden because heterosexuals, particularly those who were driven by antihomosexual religious beliefs, "could be mean and evil, especially when it comes to something like that." She noted that her neighbors' children were equally prone to this, constructing this threat as enduring across generations and therefore as immediate now as it was in the past. By passing in threatening contexts and not in others, Marge produced herself as sensitive to the situational nature of identity management: specifically, to the greater degree of openness allowed for by one context than by another.[5]

These techniques, then, needed to be situatedly deployed. They also needed to be used in various combinations and in various ways, depending upon the context. Abby changed from her "work clothes" to clothes more appropriate for the gay subculture–slacks–at a friend's home, and then changed back into heterosexually approved garb to return home. On Saturday nights, Sharon (66, A) packed her "men's outfit, men's suit and all" in a suitcase, and took the bus to a "mixed gay and lesbian and straight cocktail lounge," where she would change, then "go out and have a good time with the gay guys." Concealing and covering their homosexuality, managing the movement between regions, and being sensitive to context enabled these subjects to travel safely through heterosexual space. How subjects managed to be identifiable as homosexual to homosexuals, without being identifiable as such to heterosexuals, however, was more problematic, as we will see later in this chapter.

Upping the Ante: Surpassing the Glass Ceiling

Appropriately used, passing techniques can do more than protect the self from discrediting. As we have seen in the statements made by George and Val, they can produce the actor not only as a heterosexual person, but as one of exceptional character and merit. These accounts posited passing as a way to move beyond merely *surviving* in the dominant heterosexual culture by precluding homosexuality's negative consequences to *succeeding* in it by meeting extrasexual standards and criteria.[6] The account Val provided upon being seen at a gay bar, for example, produced her not just as a heterosexual, but as a sophisticated and hospitable one. She viewed homosexuals as deviants inhabiting "the other side," and treated this division as so significant, and the deviance of homosexuals so worthy of note, that its enactment constituted a legitimate stop on a sight-seeing tour, on which she was willing to take her friends. Patricia (77, D), citing her exemplary passing practices, described having so thoroughly assured heterosexuals of her own heterosexuality that they allowed their children to attend parties with her. Again, this constructed passing not just as a way to survive, but as a way to climb the social ladder: by acting as a seal of approval, passing led heterosexuals to reframe her from a danger to their children (read: homosexual) to their protector (read: heterosexual). Although "a lot of people" in her neighborhood suspected that there was something wrong with her because she was unmarried,

> when there was going to be a real good party someplace or a big dance and the young girls all wanted to go and their

parents wouldn't let them go: "Ah, Mama, let me go, Patricia is going to be there." "Oh well, if she is going to be there, then okay."

Patricia's account produced her as having usurped what was becoming a real threat to her social status and having passed so successfully that she actually improved it. But she also produced a moral story based on the positive resolution of the conflict between natural urges and long-term survival. Elsewhere, she framed her passing as an effort. She "never enjoyed anything so much as" attending private homosexual gatherings where she could safely forego achieving heterosexual appearances. This clarification highlights the conflict between her natural propinquity toward the gay subculture and her desire to pass. By framing her passing as a success story, however, she cast both her efforts on passing and her time away from her own "private" world as well spent. Moreover, by basing her ability to pass on diplomatic and semiotic skills, she presented passing as a skillful and valid way to achieve a safe balance between the homosexual and the heterosexual worlds.

To sum up: in these accounts, successful passing requires the effective deployment of basic techniques (concealing, covering, and managing the movement between regions), usually in combinations fashioned in response to situated demands. By passing, the homosexual can engage in homosexual relations and associations and remain merely discreditable, rather than become discredited–indeed, even enjoy the social status reserved for heterosexuals. These accounts are thus more than descriptions of the benefits of passing as heterosexual and the perils of being recognized as homosexual. Rather, they are *prescriptions* for the successful management of information about homosexuality. These prescriptions foreground the distinction between those who follow the prescribed path and techniques and those who do not. Immanent, and often explicit, in these accounts is the possibility for homosexual others to have their own successes or failures–to achieve homosexual competence by mastering the skills subjects had honed, or to become homosexually incompetent by failing or refusing to do so. Subjects treated these successes and failures as both accountable matters (realizing passing not just as an essential feature of homosexual competence, but as a standard against which other homosexuals can and should be judged) and matters of practical importance–indeed, as we will see, they saw others' sexual information management as implicating and affecting their own ability to pass. Because incompetent homosexuals made them more identifiable as homosexuals and thus more vulnerable to the threat of attack and/or rejection, these incompetents constituted a threat of their own. Informants described various homosexually incompetent "types" whose incompetence centered on the disclosure of their homosexuality, specifically, on their mistaken or motivated transmission of private, discrediting information to heterosexuals. These types are those who exhibited their homosexuality, those who "flaunted" it, and those who declared it.

Passing, Disclosure, and Their Discontents: The Prescriptive Nature of Information Management

Stigmatized Constructions

Exhibiting and flaunting are two extreme forms of the same act: making one's homosexuality visually evident by displaying signs and mannerisms recognizable by all as evidence of homosexuality. Members of the discreditable identity cohort condemned the former type for knowingly exposing themselves to harassment by *exhibiting* their homosexuality to an array of anonymous others, a practice that was often described in visual terms. Lillian (69, D) invoked the image of persons publicly and visually marking themselves with a sign when she characterized herself as having "always been very closeted about my lifestyle." She defined closeted as being unwilling "to announce my sexuality to the world" and thus as being committed to "not wearing a sign on my back." Because her sexuality was "my business, it's none of your business," she did not "go walking around and telling who I am and what I am." Ryan evoked a similar image when he described how his gay church group does and does not advertise its existence. While the group is mentioned in the church bulletin, members do not "wear badges or anything"–in short, do not publicly mark themselves as homosexuals, a practice that would publicly express an essentially "private" matter. In making this distinction, Ryan cites an aspect of homosexual incompetence ("wearing badges") to underscore the correct way of making a homosexual group's existence known: advertising the group, not its individual members. "It comes out on our bulletin: gay and lesbian support group. And we don't wear badges or anything like that but we don't hide either. It's all wide open."

Often, those who exhibited their homosexuality were described as doing so by failing or refusing to achieve gender-appropriate appearances, a deficit that made them vulnerable to the kind of attacks described in Chapter 4. Rhoda (89, D) spoke of encountering "some people, the butch people especially," in Kansas City bars in the 1930s and 1940s, whose open display of homosexuality, knowingly engaged in despite the "ridicule" they "endured," signified them as stupid. "It was so stupid of them," she said, "because the majority of the society didn't accept it, especially the ones that were butch looking. It might be what they wanted and yet–they would want it and be that way and endure the ridicule."

Discreditable subjects condemned *flaunting* (in Goffman's 1963, pp. 107–108 words, "flamboyantly or pitifully acting out the negative attributes imputed to" the stigmatized group of which he or she is a member), which they considered an especially onerous form of homosexual incompetence that was damaging to all homosexuals, including themselves. Goffman (1963, p. 110) notes that a central tenet of the stigma doctrine through which the actor comes to understand her or his stigma is an obligation to avoid and condemn "'minstrelization,' whereby the stigmatized person ingratiatingly acts out before normals the full dance of bad qualifiers imputed to his kind, thereby consolidating a life situation into a clownish role."[7] In addition to being the knowledgeable and motivated invitation to negative treatment that all declarations make, flaunting is a public presentation of homosexuality as a public affair that others are obligated to see.

Patricia (77, D) saw flaunting as both unnecessary and self-destructive. First, it ignores the more appropriate way of making one's homosexuality known: to wait until someone asks you (in her words, "we don't have to flaunt it. It's all right if somebody should ask me: 'Yes, I'm gay.' But I haven't flaunted it."). Second, it makes heterosexuals' acceptance of homosexuals less likely. She explained that should homosexuals feel the need to assemble and march en masse, they should do so while dressing "normally," as "ladies and gentlemen." Thus it is not the public assembly to which she objects, but the public display of stereotyped homosexual behaviors.

> Some of them go around and push their lesbianism or their homosexuality down everybody's throat. When you have your gay parades and the men grab their balls and say, "Hey, hey,

we're gay!"–I don't feel that that's necessary. If they could only learn to be gentlemen and ladies people would accept us much more easily. They can go do their parades and dress up normally. What we do behind closed doors is up to us, we don't have to flaunt it.

Patricia noted that flaunting poses a danger to all homosexuals seeking acceptance by heterosexuals, since only appropriately restrained behavior will encourage the acceptance of homosexuals as a group. The motivated public display of the most negative, "extreme" aspects of homosexuality becomes an image bound to be taken by the designed mass audience as typical of all homosexuals–herself included. This was echoed by other subjects as well. Gabrielle (77, D) declared that she and her lover "don't go to any gay things, gay parades" because "the media picks out the worst" images to transmit. Rodney (75, D) explained that "I don't like to see a lot of the [actions] of some of the gay guys and I'm not too keen on dykes on bikes. I think these are the extremes, I think they give the whole community a bad name." Similarly, Julius (89, D) claimed that gay men and women would not achieve integration and civil rights with "the parades and marching" that tend to lead young people to associate homosexuals with "transvestites or floozies" rather than with the larger, more legitimate group of "straight gay people" with which he identifies.

Henri (67, D) also identified with this larger group, noting that its members' declination to exhibit identifiably and typically "gay traits" makes them "invisible"–so invisible, in fact, that their numbers are unknown, even by the group's own members. "The only ones that are very visible," he said, "are the ones who are very gay and flimsy and all that. So I always wonder how much of the gay population is invisible, but I am sure it is a larger percent of it." Henri found the increasing openness of the lesbian and gay community to be unbalanced, "because all the open people are the ones that shouldn't be open, and all the ones that should be open are not." When I asked him which homosexuals should be open, he pointed to "a lot of prominent gays that are not very open, or are not open at all." When I countered that many prominent gays, such as Martina Navratilova and David Geffen, were, in fact, open about their homosexuality, he said that there were "not enough," and that "a lot of these people, like Martina, it's very hard for them not to be open because they can't pull it off the other way." In short, celebrities who were open about their homosexuality were merely acquiescing to their gender nonconformity, and had disclosed their homosexuality to the public because they would have been recognized as homosexual anyway. The resultant imbalance between the public image and the private reality of homosexuality was, to Henri's mind, "terrible, and I don't blame the ones who are not open, because I feel the same way"–that being "open" about one's homosexuality was to be open to negative imputations driven by incompetent homosexuals' domination of public opinion about all gay men and women.

While several members of the discreditable identity cohort spoke with distaste of people who flaunted their homosexuality, virtually all distinguished themselves from the incompetents and incompetencies attendant on failing to pass most clearly and adamantly when they discussed the practice of coming out, which they defined as *declaring* one's homosexuality to everybody, including heterosexuals. They contrasted this with the definition of coming out that prevailed before gay liberation, during the era in which they had identified as homosexual. Subjects explained that in their day, coming out meant entering homosexual life and engaging in homosexual relations and associations, practices of which they approved and in which they had engaged. (For more definitions, see this book's concluding chapter.) The equation of coming out with an unnecessary and unsolicited declaration to a group of heterosexuals was a central theme in discreditable subjects' talk and figured in Ryan's (81, D) presentation of a typical coming out scenario–a child's declaration of homosexuality to his family, usually at a large and public family gathering. He emphasized that the chance that the family will be accepting is slim, and that most families banish the voluntarily discredited.

> They come out to their family–sit at the table, big dinner, big entertainment, something like that, and they'd say, "I've got something I want to tell you and I want to tell everybody at once: I'm *gay*." And some of the family would say, "What does that mean?" and they'd have to tell them the truth and that's the way it would be. And some of them would explode and kick him out and disown him and others say, "Well, if you are, you're still our son and we'll accept you" and things are fine. But it was seldom that that had worked out that way.

To these informants, that actors would voluntarily subject themselves to rejection or banishment was evidence of their ignorance of or blatant disregard for the consequences of being discredited. Lillian (69, D), who considers sexual identity a "very private" matter, described being "astounded" by "these kids who tell their bosses they're gay and then in the next breath they wonder why they're fired." They are fired, she explained, "because this society, this era that we live in, is not ready to accept homosexuality as a lifestyle. It's coming a little better," she said, but will never be accepted "in my lifetime." Lillian displays an understanding of coming out as a self-destructive and quixotic declaration rendering the individual vulnerable to the negative reactions of homosexuals and heterosexuals alike. Her astonishment over younger homosexuals' inability to foresee the negative consequences of their immoderate, self-destructive, and incompetent declarations displays her understanding of her own management practices as cautious and self-protective.

Franz (86, D) explained that his homosexuality did not affect his life because his success in keeping it hidden from heterosexuals precluded negative responses on their part to it:

> It didn't affect my life so far because what my business concerns I achieved what I wanted, being gay or not being gay. It has nothing to do with being gay, because I never put it on the platter and told them, "Here, I'm gay!" So how should it affect me, it *didn't* affect me.

Franz produced himself as having mastered the key components of homosexual competence, glossing a range of passing devices into the commitment to refrain from making his homosexuality obvious, intrusive, or a topic of discussion.[8] Franz and others condemned the formal presentation of the homosexual self to heterosexuals as naive, self-destructive, and unnecessary, and the negative consequences of such a declaration to be foreseeable and, of course, avoidable by passing. That his homosexuality never affected him because it never affected his work career is treated as the ultimate sign of having successfully managed his homosexuality. In contrasting themselves with these declarations, Franz and other members of this identity cohort produced themselves as competent social actors aware of and responsive to their environment.

As we will see, these respondents saw both exhibiting and flaunting as constituting a threat to their own investment in passing: the former publicized the existence of homosexuals who would not otherwise be recognizable as such, thus expanding the semiotic competence of heterosexuals, and the latter reproduced heterosexuals' sense of homosexuals as driven by their sexual desires and unrestrained in their pursuit of them, a belief echoed by accredited informants. How, if at all, homosexuals' disclosure of their sexual identities presented a threat to their own impression management, however, only becomes clear through some subjects' assertion that the disclosure of homosexuality to heterosexuals has become an expectation on the part of homosexuals and heterosexuals alike. Gabrielle (77, D), for example, associated the term *coming out* with a perceived mandate to publicize forcibly homosexuals' private lives, and spoke of being offended by the term and its associated celebration by those committed to the practice. "It's an offensive term to me," she said, "because people have used it in the sense that, 'Oh, I'm so glad that she came out or he came out,' and 'Why don't they come out?' [My lover and I] take it as forcing, or thinking people *should*." Similarly, Lillian described her cousin's having gotten "very mad at me because I never told him I was gay," emphasizing that had he questioned her about her sexuality, she would have answered him, but that she "wasn't about to make an announcement." She interpreted his belief in her obligation to disclose her lesbianism to him as evidence of his own immaturity, which she saw as both the source of the trouble and a contrast to her own mature understanding of the relational norms surrounding hetero/homosexual relations.

> Could you believe that? I said, "I never heard of something like that." First of all, as you could hear, I'm not one to wear a sign on my back, and like I told him, "If you were that curious to know what my lifestyle was, why didn't you ask? If you would have asked me I would have told you, but I'm not about to come to you and say, 'Hey Louie, I'm gay,' so—you know. I mean, he's seventy-two years old! And I said to him, "You're a grown man, if you were that curious, why didn't you ask me? I would have told you. But I'm not about to make an announcement."

Accrediting Constructions

While members of the accredited identity cohort did not condemn those who exhibited their homosexuality, they joined the discreditable subjects in condemning flaunting. Marilyn (66, A) felt that it was "unfortunate that some people feel they have to go running around without any clothes on hardly in gay and lesbian parades." Although she admitted to having done the same thing at the Califia Collective in the 1970s, that, she said, "was for ourselves, and not in a public parade [with] TV and cameras that are nationwide that say, 'Oh, look at these terrible things that gays do'." Indeed, Leonard (72, A) explained some homosexuals' unwillingness to attend his meetings for gay seniors by their fear of being associated with elements of the lesbian and gay community with which they don't identify—for example, "the ideology of ACTUP," a group that "can be terribly embarrassing if you want to do some nice little thing and here they come marching by with signs and throwing things or something of the sort." These subjects did not, however, agree that disclosure represented homosexual incompetence. On the contrary, to them, condemnations of disclosure such as those that figure above represented a seriously flawed take on the management of homosexual identity.

To this group, passing as heterosexual produced the homosexual not as a virtuous and competent person, but as a morally deficient and incompetent one, since homosexual competence lies in the always-already necessary disclosure of the homosexual self to those who merit it, regardless of sexual orientation. Seeing homosexuality as constituting an authentic self led the accredited to view the disclosure of their homosexuality to others as essential to homosexual competence and to the authenticity of social relations, both of which, they felt, are precluded by passing. Indeed, the decision to "deceive" others through passing was taken as evidence of homosexual incompetence in and of itself. Marilyn depicted disclosing one's homosexuality to others as a moral problem, a question of authenticity ("I wouldn't be completely me"), and a decision based on degree of intimacy.

> It's also a moral problem that I've struggled with for some time, about coming out, because of being deceptive with other people if I'm not entirely myself. When I have somebody as a friend, it's somebody that I would talk over issues that are close to me. So if I have a straight friend I can enjoy their presence in going out and being social, but I wouldn't be completely *me* if I'm not out to that person.

Tex (72, A) condemned interacting with people who are unaware of the homosexual's "true" identity as dishonest to self and to other and thus as an enactment of a false self within and through that social interaction. Tex's equation of passing with trying to have it both ways displayed an understanding of this practice as a contradiction to authentic homosexuality: homosexuality's "real" status as an essential, unmanageable identity requires its interactional proclamation and enactment. Dishonesty about one's homosexuality represented by passing displays an incompetent enactment of "true" homosexuality, hence a *homosexual* incompetence; delusion about the consequences of its disclosure to the integrity of social ties displays an inability to differentiate between authentic and superficial relations, hence a basic *social* incompetence.

> It just irks me because these people aren't being honest with themselves. I think if you are or believe in one way, and you project a belief or an idea of what you are contrary to that, then you're not being honest with yourself or them because you do have to interact with other people. I mean, you can't have it both ways.

These accounts, while illuminating, describe a moral commitment to disclosure rather than its actual practice. The latter is more complex than either these accounts or those of discreditable subjects indicated. While discreditable subjects glossed the contemporary practice of coming out into an indiscriminate proclamation of one's homosexuality to everybody, the accredited understood coming out as a disclosure of homosexuality to a select group of homosexual and heterosexual contacts *if and when homosexuality is made contextually relevant*. In addition to characterizing coming out as a moral mandate, then, members of this identity cohort cited specific instances in which their homosexuality "needed" to be divulged. They presented these as evidence of the importance of disclosure to maintaining authentic relations with self and other, and of the wide array of circumstances under which the disclosure of self was required.

The accredited spoke of their homosexuality becoming *relationally relevant*. For them, the most obvious example is the adoption of a homosexual identity in the context of a traditional marriage. Tex (72, A) described coming out to his wife in 1966 as "one of the most impossible things I could do," but as essential to personal integrity: "I couldn't be myself if I was lying. So I had to tell the truth." Predictably, these accounts depicted coming out to others as an assurance of authentic relationships; homosexuality is thus made relevant by the desire to achieve them. This theme emerged in Marilyn's talk as well. She explained that the evolution of acquaintanceships into friendships requires an increasing level of intimacy and honesty that can only be genuinely manifested in the disclosure of homosexuality. Her decision to disclose her lesbianism hinged on whether she had "developed a close enough friendship that my sharing this information will not matter to them"—indeed, she explained that whether disclosure would "terminate the relationship" depended "on whom you select" to receive the information. For Marilyn, then, acquaintances become friends only if she sees in the former the "humanitarian" potential upon which her friendships ultimately rest. Without this potential, acquaintances remain just those, and the "full disclosure" upon which true friendships are built becomes unnecessary.

> You get to know them—who they are and how humanitarian they are. You know there are different kinds of friends, maybe the distinction is between acquaintances and friends. And a friend to me is somebody who I have selected whom I want to be with, whom I enjoy mutual experiences with, somebody I really would like and enjoy their presence. Acquaintance-ships I enjoy, but I wouldn't necessarily make an effort to continue the relation.

Subjects also described homosexuality being made *conversationally relevant.* In these cases, unknowing others, with whom they may or may not be intimate, make statements to which subjects feel they can only respond by disclosing their own homosexuality to them. For Mary (66, A), such a situation arose during a 1990 job interview for a job she still holds.

> I know some older people who say, "Well, yes, I'm out," but what they mean is they're out among their friends, which to me is not being out. When I interviewed for this job that I have now, they said, "Oh, so you haven't worked in five years, what have you been doing?" And I said, "Well, I do community work." And then they said, "Well, what kind of community work?" And I said, "Well, I'm co-chair of the Black Lesbian and Gay Party." And went right on with the rest of the interview. So to my way of thinking, I can't think of any other answer. Now if I were *not* out, I could probably have said uh . . .
>
> DR: Church.
>
> Whatever. You know. But that to me is being out.

Mary's account of coming out during a job interview as a trouble-free, appropriate disclosure of self produced her as a competent and reasonable social actor capable of taking calculated risks necessary for the maintenance of personal pride. By situating her disclosure within the narrative context of "normal" and professional talk, Mary demonstrated both the normality of her lesbianism and the appropriateness of her self-presentation as gay. Here, communicating her lesbianism was neither an inappropriate nor an irrelevant statement, but a means of providing information made relevant by the continuous request for details about her community experience. Her lesbianism, enacted by and embodied within her leadership position in a national organization, was understood to be relevant to areas of her life other than the purely sexual; her lesbianism thus spanned the public and the private realms and constituted a public and a private self. That Mary possessed the knowledge that this self should be divulged to potential employers was attested to by her going right on with the interview; this displayed both a competent understanding of the centrality of homosexuality to the self and its competent interactional enactment. Moreover, because Mary was hired without conflict arising over her proclamation, the account constructed passing as heterosexual as awkward and unnecessary.

This is, clearly, a stark contrast to Lillian's characterization of coming out to co-workers as an "astoundingly" naive and self-destructive move. It is also a clear rejection of the stigmatized discourse's formulation of homosexuality becoming a degrading master status—a scarlet letter—if discovered, since, in Mary's case, her lesbianism became neither a master status nor an obstacle to her social advancement. Indeed, while discreditable informants claimed that homosexuals had to pass as heterosexual to be measured by extrasexual standards, members of the accredited identity cohort rejected this claim, citing the continuation, even improvement, of their relationships with heterosexuals after they had disclosed their homosexuality to them. Sharon (66, A), for example, noted that she was "the most successful person in my company" despite her boss's sexism and the fact that she is "out" at work. Moreover, her success at her job is so widely accepted that

> I'm allowed to do anything I want. I can come and go if I have to. He knew I started the church, he knows I'm a lesbian, he told me, "Anything you want to use here for your church, you go ahead, make all the calls you want."

The conversational relevance—and ultimately inconsequentiality of—homosexuality appeared in accounts of family relations as well. "Six or eight months ago," Kate (76, A) disclosed her lesbianism to her aunt, who had introduced homosexuality into the conversation by describing mutual relatives' experience of their child's homosexuality as a "disappointment." After contesting that interpretation, Kate used the conversation as an opportunity to disclose her own lesbianism: a testament that, in the context of the discussion about the "nature" of homosexuality, disproved her relatives' assumptions. Here, too, in contrast to Ryan's depiction of disclosure to family as fatal to familial ties, the relationship survived the disclosure.

> What made me decide on the spur of the moment to do it, over supper she was talking about problems that a niece and nephew of hers are having. One kid was on drugs and that was a problem, and another kid was a homosexual and that was a disappointment. And I said, "Well, it's not always a tragedy," and she said, "I realize that, but they were unhappy." And I said, "You realize of course that I'm a lesbian." And she said, "No! Are you?" And I said, "Yeah." And she said, "Oh."

Accredited informants offered these technical and moral success stories as proof that others' failure to disclose their homosexuality to heterosexuals was misguided. While members of the discreditable identity cohort often cited their passing as preventing their homosexuality from having had an impact on their lives, accredited informants saw passing as affecting those who engaged in it: not only did passing undermine their integrity and the integrity of their relationships, it took a lot of effort, effort that was ultimately futile, since it underestimated heterosexuals' decoding capacities. This can be seen in the following statement by Leonard, who didn't "know of anybody who's gay who hasn't had his life thoroughly affected by it":

> If you think that you're hiding it from people, you're *not*. I mean, how many people do you know that are in the closet that are not really known anyway? And the people who are in the closet with all that scurrying around, throwing sand up in this direction and sand up in that direction in order to keep people from figuring out that they're gay! I mean the amount of effort that's put into *that* sort of thing? *Enormous* amounts go into that!

Similarly, Kate described her ex-lover Jan's refusal to accept the "fact" that, despite her best efforts, others knew of her homosexuality and talked about it among themselves:

> She's quite butchy in appearance now and eventually ended up having a relationship with Nell, a teacher on her faculty, and when they broke up Nell said, "Jan thinks that nobody knows, but the kids call her Lizzie, and they all know." And I said to Jan, "Do you really think that people don't *know*?" And her response then was the same she had said years before—she said, "I don't care what people *think* they know, as long as they don't catch me in the act or I don't tell them, they don't *know*." And it matters to her, it matters very much to her.

6

Contingencies and Challenges

As I NOTED in the introduction, identity discourses
supply actors with both the tools to construct, contest, maintain, and assess their own and others' identities, and with
scripts for constructing and evaluating the self and for enacting it in interaction with others. As we've seen, these scripts
dictate how to interact with heterosexuals–by either passing as heterosexual, in the case of the discreditable identity cohort, or by declining to do so under certain circumstances, in the case of the accredited one. But, as both sets of
subjects' condemnation of flaunting homosexuals suggest,
these scripts also dictate how to interact with and relate
to other homosexuals. Moreover, these scripts are designed
to optimize one's quality–and the quality of one's life–as a
homosexual, albeit in starkly different ways and according
to starkly different standards, and thus must be sufficiently
flexible to allow for their situated and creative use in circumstances that challenge their uniliteral application. Finally, these scripts must be able to survive these challenges,
including those posed by informants' decisions to breach
their demands. This chapter considers these challenges that
informants faced in pursuing their quest for homosexual
competence, and demonstrates that this competence is, in
these respondents' view, contingent upon the sensitive and

situated application of the demands made by the discourse of homosexuality through which they conduct their identity work.

Relations with Homosexuals

"It Takes One to Know One"

While, to members of the discreditable identity cohort, passing as heterosexual is a practice intended to potentiate safe interactions with heterosexuals, not to preclude associations with homosexuals as homosexual, they were aware that they could inadvertently pass in front of those to whom they wanted to appear homosexual, specifically, other homosexuals. In short, the same techniques that produce social status in heterosexual contexts may occasion social failure in homosexual ones. Indeed, two informants described having experienced this. Having associated with gay men as a heterosexual, William (76, D) began a relationship with Bobby, another gay member of his social group. When, in 1954, they spent a weekend at the Fire Island home of Max, another gay friend, William found his friends' treatment of him as heterosexual–even an interloper–to be alienating and "bothersome." Interestingly, although he found his friends' misidentification of him as heterosexual uncomfortable, he decided that he "wasn't making any big pronouncements or anything."

> Max went around introducing me as his straight friend. He knew we were living together, I don't know what the hell he thought. And it made me very uncomfortable. And a lesbian just taunted me and said, "Well, are you going to write a book about us, are you taking notes?" You know–I was their great straight friend and none of them wanted to accept the fact that all of the time I'd been gay. It annoyed me that he was introducing me as his straight friend. Anyway, Sunday morning I said to Bobby, "Please, can we go home?"

Similarly, before he established a support system of other gay men when he immigrated to the United State from Israel in 1950, Franz (86, D) found that his "manliness" convinced other men in the gay bars he frequented that he was an undercover FBI agent. His presence in a gay bar, motivated by a desire for social contact with other gay men, was misinterpreted by them as constituting a (heterosexual) threat, and was therefore frustrated. "I went to bars," he said, "and nobody would talk to me because they were afraid that I was FBI because I looked too manly, I wasn't swishy."

Despite these challenges, however, subjects saw balancing these two projects as a complicated, but not insoluble, problem. Just as Franz had discounted the work he had done to keep his homosexuality secret from heterosexuals, most subjects glossed the work required to be understood by other gays as gay into homosexuals' "natural" ability to recognize each other. Barbie (67, D) explained that, while she had never spoken of her lesbianism to her "other lesbian friends," they knew she was gay because "there's just something about it, it takes one to know one." Sharon characterized this ability as a "sixth sense" that helped her connect to the gay world in the 1950s, when she was still in high school and saw a "swishy" man reading a book entitled *The Gay Years.* "For some odd reason," she said, "the words *gay, gay years,*" inspired her to think, "I gotta be gay, that's me." Susan (75, A) said that she

> can't conceive of just going up to somebody and saying, "You know, I'm gay." It's just that you seem to fall into meeting other people, and you're comfortable with them, and there's no *denying* it. That's the way I think about it.

Others, however, spoke of this "natural" ability essential to homosexual competence as a skill achieved through exposure to and engagement with the homosexual world. When recounting their identity careers, these informants spoke of their past inability to recognize homosexual persons and actions as evidence of their having been temporarily homosexually incompetent: unlearned in the basic cultural, conversational, and sexual codes of homosexual life through whose use homosexuals may inform each other of their sexual identities. Given the importance of knowingly and willingly engaging in homosexual associations, this is not surprising: identifying–and living–as homosexual requires a basic knowledge of the signs and symbols of homosexual life. Dan (70, A), for example, described having been "completely oblivious" to homosexual life in general and to what he retrospectively sees as an obvious homosexual overture in particular.

> Looking back, you note things, but I didn't know. When I worked in New York, the storekeeper had an assistant that was a real butch man that used to screw all these actresses and everything, and he asked me if I wanted to go along with him to watch or be part of it. Looking back, I think he wanted me alone in the room, but I didn't know that at the time. I was completely oblivious. I was drafted at nineteen into the army. I used to hear the beds squeak all around me, but I didn't know what was happening, I wasn't aware.

In almost identical terms, Tex spoke of his ignorance of homosexual overtures despite his acquaintance's dropping now obvious hints about his own sexuality (e.g., "talking about the latest shows"). "In retrospect," he said, "a lot of people were trying to show me, but I didn't know, I guess I didn't *want* to know. One fellow I even went home with him and I still didn't get the idea, we played records! That's about as far as it got. He was always talking about the shows, the latest shows, you know. But nothing sunk in." Deborah (74, D) treated her relatively recent ability to recognize other homosexuals as such as evidence of her own maturation as a lesbian.

All of a sudden I was aware of knowing whether somebody was or not without knowing them. You know what I mean? I mean just by me walking down the street. It must have sort of grown on me gradually and first I wouldn't be aware and then–it really surprised me, I would look at this person and then we'd click: "Oh, there's one!" In the marketplace, walking along the street–it wasn't that I was looking for anybody, it was just a recognition. Sometimes it was mutual and sometimes not. Mostly not. I just thought, "Well, you are growing up a little more now."

This "ability" is what prevents the practice of passing as heterosexual from isolating homosexuals from each other. Rhoda, as we have seen, described having patronized a "gay bar" to which heterosexuals would go to observe the female impersonators. Although her fellow-homosexuals knew she was gay, heterosexuals' inability to recognize "normal-looking" homosexuals such as herself helped her to pass as "normal." According to this formulation, that competent homosexuals are assumed to have mastered this ability–and incompetent ones to have not yet done so–renders telling even other homosexuals about one's homosexuality unnecessary and insulting. Homosexuality is "naturally" detected and assumed by those whose competence as homosexual entails the appropriate dislike for such declarations, and their own ability to identify appropriately other gay men and lesbians. According to these subjects, therefore, to topicalize and declare one's homosexuality is to assume that other gays and lesbians could not determine this on their own, and thus to deny the homosexual competence of other gays and lesbians. Kate, for example, described the outrage with which Billie, a lesbian with whom she and Jan had socialized "for years" in the 1950s, exhibited when, "several years" after Kate retired in 1982, Kate broached the subject of Billie's long-term lesbian relationship with Melanie.

We were friends with them for nine years approximately. And
after Jan and I broke up I continued teaching at Adams Clay
and Melanie was teaching there even at the time when I retired. And several years after I retired I met her at some party
or function or dinner or something. And I decided hey, it really is time to come out to this one, time to get this thing clear.
And I said something to her about, "Billie, I really should
ask you what's your formula. You did a hell of a lot better
than Jan and I did." And she looked at me sort of blankly as
if she didn't understand or I'd suddenly started speaking to
her in Esperanto and I said, "After all, you've been together
how long now?" And she said, "I don't know what you're talking about." And I said, "About your being together so successfully!" And she said, "You know, I think you're insulting me!"
And she glowered at me, and she has never spoken to me
since. Go figure.

This theme emerged in subjects' accounts of others' perceived challenge to their own homosexual competence, displayed in their expectations that subjects come out to them
(i.e., Lillian's umbrage at her cousin) or in others' coming
out to subjects. Manny (77, D) described refusing to partici-
pate in his nephew's attempt to come out to him in the 1960s:

I have a nephew that's gay in Montreal, a college kid. And he
came out to his mother and father when he was in college. I
went home, and the mother said, "Manny, call Josh. Manny,
call Josh." I said, "OK, I'll call Josh." So I'm leaving Montreal
and I didn't call Josh. So Josh calls me: "Uncle Manny? You're
leaving–I'm gay!" So I said, "What do you want me to do?" You
know?

Here, Manny contrasts his nephew's insistence that he be the
recipient of his declaration with his own understanding of it
as a pointless exercise–an interpretation he communicated
to Josh by asking him what he was supposed to do about
it. By rejecting the role his family requested of him, that of
willing participant in the practice of coming out, Manny dis-

tances himself from the discourse of disclosure in which they are participating.

Predictably, the accredited did not concur with Manny's stance. On the contrary, because they considered homosexuality to be relevant in the context of close relationships, these subjects depicted the refusal of intimate others to come out to them as an insult to the relationship. Sharon, for example, portrayed her (homosexual) brother's failure to discuss his homosexuality with her as an astonishing, almost "unbelievable" lack, and contrasts her brother's incompetence with her own competent actions:

> My brother is not married. He has never said anything to me about being gay. *Ever.* Can you believe it? And he and I were just this close, we grew up like twins, there was a year difference. Yet he will not tell me he's gay. He knows about Vivian and I, in fact I sent him a copy of my will telling him if anything happens to tell Vivian whatever he wants and she'll give it to him and she's getting this and this.

Indeed, in stark contrast to Manny's account, Abby (70, A) welcomed the possibility that a younger relative might adopt a gay identity and call upon her for help:

> For some reason or other, I thought, one of my great-nieces is going to turn around some day and say something to me. And if she does, then I will tell her flat out, and I will tell her where to go and what to do, and steer her away from any of the pitfalls that I possibly can. And if I have to run interference for the rest of her family and mine, I will.

Managing Associations

The stigmatized are caught between a desire to associate with their own and an awareness that these associations might discredit them. In Goffman's (1963, p. 47) words, "The issue is that in certain circumstances the social identity of those an individual is with can be used as a source of information concerning his own social identity, the assumption being that he is what the others are." My subjects described heterosexuals' interpretation of any association with "obvious" homosexuals, or with groups that could be interpreted as such, as evidence of homosexuality. Put simply, because association with others can be understood by observers to represent the possession of similar characteristics (what Goffman termed its "informing character"), gay men and lesbians who would not or could not master these management techniques, and would not or could not accept the norms surrounding disclosure of identity–in other words, those who exhibited or flaunted their homosexuality–were seen as threats to the self's ability to keep one's homosexuality secret, in other words, as capable of "blowing one's cover." Indeed, as we have seen, gender inverts were readily recognizable as homosexual by subjects themselves, even before they had connected with the gay subculture. Moreover, as we've seen in Patricia's recognition of a girl's lesbianism by reference to her association with her "butchy" girlfriend in Chapter 2, these inverts implicated the identities of their "normal-looking associates." Subjects avoided these discreditable associations and embraced those that served as a cover. George (75, D) told me he wanted to have a gay man as a roommate, but "not a nelly person" because "the neighbors and things, I guess, pick up on it." Lillian (69, D) also avoided "women who look gay":

> I don't like to be around a woman who looks gay. I don't want to be walking down the street per se with someone that's–you know what I mean? I don't want anyone turning around and pointing their finger: "Oh, look at those two."

Managing associations often overlapped with managing the movement between regions. Abby described having geographically maneuvered her relationships with her recognizable gay lovers in the 1950s and 1960s, only being seen with them in certain areas of Manhattan and not others. Underscoring the important of place in shaping the perceived meaning of associations, Abby said that being seen with her "obviously gay" lovers in the Village did not pose a danger to her because heterosexuals who might recognize her did not frequent that area, while they did frequent midtown Manhattan. "At that time," she explained, "I was very conscious of how people looked. And I never went beyond 19th Street with some of these people. I wouldn't have them meet me up at the Port Authority or anything like that."

The concern with avoiding being seen with obvious homosexuals can easily translate into avoiding any associations that could be interpreted as evidence of homosexuality, including those with passing homosexuals. Franz (86, D) explained that some gay men don't socialize with men in public because "they figure if they see three, four men together they must be gay. That is the mind of the gay people: when they get three men together, then here is a restaurant, a gay restaurant." "The mind of the gay people" refers here to the collective awareness of the informing character of all-male associations, interpreting them as indicating homosexuality on the one hand and a homosexual gathering-place on the other. Franz's subsequent claim that this equation is specific to men, and that the same conclusions are not drawn about women who congregate in public, suggests that women are not prone to limiting their same-sex associations out of fear of their informing character. This suggestion, however, was not borne out by the accounts of my female informants, several of whom described limiting, even terminating, romantic relationships because of real or potential suspicion. Abby (70, A), for example, explained that, when she was in her twenties (and committed to passing), she and her lover had decided not to live together. Given that both she and her lover were living with their parents, the only "valid" reason for their leaving home would have been heterosexual marriage.

> The first woman that I really had a relationship with, we both lived at home. We had absolutely no reason, or no valid reason, when we discussed it, to live together.

> DR: You thought people would think you were gay because you had an alternative.

> Or whatever, yeah. That your parents would wonder why you wanted to, when you had this cushy lifestyle.

In a similar account, Rhoda (89, D) explained her decision to break up with her lover, Betty, with whom she was going to live, in the 1950s, because Rhoda's ex-lover told the head of a business association to which Rhoda belonged that Rhoda and Betty were gay. Although Rhoda denied the charge, she and Betty decided to break up to preserve Betty's "marvelous [read: heterosexual] reputation."

> It scared Betty, so she said she couldn't live her life like that—people will talk about her reputation and everything. I said, "Betty, it's not worth it. I love you and you love me but it's not worth it, us going on together and having our home together and everything." I didn't want to hurt her reputation. She had a marvelous reputation built up.

Despite the precautions discreditable subjects described taking, however, they knew that they could not completely control their associations or others' interpretations of them. As in the cases of Val and Manny, who were seen in obviously gay spaces, there were times when subjects found themselves in the company of obvious homosexuals, and, if heterosexuals noticed their co-presence, they had to either account for it or pass despite it. Rhoda (89, D) found her heterosexual friends, who did not know she was gay, ridiculing gay men and women, a practice in which she did not engage.

So many people did not know that I was gay, and I associated with a lot of good people who were not gay. And especially with the very feminine boys [they] pointed their fingers at them and talked to me about them, thinking I wasn't gay.

When I asked her if she was trying to come across as not gay, she answered, "No, I just was natural. They knew that I was the type that wouldn't ridicule gays or normals, so they didn't expect it from me." Her heterosexual friends thus sustained their understanding of her as heterosexual despite her declination to ridicule obvious homosexuals, a decision that could have resonated as acceptance of, even identification with, the ridiculed group, but which she successfully reframed as evidence of a general kindness and a tolerance of deviants, whether gay or normal—a practice that, as we have seen, produced her as not only "normal," but as a normal person of good character. That she found passing "natural" allowed her to witness even "good" heterosexuals' contempt of gays without suffering that contempt herself, and this confirmed her view that failing or refusing to pass results in the loss of the actor's status in the eyes of others, even close friends.

Two members of the discreditable identity cohort, however, spoke of having participated in the ridiculing of obvious homosexuals as a way to pass as heterosexual. Marge (81, D), for example, explained that when she was among people who "considered everybody [else] straight" and "made derogatory remarks [about] gay people," she joined in the derogation because "you couldn't let them know how you felt about things. I myself have been guilty of doing that."[1] Similarly, when Ryan (81, D) and his co-workers saw "some real nelly thing come in the store, we'd all laugh at him when he went out. I didn't want to be that type of a person. I didn't want people laughing at me. So I stayed away from it."

This is not to say that subjects necessarily isolated themselves from other homosexuals. On the contrary, subjects described rich homosexual friendship networks. They tended, however, to associate with *passing* homosexuals, a practice that served as a cover in itself. Patricia (77, D) spoke of dining at restaurants with her lesbian and gay male friends; since all would dress ("to the nines") according to gender norms, they passed as a group of heterosexuals.

> This is the thing that all my life I had to cover. I had to play the two roles. I had the few friends who were gay and we would have our little private parties but when it was outside we were the nicest ladies you ever saw. We'd dress up to kill. High heels, hose, silk hose, beautiful dresses, gloves, the hat. I didn't mind dressing, but I never enjoyed anything so much as having our little parties that we had when I could wear my pants. I wore nice looking clothes though, even in the pants so that they'd look lady-like. I did that also to cover up because they would see us dressed like [ladies] and as soon as there were a whole bunch of us and we'd walk like ladies, we didn't have to worry. So that covered up a lot.

Similarly, Marge (81, D) explained that, despite her association with other homosexuals–including her lover, and often in her and her husband's own apartment–her husband did not suspect she was a lesbian because her gay friends all conformed to gender norms. Although she eventually told him she was gay,

> at first [my husband] didn't know what was going on, he thought we were just really good friends and although he didn't drink he used to buy alcohol for my friends who were mostly all gay, the guys were so manly.

Some of the accredited had, of course, engaged in this passing practice in the past, when they had lived as stigmatized homosexuals, avoiding obvious homosexuals and/or working to avoid drawing attention to themselves as homosexuals when out with other homosexuals in public. Abby, as we have seen, limited her public association with her obviously gay lovers to lower Manhattan. But their current, accredited homosexual identities and affiliations recast their past practices as deficient–as retroactively homosexually incompetent from the vantage point of currently held beliefs. Abby credited the connections she made after she immersed herself in lesbian life in the 1990s (again, after a decadeslong hiatus) with a newfound comfort with her lesbianism, and credited this comfort with her new declination to limit her associations to passing homosexuals. "For the first time in my entire life," she explained, "I am so comfortable with being who I am. I never even think about it anymore. It feels great! I never worry about what other people think." She characterized this as "a major step": while she doesn't "walk around the street, or walk into the market, and say, 'Oh by the way, I'm a lesbian,'" she is "not uncomfortable with it anymore. I never worry about who I'm with, what they look like or *anything*."

Similarly, Marilyn considered her relatively public openness about her lesbianism to be remarkable, given her past fears of being identified as gay. She described having attended a local festival over the previous weekend with other members of a social club for lesbian seniors and having "found myself talking about being gay and lesbian without any thought about it until I stopped and looked around–I said, 'Hmm!' But here I was in public talking about being gay and lesbian. I might not have done that at one time, but I felt comfortable doing it on Sunday and I didn't care–well, I mean, it was easy to do and not something I censored myself doing, which at one time I might have." Indeed, Mary (66, A) listed other gay women's commitment to passing as one of the obstacles to finding a lesbian life-partner, since she "wouldn't want" to become intimate with someone whose basic approach to homosexuality was so different than her own–in other words, who had adopted a stigmatized homosexual identity. Thus, just as Marilyn and Abby had begun to associate with gay women in ways that made them more easily identifiable as lesbians, Mary avoided associating with women who declined to do so.

> I even dated one woman who was about twelve years older than I am. But [her] attitudes and things are just so much different than mine. And that's such an individual thing. And you know, I could find somebody your age whose attitudes and things would be so much different that I wouldn't want, you know. This particular woman said she'd always been out, but in reality, she was one of those people who say well, you know, whoever she was was nobody's business but hers.

For the discreditable, though, this passing device remained abidingly rational. Ryan's (81, D) assessment of his life spent managing associations with other homosexuals stands in stark contrast with Abby and Marilyn's statements.

> I oftentimes think if I had my life to live over, I would probably do it about the same as I did because I think I've been smart to stay away from it and not make myself obvious. When you were working you had to be very careful that way. We would have some people come into work, we would hire them, why, I don't know, because it was obvious they were gay. And they would get them in there and just make fools out of them. They'd try to make them do the dirtiest work and the hardest work. Well, they didn't pull that on me. And I think it was because they weren't sure about me.

As these accounts demonstrate, passing as heterosexual is not an isolated practice. On the contrary, informants explained that a key method of passing is managing one's own social relations, specifically, avoiding homosexuals with deficient management practices and embracing those with adequate ones. Managing identity involves recognizing and

avoiding the deficient management practices of other homosexuals–a practice designed to preclude a situation in which
what Goffman (1963, p. 50) terms "the decoding capacities"
of others could be fruitfully applied. While the ease with
which this can be done depends in great part on the relationship in question–it is easier to keep certain associations secret from business associates, for example, than
from family members who live in the area–that it needs
to be done remains unquestioned throughout discreditable
subjects' accounts. Indeed, in these accounts, the distinctive
formulation of homosexuality as a discrete aspect of self that
can and should be managed through passing as heterosexual survived a range of challenges, not only by gay liberationist formulations, but by circumstances and experiences
that seemed to contradict the validity, and/or applicability, of
the formulation itself. Accredited informants also described
maintaining their commitment to their standards of homosexual competence in the face of their own failure to enact them.

Deviant Cases

As I noted in the introduction, subjects oriented to the discourses of homosexuality as ideal types composed of mutually elaborating prescriptions on the one hand and resources for enacting them on the other. Accordingly, they
were aware that there were times when these prescriptions
and resources needed to be creatively reshaped to fit particular circumstances. They were not, in short, inflexible
demands to be met regardless of circumstances, but tools
that became useful only if used by people who were sensitive to context and applied in ways that made the best of
those circumstances, and, in rare cases, these contexts and
circumstances demanded that the prescriptions provided by

the discourse to which they were committed be suspended. Moreover, there were times when the pursuit of these prescriptions had negative consequences. Members of both identity cohorts offered instances of these exceptions to the rule, but did so to display their awareness of the contingent and complex nature of passing as homosexual, not to contradict the validity of the "recipes of being" through which they enacted their homosexual identities.

Disclosure

Although members of the discreditable identity cohort saw passing as clearly essential to homosexual competence and coming out as constituting homosexual incompetence, two of these described having voluntarily declared their homosexuality to heterosexuals—specifically, their siblings. Rather than challenge this equation, however, these accounts concretized it: both subjects specified that it was extraordinary circumstances, not a basic commitment to disclosure, which made these declarations necessary. Jan (68, D) explained that she told her sister she was gay because the sister was in the process of moving in with her. Since Jan was beginning a relationship with Carol, she preferred that her sister learn about her lesbianism by "discussing" it, rather than by observing Jan and Carol's interactions. Jan's declaration was thus constructed as a responsible means of preventing trouble in the home posed by new and unforeseen circumstances, rather than a commitment to disclosure regardless of the context in which the actors in question might find themselves. Note that Jan had not disclosed her lesbianism to her sister before she moved in, despite their unusual closeness.

> My youngest sister, the one who died and with whom I was so close, between husbands she came to live with me. This was about eight years ago I guess. She lived with me for two

years. When she appeared I said—I had just met Carol—"I want to discuss this with you. You're going to be living here."

Similarly, Franz (86, D) described disclosing his homosexuality to his sister, with whom he lived after he immigrated to the United States from Israel at the age of forty. The move was a difficult one for him: separated from his lover and from his community, he became so depressed that his sister became concerned. When she asked him what was wrong with him, he explained that he was gay and that he missed his friends. Here, coming out is presented as made necessary by unusual circumstances on the one hand and the nature of the relationship on the other: to have answered his sister's question in any other way would have escalated both his sister's concern and his own depression.

> I was very depressed the first day, because I left a guy and I left a lot of friends. I left a whole community—we were sticking together. For instance, Friday nights we went to one guy's apartment on the roof, and all the gays were meeting each other. So I missed it, I said, "Who am I here? A stranger." So my sister forced me to—"What's wrong with you?" So I told her that I'm gay.

Again, discreditable subjects understood passing as heterosexual to be the best response to the range of threats to person that would be carried out if their homosexuality were to be discovered. This stance suggests that should these dangers significantly wane or even disappear, passing would be less necessary, perhaps even not required at all. This possibility was, in fact, seen as having come about by three subjects who had identified as homosexual before the advent of gay liberation and "went public" with their sexual identities, not in response to specific demands, as was the case with Franz and Jan, but in response to what they saw as the suspension of the heterosexual threats to person outlined in Chapter 4. To a great extent, this relative sense of safety had to do with their having all worked in relatively gay-friendly environments. Michael (78, D) was a well-known and influential screenwriter in New York and then in Hollywood,[2] Gabrielle (77, D) was a very wealthy investor in Los Angeles, and Phoebe (79, D) worked in a social work office, where

> there was always a spirit of inclusiveness. Whenever they had an office party they [would] say, "Bring your meaningful other." Nobody ever paid attention to it. If it was in writing it was, "Bring your significant other." It was very accepting. . . . We had a lot of gay couples in our office as it grew larger, the personnel man was gay, and his boyfriend, [who] didn't work at the office, and two or three gay supervisors, and others like that.

Despite this openness at work, Phoebe had passed with her neighbors until she retired in the 1980s, at which point she began to socialize with them on a more regular basis, becoming heavily involved in her neighborhood association. She also met a woman who was interested in her, and who "really taught me the word *lesbian,* and she taught me about coming out, and we were both on the board of the Rainbow Coalition" (a gay organization). Since her neighbors "already liked me," and since "we have a lot of gays" in her neighborhood, she "gradually" began to disclose her lesbianism to her heterosexual neighbors–when it became conversationally relevant. This began with the following exchange with her neighbor, "one of my best buddies" and a fellow member of her neighborhood association, Claire:

> I had been to some COOL meeting or something, and I was going in front of her house and she was out in front on a Sunday afternoon, and she asked me, "Where have you been, Phoebe?" I said, "I was in a meeting of COOL," and she said, "What is that?" I said, "The Coalition of Older Lesbians." She *laughed*, she thought that was so funny. Then a couple weeks later she told me that her dad had been gay, and he was a college professor, and a great [guy].

The resemblance between this account and that offered by Mary in Chapter 5 is striking: neither woman raised the issue of homosexuality until the heterosexual party asked questions that called for the disclosure of that information. Indeed, the heterosexual person in each case asked *two* questions: in Mary's case, what had she been doing (to which she had answered "volunteer work"), and then what kind of volunteer work it was; in Phoebe's case, where she was going (to which she answered, "to a meeting of COOL"), and then what COOL stood for. Each woman, then, "gave" the heterosexual an opportunity to change the subject, to steer the conversation in a direction that would not require the disclosure of homosexuality. Moreover, Mary's account was, in large part, a success story, and Phoebe's was as well: instead of producing tension, her disclosure produced laughter and Claire's subsequent disclosure of her own father's homosexuality. Furthermore, because of the high percentage of gay men and lesbians in her neighborhood, Phoebe didn't "think it was much of a tragic thing for my neighbors."

Michael pointed to social changes in the status of gay men and women as grounds for the suspension of passing techniques, on both his part and the part of others. According to him, "There is no longer, in my opinion, any reason to be in the closet," because "I don't think it is a stigma anymore, not unless you're terribly bigoted or Jesse Helms, or something. I think it is part of society, it's here to stay, as you hear in parades."

It has ceased to be traumatic to be gay. "So you're gay!" That's the attitude I get from most people I know. I can't think of anybody I would be unwilling to tell that I was gay, if they didn't already know, and I can't think of anybody that I care who knows. That was not true in the University of Wisconsin. We used to whisper about gay people when I was at the university, now they are all over town. I cannot think of a

single soul that I would not be willing to tell that I was gay, if
they wanted to know. I don't think I would volunteer it, but it
wouldn't bother me in the least. In my opinion people don't
care as much whether you are gay or not as they used to.

Indeed, Michael described telling young gay screenwriters
how open Hollywood is to homosexuals, encouraging them
to disclose their sexuality to film producers.

When I taught writing at UCLA I always bring this up the
first night. I said, "I know about forty producers in this town,
and you could walk in and give them your script, and he will
read it, and then you say, 'Sir, by the way, I should tell you
I'm gay.'" I said thirty-nine out of the forty are going to say, "I
don't give a damn. Let's see if the script is any good." And that
was not true [in the past]. I can't think of anybody that would
care very much if I am gay or not.

Negative Consequences of Passing

While discreditable subjects saw passing as heterosexual as
clearly essential to practical, psychic, and emotional survival, several were cognizant of rare instances in which it
had negative consequences. One such consequence was inadvertently passing among homosexuals. But three other
(interestingly, male) informants spoke of rare instances in
which passing among heterosexuals was a problem. Passing
posed a particular problem for gay men who were attracted
to heterosexual men; just as the latter's recognition of the
gay man's interests could be dangerous (see Chapter 4), their
ignorance of the subtle nuances of gay courtship, which prevent them from recognizing those interests, can be frustrating. Rodney (75, D) expressed this when he described his
new sexual interest's failure to grasp his intentions:

I have a real hang up on someone now that is straight. I think
he's thirty-one. I'd love to have a connection with him but he
doesn't know that I'm gay, I guess. My god, the things that I

have said, within limits, you would think that he would have tumbled long ago, but I don't think he's tumbled to the fact that I'm gay.

Furthermore, even if he were to connect with the young man, the fact that Rodney's reluctance to disclose his sexuality to heterosexuals extended to members of the medical profession posed another obstacle to pursuing the relationship: he could not, he felt, ask his doctor for guidance on how to have safe sex. Because homosexuals are "not part of the mainstream," he explained, "you hesitate even if you wrote a professional person. My doctor doesn't know that I'm gay. I've mentioned earlier this young [man]–if he were available I would like to go to the doctor and say, 'Is there any way that we could make contact that's gonna be relatively safe?' " Passing can thus close off opportunities to raise issues relevant to one's homosexual circumstances and concerns.

Others raised a related problem: the inability to protect the self from the intrusion of unwanted heterosexual expectations and demands without identifying oneself as homosexual. Manny (77, D) described receiving unwanted romantic attention by heterosexual women when eating at the local Jewish senior center.

> The women don't know that I'm gay, and two of them have a terrible crush, but I act like I don't know what they're doing. Last week one of them told me–the other woman didn't show up–she said, "You know that she's got a terrible crush on you." I said, "Yes, I know," but I act like I don't know. Anyway, that's the story.[3]

Similarly, Brian (74, D) cited the tendency of his heterosexual friends to think of him as more lonely than he actually was. Having worked to achieve a heterosexual front with them (by, for example, elaborating his relationship with his "little old lady friend in Glendale" into a romantic one, and presenting himself as divorced), he found their misplaced concern for him troubling.

> I think now they think of me as being lonely, more so than–
> they don't know I'm gay. And there's no reason to let them
> know. I'm not going to get into that. It's just, you know, they,
> "Oh, he's been divorced, had an unfortunate marriage and
> now he's lonely" or something. So they do nice things for me.
> It's all right, and we have a good time, but they bother me.
> I think sometimes they're feeling sorry for me because I'm
> divorced, don't have a wife now, I'm alone. It bothers me that
> they do, because it doesn't bother me like they think it both-
> ers me.

Again, these are deviant cases. Instead of challenging the commitment to passing made by members of this identity cohort, they confirm it. Passing is designed to improve relations with heterosexuals and potentiate associations with homosexuals, not damage or preclude them, as did the examples cited above. According to these actors, passing is a key mode of being, adopted to protect the self from the threat of rejection or banishment, and any negative consequences of passing can and should be overcome or disattended.

The Discredited

In stark contrast to the subjects discussed above, four members of the discreditable identity cohort had been recognized–and discredited–as homosexual.[4] Their homosexuality was thus not a *discreditable* aspect of self, but a *discredited* one. Yet rather than inspiring the subjects to question the legitimacy of equating successful passing with competence, these subjects continued to orient to passing as a desired goal whose accomplishment merits praise and whose failure merits condemnation. Different causes of discrediting, however, had different implications for self. For Manny, who, at the age of nineteen, was seen by his co-workers who had come to a gay bar to see a drag show, his discrediting was due not to his own failing but to a highly unlikely circumstance: he was, he explained, "just there."

> This gay bar, a lot of the boys would be in drag, and it was a big thing, where the straight people would come. And at that time I was out of the garment trade, and one time the buyers from the dress department came. They came in a crowd of five or six, but two of them were the big buyers, and of course [they] saw me, so I was *ruined*, absolutely *ruined*. Well, you know, it's a terrible thing. I was just *there*.[5]

While working at the telephone company in the early 1940s, Val (74, D) attended a party thrown by some female co-workers, where she got drunk and made an open pass at another woman. This indiscretion "went all over the telephone company" and resulted in one of her co-workers teasing her about the incident. When a lesbian co-worker alerted her to the dangers such an impression posed, Val became committed to passing–to, in her words, "becoming covert." Her discrediting became, in her mind as well as in the mind of the gay woman who guided her in the wake of the discrediting, a function of her ignorance regarding the appropriate way to express her desire for women, and thus a product of a temporary homosexual incompetence. This incompetence thus resonates with the inability to recognize other homosexuals (see above) as an immaturity corrected by a gradual immersion in the homosexual culture and a gradual familiarity with its codes of conduct.

> So then one of the women–there was a couple of them, one worked for the telephone company and one worked somewhere else, and they lived together, and I think they were gay, but there was no evidence of it–and the one girl called me over and told me, "There is this [rumor] going around, and you have to be very careful." She sort of scared the pants off me, and made a Christian in that area of me. I learned right

then and there that you aren't out to everybody, and you're very covert in your actions.

In contrast, Maria's (64, D) discrediting was due to her declination to dress in gender-appropriate ways. Never comfortable in girls' clothes, she began wearing men's clothes when she started working during high school. "I started buying my own clothes and everybody knew, based on my clothing, my attire. Nobody ever knew before, that I liked girls. I kept it to myself." Declining to conceal her lesbianism from an early age, she has been discredited throughout her adult life: she considers herself out to "the whole world."

> Like Patricia's not out completely. Did you know that?
>
> DR: Nobody's out to the whole world.
>
> I am.

Here, Maria displayed an understanding of "being out" as a matter of degree—Patricia is "somewhat out," while she is out completely. Moreover, Maria considered her discrediting to be evidence of her own incompetence: her dress being something under her control, her discrediting can be traced to her own, knowing actions. This has significant implications for her interpretation of other, "competent" homosexuals' attitudes toward her. As we have seen, discreditable subjects tend to avoid homosexuals who failed in this control and to see their avoidance as morally right as well. The legitimacy and intelligibility of this avoidance was also agreed to by Maria—a discredited subject who is herself avoided because of the "obtrusiveness of her stigma."

> She picks her friends very carefully. And I don't think I seek her [out] because she's not *out* out, you know, and I'm a very obvious lesbian. And I find that a lot of lesbians don't wanna [hang] too much with [obvious lesbians]. They're not *out* out. And so there are functions that they attend that they would

never ask you to go to, because I just don't fit in. And I don't
blame them. I'm not, you know, I understand that there's
places where I just don't fit in, because of the way I am, my
attire and everything else.

While Maria used her own discrediting to reproduce the
legitimacy of the stigmatizing discourse, she respecified that
discourse's features to accord with her status as someone
who has failed to uphold its central tenet. Maria displayed
an understanding of her own lesbianism and the position
in which it places her in the lesbian world: since the way
she is is homosexually incompetent, incapable of mastering
the management techniques adopted by other lesbians, she
cannot expect to fit into a social world grounded in the successful identity management necessary to avoid being out
to more than a select few, or "*out* out." Furthermore, Maria
condoned the fact that competent lesbians should construct
their social worlds around this secrecy and the exclusion
of those who threaten it: she made it clear that she doesn't
blame them for what is obviously a necessary and reasonable protective avoidance of her own failure to pass. Thus,
in contrast to the discrete and manageable aspect of self of
other lesbians, Maria understood her own lesbianism as a
discrete yet unmanageable stigma, one that other lesbians
understandably wish to avoid. As such, she constructed a
secondary stigma for herself by accepting the stigmatization
of homosexuals who cannot or do not appropriately manage
their own stigma.

It is important to note that, while Maria treated her lesbianism as an unmanageable aspect of self, in large part due
to her obvious gender nonconformity, this nonconformity
did not in and of itself always produce a similar assessment
of the manageability of sexual identity. This is most obvious in the seemingly contradictory accounts of Constance,
a long-time friend of Maria's, who was butch "ever since I

can remember," and who understands her public presentation of her butch identity to be a proclamation in itself, as did Maria. As Constance (74, D) put it, she "never hid," and has "always been out. I always dressed real butch ever since I was knee high to a grasshopper," adding that she was "not *ashamed* of it. I may be an old bag, but honey, I'm still not ashamed of it." Constance gave numerous examples of this, noting that her butch persona and dress were her own business. "It's my life," she said, "I don't bother nobody, I don't ask anybody for anything," positing her butch identity as benign, and rejecting the notion that it was either an imposition or a demand. She also stressed that, with the exception of two older neighbors and a boy for whom she baby-sits, "everybody around here knows it." She displayed some ambivalence, however, over whether her butch identity constituted a master status, identified her as lesbian to all observers, or made her vulnerable to harassment or attack. Having asserted that "everyone knows," she invoked the possibility of others' inability to read her butch persona as lesbian when she echoed other subjects' statements that if anybody ever asked her if she were gay, she'd answer in the affirmative. She also described having kept her lesbianism hidden from the parents of the ten-year-old boy for whom she cares.

> When she works I take care of him, just when he comes from school and he sleeps here. And a lot of time she works on Sundays. Saturdays, Sundays there are times when I can't even go out myself, 'cause I will not take him to a gay place. Because his mother and her boyfriend or lover or whatever it is, that's a family there. And I don't want him to go with me and then come out and talk about it.

Most important, she explains Maria's having been harassed by the police as due to Maria's being a "trouble-maker," not to her being butch, since Constance was butch as well, and would never get harassed or arrested when in Maria's company.

> We used to hang around every darn bar, they were straight bars, and Maria used to get in so much trouble. I never got harassed. She did, but I never did. She used to get thrown in jail, and we were out together! We were inseparable.
>
> DR: So you'd be walking down the street and they'd pick her up, but not you?
>
> No, because she was a troublemaker.

The "Failed" Accredited

I have shown that those orienting to their homosexuality as a stigma to be managed continued to orient to it this way even when they had failed to pass. A similar pattern can be seen among those accredited respondents who, having had failed to live up to gay liberation's mandate to disclose their homosexuality, continued to orient to this mandate as valid. Marilyn (66, A) described her decision to keep her lesbianism secret from her mother:

> Personal is political, I can remember that phrase. But I was too much of a wimp. I did not come out to my mother, I had a great conflict. She passed on in 1981, I never came out to her. I felt that she would feel guilty, I felt that it would be too hard for her to handle, that she would feel that she was responsible in some way for my being gay. I came out to my female cousin and she's the only member of my blood family that I came out to.[6]

Since lesbian-feminism insists upon public disclosure as essential to liberation, Marilyn characterized her decision to keep her lesbianism secret from her family as fueled by weakness. Her mother's potential unease, while informed by heterosexist understandings of lesbianism, was more influential in her decision than were the requirements of her newly found identity.

The accredited maintained their commitment to this mandate to disclose even when they had partially upheld it, responding to homosexuality being made conversationally relevant by standing up for homosexuals in general, yet declining the opportunity to identify themselves as gay. Abby (70, A), for example, while proud of having defended her gay friends, characterized her failure to take advantage of the opportunity to come out herself as a "cop-out":

> Somebody did say something at a family gathering once and I jumped right in. I said, "I don't want to hear anything like that about my two close friends who are gay. I have a lot of gay friends." And that was a cop-out because that would have been a perfect opportunity to say, "You're talking about me."

Thus, in stark contrast to the discreditable subjects' accounts, accredited respondents constructed homosexual competence as the commitment to and successful accomplishment of the disclosure and enactment of homosexuality necessary for personal and political integrity. Consequently, while Goffman (1963, p. 107) wrote that "the stigmatized actor exhibits a tendency to stratify his 'own' according to the degree to which their stigma is apparent and obtrusive," here we see that the accredited–who reject the stigma–can be seen to stratify their own *according to the degree to which the formulation of homosexuality as stigma is adopted, enacted, and legitimated.* In the course of telling me that the commitment to passing was made by younger generations as well, Mary (66, A) gave an example of "someone your age whose attitudes would be so different that I wouldn't want [her as a lover]. This particular woman, she said she'd always been out, but in reality, she was one of those people who say well, you know, whoever she was was nobody's business but hers." Accredited subjects assessed themselves according to these standards, and distinguished themselves from a set of incompetent homosexuals who could not or would not recognize and embrace their essential, positive, political homosexual identity. These subjects reproduced themselves as members of an accredited group whose accreditation depended upon their distancing of self from, and condemnation of, homosexuals adopting and enacting a stigmatizing discourse.

Conclusion

The discourses through which informants identified as homosexual, and through whose properties they formulated and constructed selves and worlds, have deep implications for acting as a particular self within distinctive worlds. In both identity cohorts, standards for appropriate action were treated as standards for the evaluation of self and other. These evaluations drew upon and elaborated homosexual "types" on the one hand and the preferential ranking of them on the other, and, because association with incompetents threatened the goal at hand, this ranking then informed relations between homosexuals. These actors were deeply involved in the production and use of these standards of competence and incompetence as a feature of the production of both personal competence and integrity and a world ordered according to fundamental precepts.

The discreditable identity cohort saw its goal not as avoiding enacting homosexuality, but enacting it in particular ways—passing with heterosexuals and associating with homosexuals as a homosexual. This was accomplished through the use of certain passing techniques, the appropriate use of which required a sensitivity to context. Immanent in subjects' success stories is the possibility of those who failed or refused to achieve this goal: subjects typologized them (as inept at best and motivatedly self-destructive at worst), distinguished between their incompetent actions and their own competent ones, and produced themselves as competent for having done so and for having avoided them in the interests of passing. This avoidance was seen as reasonable by all members of this cohort, including Maria, who had herself been avoided for being homosexually incompetent.

For the accredited, the goal was not to pass as heterosexual, but to achieve authentic relations with self *and* (homosexual *and* heterosexual) others, a project that centered on disclosing one's homosexuality to others when it became relevant–which, in the context of close relationships, it invariably did. Failure to do so both debased the relationship (again, with self as well as with other) and constituted a homosexual incompetence driven by an unreasonable fear of

Table 7   Discourses of Homosexuality, Final Version

	Homosexuality as Stigma	*Homosexuality as Status*
Relation to self	aspect	essential
Implications for self	discreditable	accrediting
Appropriately enacted in	private	private and public
Heterosexual threat	to person	to self
Relation of heterosexual to self	oppressor	moral seducer
Desired goal	social integration	moral status
Required action	pass	disclose
Homosexual competence	passing	disclosing when relevant
Homosexual incompetence	disclosing	passing

rejection on the one hand and a failure to appreciate the moral consequences of passing on the other. These subjects further explained that homosexuals committed to passing were deluded about the efficacy of their efforts (as well as about their need for them). Here, too, standards of action were treated as standards for evaluation–specifically, for evaluating the integrity of homosexuals, including themselves. Finally, the goal of disclosing one's homosexuality when relevant was described as difficult, and subjects gave instances in which they themselves failed to do so; despite this, subjects continued to treat this disclosure as a desired goal. Thus, the discourses through which subjects conduct their identity work must be elaborated once again to reflect this chapter's findings–see Table 7.

Conclusion

Challenges and Opportunities

Methodological Challenges

This book's goals–to uncover the impact of historical and life-course factors on homosexual identity work in later life– implicates a locus of methodological issues, both conventional and interactionist. The first is the question of *representativeness* (of more concern to those who wade in positivist waters than to those who don't). Difficult to achieve under the best of circumstances, it is especially difficult–even, according to Weston (1991, p. 9), "an impossibility"–to secure a representative sample of a group whose criteria for membership is unclear.[1] Clearly, a larger number of people have same-sex experiences than identify as gay or lesbian. Even if we were to define these people as homosexual (which is clearly problematic), our burden would not be significantly lightened, since we would then have to wonder whether we have only managed to record those people who have admitted to these acts.

Happily, this book is not concerned with securing a representative sample of homosexual elders, but with uncovering the range of, and patterns among, identity practices in which these actors engage. Accordingly, in addition to snowball sampling, I engaged in "spectrum sampling," searching for subjects with experiences and circumstances that differed from those I had just encountered, and designed to challenge the ideal types that emerged. Despite my best efforts, however, I did not secure as diverse a sample as I would have liked. African-Americans are underrepresented, and Asians are not represented at all–a particularly egregious absence, given the large Asian population in the area. Others I wish I could have located include those in nursing homes (I only found one) and men who were "recognizably gay." I also wish I had interviewed more people who had identified as homosexual through the accrediting discourse (of my thirty-five subjects, only seven had done so), and can't help wondering whether I would have learned anything new from those few people who declined to be interviewed.

Despite these difficulties, I had little trouble securing a heterogeneous sample: my subjects ranged in age from 64 to 89, with an average age of 73.5, and 37 percent of the sample is 75 or older (14 percent is 80 or older); while over 75 percent lived alone, others lived with lovers, roommates, or family members; and income ranged from below $10,000 to over $100,000 annually (with male subjects averaging $29,500 and female subjects averaging $24,700). Roughly one-third had been heterosexually married (7 women and 3 men) and of those, 2 men and 2 women have children. One subject is African-American, and 4 are Latino/a. While all were given new names, I have tried to capture as many details of their lives as possible, and only changed information that would be clearly identifying.

Second, the book can be easily critiqued for *tacitly equating the histories and circumstances of gay men with those of gay women.* But the social worlds of gay men and women were, arguably, as intermeshed as they were distinct. Until the late 1960s, male and female homosexuality were constructed in similar terms (specifically, through the lens of gender inversion), and while men and women had–and have–very different venues for homosexual interaction, their worlds often overlapped (in bars, restaurants, and private homes) for practical and strategic reasons. Moreover, the issue of sexual nonconformity and how it plays out in old age, after a lifetime of adaptations and interpretations, is of great moment to men and women both. How different opportunities and constraints affected identity careers is not a methodological problem to be worked out, but a phenomenon that informed–and continues to inform–the practical and moral worlds of gay men and women of all ages, and at all points in history. These differences–how gay men and women were differently constructed and regulated–are both part of the topic of inquiry on the part of the analyst and part of the project of everyday life as a homosexual discovering, interpreting, negotiating, and constructing both the world and the self in it.

Third, that *language and phrasing* mean different things to different people posed the most practical and immediate problem within the interview itself. My search for informants' identity careers was initially bogged down in the symbolic baggage associated with the term *coming out,* a term I considered to be fairly neutral, but to which subjects responded in a variety of ways, not all of them welcoming. In the argot of the post-Stonewall gay world, coming out is an umbrella term referring to the process of coming to understand, accept, and proclaim one's homosexuality to oneself and to others. Modern usage posits degrees of coming out, the first being an admission to self, the second an admission to other gay men and women, the third an admission to a range of heterosexual intimates (starting with friends and family and expanding to include co-workers, neighbors, and the like), and the last being a proclamation to those one has never met. These degrees are often sequentially linked, and common knowledge asserts that, given the constraints on sexuality that characterized the pre-Stonewall era, men and women experiencing same-sex desires in the past were fortunate to have achieved the first of these disclosures, even more fortunate to engage in the second (indeed, fortunate to have found other homosexuals to begin with), and effectively precluded from engaging in the third and fourth types of disclosure.

These assumptions are, to put it mildly, problematic. Disregarding for the moment that the nature and consequences of same-sex desire were so different in the not-so-distant past as to render unrealistic the expectation that there would be a discernible "it" to disclose to self and others, coming out has only recently come to mean the public disclosure of one's homosexuality to heterosexuals. In fact, the different meanings of the term made asking subjects when they came out a difficult, even contested, undertaking. Indeed, some subjects took umbrage at the very question, assuming that I was asking them when they had declared their homosexuality to heterosexual strangers, something which, they emphasized in the strongest terms, they had never done, and never would. Consequently, I asked subjects if they had ever heard of the term, and, if so, to define it for me.

Answers included "not hiding the fact that you're homosexual"; self-recognition as homosexual; "becoming sexually active as a lesbian" (Kate, 76, A) or gay man; "becoming active in a gay community" (Val, 74, D); and variously disclosing one's homosexuality to other gays, to heterosexuals to whom one is close (especially family), and even, according to some, to "people in general" or "the whole world." I then asked them if *coming out* was a term they felt applied to them, and why. Given the range of definitions they had given, each interview then took a distinctive path, providing accounts of, among other things, entering gay life, having a first same-sex encounter, or coming to understand themselves as homosexual. My asking questions about coming out did not serve to elicit a singular type of answer, but was, rather, a device to get subjects talking about what they saw as turning points in their identity careers, which invariably included how they came to identify as homosexual.

Another, unavoidable problem is *the creative nature of memory*, especially when expressed in narrative form, and the alleged difference between accounts of the past and the objective reality of those pasts. This is, arguably, an even more significant obstacle when working with coming out narratives, since, as Plummer (1995) has shown, the coming out story, like the coming-of-age story, provides its own narrative restrictions, topics, and devices. As Carr (1999) and other interactionists have shown, when working within the conceptual sexual scheme of a static, "essentialist monosexuality," memory reorganization is needed to produce a homosexual identity in the face of previous, seemingly contradictory experiences and decisions. Producing a relatively stable, intelligible self that emerged over time requires the actor to selectively privilege certain past actions and orientations as representing the "true" self and/or "true" path, and to view other actions and orientations as deviations from them. Hence the retroactive characterization of previous heterosexual engagements as "less emotionally significant or satisfying than their present (or future) experiences, as 'just a phase,' or as 'false consciousness' relative to their 'real' or 'true' sexual selves" (Carr 1999, p. 8). Subjects' identity work, then, is evident not only in their statements *about* the consequences of their homosexuality, or about homosexuality in general, but in their narrative constructions of the process through which they came to identity as homosexual in the first place.

While mindful of the pitfalls of presenting accounts of the past as neutral depictions of actual events, I do not see them as invalidating subjects' claims. This book approaches its informants' narratives as narratives–not as statements about the past that can be independently corroborated and that can function as objective independent variables. There is, of course, no way for me, or for any other author relying on narrative data, to corroborate my respondents' claims, but even if there were, this would not provide us with any more insight into their identity careers or identity work, since these are intermeshed and available only in the form of their expression. The goal of this book is to capture subjects' engagements with various discursive representations of homosexuality; the fact that they recount and assess their own, past engagements with them only provides for richer data. Put bluntly, subjects aligned themselves with different discourses of homosexuality that prevailed in different historical eras, situating themselves in these eras and offering distinctive sets of standards for the appropriate responses to the historical circumstances they faced. Their accounts of the identity work they conducted in specific historical circumstances are thus moral claims as much as they are descriptions of past actions, and these claims are intelligible when viewed through the lens of the discourses with which they affiliated.

Yet another factor that influenced the course of the interview and, ultimately, the data itself was *my own presence and actions as a researcher*. I often felt a tension between my role as interviewer/researcher and my connection to the matters we discussed. My personal involvement with, and stake in, the ongoing discourse about homosexuality, and my knowledge about the homosexual world, made it perhaps easier for me to understand and pursue topics that informants raised than it would have been if I identified as heterosexual. In short, I was "in the life"; while my own, queer identification placed me in a distinct relationship to subjects' homosexual identifications, the discourse framing me and them as sexual deviants reemphasized our commonality in the eyes of others, and this commonality often shaped the interview. I was also, of course, separated from my subjects by at least one generation. This created a space for the transmission of subcultural knowledge from "old-timers" to a perceived neophyte, a relationship that was a useful venue for the production of meanings about homosexuality, identity, and social change. Differences between my informants and me gave them the opportunity to situatedly produce themselves as older gay men and lesbians engaging in the intergenerational transmission of "expert" knowledge of self, homosexuality, and the homosexual world.

This tension sensitized me to differences among subjects, a benefit that stands in contrast to the claims of those who see these pushes and pulls as undermining methodological integrity. Underlying criticisms of qualitative research is a concern with the impact of otherness on the interview itself. Do differences between interviewer and interviewee potentiate or preclude insight into members' meanings? Standpoint theory (see Harding 1991; Smith 1990; and Stanley 1990) claims that members of oppressed groups have difficulty articulating their experiences in dominant terms, partly because those terms are enmeshed in a project to preclude the coming to consciousness and expressiveness of their experiences. According to this approach, otherness is a methodological liability, and people who are not members of an oppressed group must work to capture that group's social world.

In the case of these interviews, however, differences between my subjects and me (our histories, understandings of past and present, and homosexual careers and politics) emerged not as obstacles to understanding, but as opportunities to explore homosexual identity work through contestation or lengthy discussion. Informants were remarkably attendant to my understanding of their talk, pointing out, correcting, and even mocking my blind spots and my often unwitting but sometimes strategic misinterpretations. They validated some of my interpretations of their talk and invalidated others, sometimes quite heatedly. Consider these three interactions:

Manny (77): I have another niece, who's married, and they're orthodoxish, and it's her brother that's gay. Many years ago, I went to Montreal, and I went to their house. And I had a glass of water, and the husband, as soon as I put down the glass, grabbed the glass and ran into the kitchen and washed the glass, that, because I drank, you know what I mean?

DR: Yeah.

And it was only because I'm gay, and he is a . . .

DR: Orthodox.

No, not that he's orthodox. He's a moron.

DR: He's a bigot.

Yeah, a bigot, that's the word to use.

DR: Jeez.

* * *

Jeannine (66): Well, I think somebody called us fairies, and then we talked about it, and we thought we'd heard the term *homosexual* at some point, so we looked it up in the dictionary. And homosexual, as I recall, is in *Webster's Unabridged*, and it was basically "a homosexual is a person who has a sexual relationship with a person of the same sex."

DR: Did you think the implications were, "Oh, this must be me"?

Well, I was annoyed, because it appeared that I would never be able to follow the major mode of what women were expected to do. Get married and have kids. And I was just kind of annoyed, because it put me out of the norm.

DR: So you were annoyed because you found that it precluded involvement in . . .

No, I was annoyed because it put me beyond the pale, basically. Yeah. Because it segregated me, in effect.

* * *

DR: So do you consider yourself to be out now?

Marge (81): How?

DR: I don't know, you tell me.

I'm not *with* anyone, I mean how would I know whether I would be out or not? When I was with her I wasn't, when I was in New York I was.

Subjects corrected my interpretations of their talk on the spot, underscoring my own assumptions about the sources of bigotry, the felt implications of membership in a stigmatized category, and the nature of being in or out of the closet, respectively. These corrections, while untheorized by the informants quoted above, nonetheless guided the interaction along lines that were intelligible to them and that were clearly intended to be intelligible to me. Sometimes I realized then and there that I had misinterpreted their talk, and sometimes I only realized it when I analyzed the transcripts. Sometimes, in fact, I engaged in a debate over the "true" nature of these and similar constructs, committing the cardinal sin of "taking sides," but these instances also served as opportunities for subjects to clarify and contest various stances. The transcripts I analyzed were riddled with these corrections, some of which were about important fissures in the ongoing debate about homosexuality and self, and all of which can be seen as minute, situated, ongoing attempts by subjects to make their points of view and experiences understood.

Thus, distance often served to bring me closer to respondents' meanings than it did to mask them. This often played out in unpredictable ways. While I was, for example, least biographically "other" to Kate, an "out" lesbian who was educated, middle-class, left-wing (and raised in a left-wing home), healthy, a teacher, and from the East Coast, I felt very different from her because she was antimale, antibisexual, antiqueer, and involved with the Jewish community–all things I am not. Our differences in outlook overshadowed our structural similarities, whereas the opposite occurred with Dan, a left-wing, feminist gay man.

Finally, qualitative research stresses the reality of *the interview as a collaborative product rather than as a neutral means of collecting objective information* (Holstein and Gubrium, 1995). The interview itself is thus an "identity occasion" in which subjects produce themselves as gay, lesbian, and old in response to, and as a way of shaping, the immediate exigencies of talk. As a consequence, the interviews acted as an arena in which I questioned "informants" on the one hand and encouraged the situated construction and display of homosexual identity on the other. While the interviews covered the same basic topics in roughly the same order, they were concerned both with capturing "information" and with deeply engaging those areas related to homosexuality that subjects raised themselves in the process of telling me "how it was" and "how it is." Moreover, all interviews are begun with both sets of actors' assumptions about the interview's goals somewhat in place. My subjects knew that age and sexual identity were aspects of self in which I was most interested, and that I was much more interested in their stories than in those of "famous" gay activists, to whom many subjects tried to refer me. Because the interview foregrounded the presence of homosexuality in subjects' everyday lives, I risked missing their more pressing concerns in exchange for extensive data about their homosexual identities. This is not an insignificant risk to have taken, since the felt relevance of homosexuality to self can tell us much about members' understanding of the nature of homosexuality. I compensated for this in two ways.

First, I asked subjects to assess the consequences of homosexuality for their lives. Responses ranged from those that depicted homosexuality as having a minimal impact on their lives to those that depicted it as "all there is." These assessments were both findings in themselves (some responses were characteristic of one identity cohort, and some of another) and reminders that the centrality of homosexuality may very well have been a feature of the interview rather than a reflection of practices engaged in outside of it. Second, I asked standard questions and allowed for digression. At the outset of the interview as well as throughout, I encouraged subjects to discuss experiences, ideas, and concerns they felt were important. The structure of the interview helped me do this: beginning the interview with questions about income or education, for example, often produced life histories and detailed narratives about particularly salient aspects of these histories. More open-ended questions (most notably, about coming out) produced these narratives as well. This allowed us to revisit moments in the interview and in subjects' own biographies in order to elaborate and question what was being discussed at the time.

The result is that the accounts that I unpack throughout this book may vary in significant ways. They may refer to specific circumstances and not others, to particular sets of actors and not others, and to particular periods of time and not others. Were these accounts unambiguous responses to specific questions about these circumstances, actors, and time periods, I could compare the answers to each question to produce a seamless, solid statement about subjects' understandings of discrete circumstances and events. These accounts, however, were not always produced in response to particular questions, but often emerged in the course of discussing other issues and events—were often, in fact, tagged as "tangential" by the subjects themselves. Descriptions of harassment by heterosexuals, for example, were made in the context of discussing past and present circumstances, the consequences of homosexuality for self, encounters with discourses of difference, and concerns about the future; each of these topics, in turn, inspired a wide range of other topics and concerns. This might by seen by more traditional sociologies as a problem of standardization that precludes a consistent understanding of subjects' lives, but I would argue that the consistency of assumptions and concerns *across questions and topics and endogenously produced by subjects themselves* speaks to their status as members' meanings that are central to their orientation to—and production of—distinctive social worlds.

Caught in the Web of Change: The Challenge of Capturing Lives Over Time

Groups that underwent a radical reconfiguration since the Second World War provide an especially promising insight into the intersection between identity and social change. How different ethnic and racial groups understand and organize themselves, for example, is very different now than it was before the emergence of the identity politics of the civil rights and Vietnam War eras, and of the global economy, among other things. Individual and group identities can change over great spans of time, as in the case of the "creation" of the notion of childhood, which took hundreds of years (see Aries 1960), but they can also change over shorter periods, often within an individual's lifetime.[2] Indeed, the alleged nature of group membership can change several times during an actor's life, as can be seen in the radically shifting discursive construction of gender and sexuality in the United States since the First World War.

While any one of a number of groups can be studied for the impact of the relatively rapid social and cultural changes of the modern and postmodern worlds upon the self, some may argue that sexual minorities are the most obvious choice for such study. Scholars such as Arlene Stein (1997), Valerie Jenness (1992), Vera Whisman (1996), and George Chauncey (1994) have all examined how the reshaping of sexuality and sexual identity over the past century influenced lesbian and gay identities. Others (see Devor 1997; Elkins 1997; Gagne et al., 1997; King 1993; Mason-Schrock 1996) have studied transgendered and transexual identities almost unimaginable a generation ago. That such research has been conducted is no surprise: it is, after all, in keeping with a central theme in sociology, namely, the relationship between self and society, and with one of its central foci, namely, the historical emergence of categories of people as a consequence of large-scale social change. Consider Marx's concern with the new bourgeoisie and the alienated man (both products of capitalism), Weber's writings on rational versus charismatic leaders and on the rise of the bureaucrat, and Whyte's (1956) work on the rise of the organization man. All describe new categories of people, with new modes of action, experience, emotion, and assessment. What is surprising, however, is that no one has yet considered the impact of the twentieth-century reinvention of sexuality on a group that lived through, and was directly implicated by, that reinvention–namely, lesbian and gay elders.

To be fair, there has been some research conducted on this population. Indeed, the 1970s and 1980s saw a mini-explosion of work on this topic (see, e.g., Berger 1982; Kelly 1977; Kimmel 1978, 1979; Friend 1980), and compilations of life histories of older gay men and women (see Adelman 1987; Coleman 2000; Gershick 1998; Jensen 1999; Vacha 1985) are now more readily available than ever. But the first wave was essentially a defensive one, designed to disprove stereotypes of homosexual elders as isolated and full of self-hatred,[3] life histories tend to present narratives without analyzing them, and more recent scholarly work on lesbian and gay elders (see Brady 1999; Baron and Cramer 2000; Cahill et al. 2000; Dorfman et al. 1995; Fredrikson 1999; Quam and Whitford 1992; Shernoff 1997) tends to adopt a gerontological, "problem-solving" approach.[4] What is missing from these works is an analytic appreciation of the sense-making work in which this generation of gay men and women engage as they consider the impact of their sexuality, and of the various regulations of that sexuality by heterosexuals and homosexuals alike, on their lives. How, if at all, did these actors respond to new definitions of homosexuality or to the startlingly new claims about sexuality in general, and homosexuality in particular, made by gay liberation and lesbian-feminism, all of which emerged in the middle of their lives? How diverse are their experiences and understandings? If they are not infinitely diverse, if we can discern some pattern to their beliefs, actions, and interpretations, how are these patterns to be explained?

This book has examined how lesbians and gay men born before 1930 make sense of their own and others' homosexuality, and how they organize their lives around it, in the context of the radical reformulation of sexuality that occurred over the course of their lives. It has treated identity

as an historically and culturally shaped product of and resource for interpretive work, and thus as a phenomenon to
be approached with a sensitivity to historical, cultural, and
interactional contexts. In the preceding chapters, I traced
the paths my informants followed on their way to adopting
homosexual identities, and linked their interpretations of,
and moral standards about, homosexuality to those paths.
Through their identity careers, subjects came to understand
the nature and implications of their desires, and determined
(in the sense of understanding *and* of creating) their quality and social standing. I found substantial–but not infinite–
variation in these careers. Some informants adopted a gay
identity before, and some after sexual contact; for others,
it was their difference from established gender norms and
identities, not same-sex desire, which led them to identify
as homosexual. Most did so because vague desires found
a definition that had been unavailable before, while for a
small group of others, the definition existed before the feelings that emerged–thus it was the feelings that were new,
not the category that explained them. These subjects saw
identification as a decision–knowing both sides of the aisle,
so to speak, they chose homosexuality for the relative benefits it provided at the time. There was also variation in the
fate of these identifications. For most, their identification as
homosexual was stable over time, but others moved in and
out of gay life and gay identity, often with pit-stops in bisexual identity, but also with stops at the land of asexuality,
later redefining themselves as homosexual as new personal
social, or societal circumstances arose.

Discourse, of course, loomed large in these careers. Although how and when respondents encountered a discourse
that explained their same-sex desires varied, the discourse
itself did not: all initially encountered the discourse stigmatizing same-sex desire and positing it as evidence of ho-

mosexuality. This discourse provided an identity peg, producing an intelligible yet devalued self. Caught between the benefits and liabilities of identifying as a stigmatized homosexual, most identified as such, adopting the stigmatized– and stigmatizing–meanings associated with that identity. These actors described their identification as gay as a relatively straightforward matter, devoid of trauma. Others, however, engaged in distancing techniques to weaken or modify the relevance of this formulation of self to their own actions and desires, and this presented a critical juncture in informants' identity careers, strongly influencing the identities they ultimately adopted. Respondents varied in the length of time they spent engaged in these distancing practices (some did so for many years) before changing contacts and contexts inspired identification as one of two particular types of homosexual: a stigmatized or an accredited one. For the smaller group that had distanced itself throughout the late 1960s, these changing contacts and contexts had been supplied and shaped by gay liberation and/or lesbian-feminism.[5]

These identity careers placed respondents in one of two identity cohorts–one that viewed homosexuality as a stigma or one that viewed it as a source of status–and it is this identity cohort membership, representing the adoption of an historically specific discourse of homosexuality, that shaped their identity work. While all subjects saw their worlds as defined and constrained by heterosexuals and thus as organized around conflict with them, for example, the nature of the conflict differed on the basis of identity cohort membership. For those who identified as homosexual before the advent of gay liberation, heterosexuals posed a threat to homosexual persons through the denial of essential resources, including civil liberties and social inclusion. For those whose identifications were made during or after gay liberation, however, underlying the heterosexual threat to person was a threat to the authentic homosexual self: the demand that homosexuals protect themselves from the former by suppressing or denying the latter.

These are not insignificant differences. They point to yet another set of practices affected by identity cohort membership: specifically, the actions and evaluations through which subjects navigated and succeeded in these worlds. Because their worlds were organized around two distinct threats, informants spoke of using distinctive, even competing, strategies to survive them, and of adopting competing understandings of how one should *act* as a particular type of homosexual in a particular type of world. For discreditable informants, threats to person mandated passing as heterosexual to avoid public attack and personal rejection, while for the accredited threats to self mandated disclosing one's homosexuality to others in public and private settings. But while subjects described these actions in some detail, they also presented them as prescriptions for the appropriate understanding and enactment of homosexuality which they followed but which other homosexuals did not. Thus, the accredited condemned homosexuals who did not recognize the true heterosexual threat as one to self, while the discreditable condemned those who failed or refused to pass as heterosexual. These and other fault lines express competing, endogenous standards of *evaluation* of homosexual self and other. Producing the self as a member of a particular homosexual order required and constituted what I termed *homosexual competence*: the mastery and appropriate application of local knowledge about what homosexuality is and how it should be enacted, evaluative criteria distinctive to each discourse and to which subjects were emotionally attached. What constituted homosexual competence and incompetence, however, varied according to the discourse grounding subjects' identities. For the discreditable subjects, homosexual competence consisted of passing as heterosexual and homosexual incompetence of coming out, while for accredited subjects the opposite was true. Homosexual competence emerged in respondents' tacit presentations of their own past actions as reasonable and in their direct claims to it. I attended to the challenge that naturally arose–to determine whether past actions and evaluations harmonized or conflicted with present ones–by considering subjects' retrospective assessments of these actions and evaluations that figured anywhere in the course of the interview. We have seen that members of the accredited identity cohort often spoke of their past passing practices as having seemed reasonable at the time, but as really being unreasonable given the real threat to self that these practices posed. In contrast, discreditable informants saw their past actions and evaluations as representing their lifelong, competent take on and response to the world. Just as subjects variously distinguished themselves from or claimed fellowship with other homosexuals to produce themselves as competent according to stigmatized or accrediting standards, they differentially distinguished themselves from or aligned themselves with their own past actions. Subjects' attempts to achieve homosexual competence also implicated their social relations on a number of levels, the most obvious being the avoidance of those they considered homosexually incompetent. For all those I interviewed, homosexual competence entailed both the ability to distinguish between the competent and the incompetent and the continuing commitment to achieve membership in the first, in part by condemning and avoiding both the actions and orientations of the latter category and of those who enact them.

In this context, homosexual competence functioned not as a set of inflexible rules but as a status that was achieved, often in typical ways, but sometimes in local, situated, creative ones. Because the perceived challenges homosexuals face are both ubiquitous and idiosyncratic, homosexuals cannot prepare for every contingency; while they may rely on certain relatively well-known techniques for meeting these challenges, they must primarily rely upon their ability to engage basic understandings within unfolding and contingent situations. Indeed, the very selection of these techniques requires an ability to read and assess the situation at hand. For example, while members of the discreditable identity cohort oriented to the project of passing as coherent and mandatory, they were aware of circumstances under which passing may have negative consequences for self and other, and, indeed, noted situations in which they themselves disclosed their homosexuality to heterosexuals. These instances, however, confirmed rather than contradicted the nature of passing as morally necessary. Similarly, accredited informants oriented to the project of disclosing their homosexuality–when made relationally or conversationally relevant–to heterosexuals as a goal whose achievement constitutes homosexual competence even when they themselves failed to enact it in circumstances that demanded they do so.

These findings expand our understanding of modern and postmodern identities in two ways. Giddens (1991) writes that the twentieth century was one of continuous changes that implicate family and personal lives. Without the meta-narratives that dictate morality and codes of action, actors experience their freedom from uniformly legitimated ideologies as risk, because each decision must be evaluated on a case-by-case basis. All decisions are made reflexively, including the decision to adhere to the same traditions that actors had upheld in unreflexive ways in the past. In the postmodern world, the self becomes an active project rather than a taken-for-granted resource, and actors pursue self-fulfillment and improvement–spiritual, psychological, and corporeal–in a context of increasingly plentiful options. In Giddens's (1991, p. 5) words, "The more tradition loses its hold, and the more daily life is reconstituted in terms of the dialectical interplay of the local and the global, the more individuals are forced to negotiate lifestyle choices among a diversity of options." The decline of absolutism thus calls forth an uncertain self, one beset by self-consciousness and self-doubt, as actors are continuously saturated by competing–and consumerist–directives for self-formation and self-expression.

Because living as a gay man or lesbian over the course of the twentieth century clearly involved a higher degree of reflexivity than one would have imagined existed seventy or eighty years ago, however, this group can be seen to have experienced this postmodern condition throughout the course of their lives. While academic discourse has only recently turned to the increasingly problematic nature of identity in a postmodern world, these elders' accounts suggest that, for them, identity has been problematic for a long time, even in the modern era. Indeed, they can be seen as having bracketed identity in an era in which, we assume, identities, and their implications for daily life, were relatively simple matters. What we think of as new and distinctive has, for this group, been in the offing for a while, even before Stonewall, as the tensions between the Freudian and the inversion models of homosexuality clearly show. Indeed, that Tony and Rodney chose between these formulations to produce a liminal heterosexuality based upon these constructs' utility to their specific circumstances (see Chapter 1) suggests that, for this group, at least, the ability to "negotiate lifestyle choice among a diversity of options" presaged the explosion of such options in the late twentieth century.

Second, the book suggests that, for this group and, perhaps, for other stigmatized groups as well, demographic categories explain beliefs and practices much less compellingly than does identity cohort membership. We are so smitten with the race/class/gender triumvirate that we tend to elide actors' engagement with history in ways that may be affected by these factors, but not reducible to them. Indeed, I was once criticized after presenting an embryonic version of this book at an American Sociological Association annual meeting for having given less weight to race and ethnicity than I gave to identity cohort membership in explaining my subjects' identity work. When I explained that my conclusions were borne out by my data, I was told that I was either analytically incompetent or deliberately distorting my findings. Of course, I have never argued that race, class, sex, or gender were unimportant—witness Michael's relative ease with being out in Hollywood, or the fact that women had much easier access to the liberationist discourse than did men—but what sticks out most clearly as an explanation for the differences in my subjects' homosexual identity work is the historical era in which they identified as lesbian or gay. This, of course, was clearly linked to whether they were still engaged in distancing during the late 1960s, when gay liberation and lesbian-feminism emerged, and the consequences of this for how they responded to the new, accrediting discourse these movements offered. For those who had identified through—and invested in—the stigmatizing discourse, the accrediting discourse represented both a threat and an insult to the lives they had built, not an opportunity for better ones. (For an earlier work on stigmatized homosexuals' response to the "colonizing influence" of gay liberation, see Grube 1990.) For those who had declined to identify as homosexual through the stigmatizing discourse, however, gay liberation and lesbian-feminism provided both a radically different homosexual identity and a radically new way to relate to heterosexuals and homosexuals. It also, of course, placed them in a distinctive and conflictual relationship to members of their own generation who maintained their affiliation with the discourse that stigmatized homosexuality.

These findings also have implications for other generations of gay men and women and for other groups for whom identity is negotiated within a changing social and discursive context. That discourses explaining sexual desire have become more plentiful and more readily available than was the case even twenty years ago, for example, makes the identity careers and identity work of those born during or after gay liberation and lesbian feminism, the emergence of AIDS and the new sexual activism, and queer theory and queer politics very different than were those of my informants. Only two years ago, the cover story in the *New York Times Magazine,* entitled "Lonely gay teen seeking same," described a young man negotiating his identity by accessing information and gaining social contacts through the Internet, stating that, "For homosexual teenagers with computer access, the Internet has, quite simply, revolutionized the experience of growing up gay" (Egan 2000, p. 113). Contrast that with the difficulty my respondents experienced in encountering a discourse of difference on the one hand and gaining access to the gay world on the other, and it becomes clear that future gay men and women will most probably devote much less time to this stage of their identity careers, and therefore spend a greater proportion of their lives as self-identified homosexuals. Moreover, the messages provided by the liberationist (and consumerist) discourse of homosexuality to which they now have relatively easy access are rapidly changing as well. For example, the inclusion of gay marriage and family, same-sex partner benefits, protection from hate crimes, and explicitly gay voting blocs are major threads in the current tapestry of rights that twenty-first-century gay men and women are now called upon to claim, and there is a strong possibility that at least some of these will achieve legal status in the course of current teenagers' lifetimes. Consider as well the dizzying potential of the homosexual "baby boom" of the 1980s and 1990s for the identities and everyday lives of currently middle-aged gay men and women in old age, and the identity cohort membership of future homosexual elders becomes even more significant.

The same argument can, of course, be made for other groups, stigmatized or not. Consider the implications of identifying as a member of any one of a number of groups that twentieth- and twenty-first-century identity politics worked to destigmatize, even valorize (the obese, alcoholics, drug addicts, children of interracial marriages, the learning disabled, the divorced, battered spouses, unwed mothers, Vietnam veterans and draft-dodgers, pacifists, victims of rape, incest, and poverty, and those diagnosed with cancer or AIDS), and of identifying as a member of a nonstigmatized group whose significance and parameters have changed over the past forty or fifty years (parents, teenagers, athletes, liberals and conservatives, members of the military, Jews, priests, academics, even members of the English royal family) in different historical eras. What divides one historical period from another will, of course, vary. For teenagers, it may be the massacre at Columbine; for the royal family, the death of Lady Diana Spencer; for those diagnosed with HIV, the advent of life-extending medicines; for priests, the current groundswell of accusations of child molestation; and, for any one of a number of groups, the attacks of September 11 and the resultant reconfiguration of patriotism, citizenship, and civil rights. Regardless of the specific fault lines that determine identity cohort membership, however, the fact that one never steps in the same river twice underscores the historicity of identity and its implications for a lifetime of decisions, opportunities, and accomplishments, and for the standards for evaluating these lives from the vantage point of old age.

Appendix

Informant Profiles

Discreditable Identity Cohort

Barbie (67): Single white female born in Midwest, now living in apartment. Received her BA and attended one year of graduate school; retired from her job as a schoolteacher in 1981. Annual income: $22,000. Had major surgery "about 1989," when she was diagnosed with cancer, and has heart trouble, but is allergic to the medication, and so has "to take it easy. I can't do too much." After a three-year stint with the telephone company after high school, she joined the army in 1951 and identified as a lesbian when she "met our kind." Left the army in 1954 to attend college, then taught in the Midwest, where she "never got close to anybody, men or women." She became lovers with a woman from the service after "running into" her while shopping, and they moved to California "as a couple." They broke up several years later. Currently "coming out of bereavement" over the death of a longtime friend she had met in 1969 at an AA meeting, and with whom she had shared a strong commitment to Christianity. Over the years, they had been lovers and had lived together "off and on." Although she is close to some heterosexual members of her "church family," she is "not really close to anybody [since] I lost her."

Brian (74): Single white male born in 1922 in the Midwest, living in an apartment. Retired in 1992 from career in banking. Annual income: $24,000. Had two years of college, then four years in the navy during the Second World War; identified as gay in 1946 and moved to Los Angeles in 1946 to "be in a gay lifestyle." Married a lesbian in 1952, at age twenty-nine, to pass as heterosexual at work and in context of his family, which remained in Iowa, and divorced in 1954. Socializes with gay men his age he meets at his gym. Close to his seven nieces and nephews, and to their children; closest to a fifty-year-old nephew living in New York, who is his heir.

Constance (74): Partnered Latina born in 1922 in Los Angeles, now living in rental house. Raised in Catholic orphanage, finished eleventh grade. Retired on disability in 1978 from janitorial job in hospital. Annual income: $8,000. Identified as lesbian in late teens; between 1941 and 1953, raised eight nieces and nephews after her sister died—supported them by driving a meat truck. Met Jane, "my second wife," in Baltimore in 1960s, where she was working as a bartender. Was with her for twenty-two years, then moved back to Los Angeles in 1987 because of problems in the relationship and because she felt that her family could help her with her growing health problems. Jane is still living in Georgia, where she and Constance had moved, and is dying of lung cancer. Constance does not feel that she can move to Georgia to care for her because "I have a bad heart. I could just drop dead any time. I can't do without this medicine. And if I go over there I know darn well that I won't have the coverage that I have here." Besides Jane, is closest to two gay women in their forties.

Dan (70): Single white male born in Brooklyn in 1926, living alone in an apartment, working full-time as a counselor for gay men. High school graduate, business school, and two years of fashion school. Writes a column for a gay magazine. Retired from city job in 1982. Annual income: $40,000 to $60,000. Identified as gay in the early 1950s after being kissed by a man: "That's when I became aware, when he kissed me in New York." Moved to Los Angeles in 1952 and to San Francisco in 1968; returned to Los Angeles when he retired. Founded social club for gay men over thirty-nine that folded in 1993. Has a network of gay male friends; is close to a female cousin ("we're like sisters"), but has "no feeling for family."

Deborah (74): Single white female born in 1921 in California, now living in own house. Retired from teaching career in 1978. Annual income: $13,520. Bachelor's degree. After college, worked in a psychiatric hospital, then joined the Women's Army Corps in 1942 and was shipped to New Guinea, moving back to Los Angeles after the war. Identified as gay in 1948, when her female roommate seduced her. Met Patricia at a gay party soon thereafter; they became lovers and lived together for "seven or eight years." After they broke up, Deborah became involved with another teacher, with whom she lived for ten years until, in the late 1960s, her lover left to "be really active in the women's movement." Closest to Patricia and to a heterosexual neighbor, and "sometimes hears from [her ex-lover] who's into consciousness raising. There's a feeling there that always stays. But people grow and they grow in different ways sometimes and sometimes they grow apart. And I think that is OK too."

Franz (86): Single white male born in 1910 in small village in East Prussia, now living in apartment. Annual income: $30,000. Left home at age fourteen to apprentice in the food industry because his parents could not support their eight children during the period of "very bad inflation." Identified as gay in his late teens which he had sex with a man. Worked in a department store in Germany until the fall of 1933, when he joined a Zionist training camp in preparation for his immigration to Palestine to escape the growing Nazi persecution of Jews. He arrived in Palestine in 1934 and found a thriving gay community. Met a man named Tomas, and was his lover for fifteen years until Franz immigrated to the United States in 1950. Met Gareth in 1956 and began a long, only intermittently sexual, friendship with him ("we were joined together for twenty years"); Gareth is now in a board and care home suffering from dementia. Franz retired from job as the manager of an import-export business in 1976 "when I had my first open heart surgery." Goes to senior center for lunch every day, is active in his gay synagogue, and has been volunteering at the Braille Institute for twenty years. Suffers from back problems, and eyesight is failing; has had two heart surgeries. Is closest to Gareth, his sister, and his nieces and nephews, all of whom live in the area.

Gabrielle (77): Partnered white female born in 1918 in Manhattan, now living with Betty, her lover of thirty years, in an apartment. Career in film and other investing, political fund raising, and restaurant/club management; retired in late 1980s when she had major back surgery and lost all her money in the oil business. After they "ran out of principal" in 1993, sold their house and moved to current apartment; now living on her social security and that of Betty, who was a well-known television actress in the 1950s and 1960s. Combined annual income: $20,400. Identified as gay in the late 1940s when she fell in love with Betty, even though she finds sex with men more fulfilling. She and Betty have a wide circle of heterosexual and homosexual friends, and are involved in women's tennis, but have lost many friends to AIDS; this, and her forced retirement, have made Gabrielle depressed. Closest to two gay male couples she has known for twenty to forty years, and to her niece and nephew.

George (75): Single white male born in 1920 in Canada, living alone on social security in a mobile home that he owns himself. Laid off from job as professional writer in 1988, and has been unemployed–and searching for work–ever since. Annual income: $7,308. Two years of junior college. Identified as gay in the early 1940s, when he fell in love with another young man. Best friend is an openly homophobic neighbor; older sister–the only family member with whom he remains in contact–lives in a nearby nursing home, but had lived with him before her health problems forced the move. Lover of twenty-two years died of AIDS in the early 1990s. Visits his sister every week.

Henri (67): Single white male born in 1928 in Canada, now living in condominium. Annual income: $20,000. For the twenty years before retirement in 1990, was in real estate; for the previous fifteen years, was a hairdresser; before that, was a professional dancer. Identified as heterosexual until age nineteen, when he had a sexual encounter with another male dancer. Became disenchanted with homosexuality in his late twenties when he had not found a long-term relationship and married a woman in 1959, when he retired from dancing and began hairdressing; they remained married for seven years, but divorced because she did not want to have children. He dated a few women after the divorce, but found that they did not measure up to his ex-wife; he then "went back to gay life" in 1968. Closest to a gay man his own age; attends a social group for gay seniors.

Jan (68): Single white female born in 1925 in Oklahoma, now living in condominium. Master's in education. Retired in 1993 from job as assistant principal of high school. Annual income: $45,000. Identified as gay in 1950 when, having seen the series of relationships she had been having with women (including a several-year affair with Kate) since her teens as "just a phase that I was going through," she decided to avoid further sexual encounters and relationships with men after she had a traumatic abortion. After a three-year stint (and a short affair with a woman) in Oklahoma, Jan returned to Los Angeles, where she got back together with Kate, a relationship that lasted until Jan fell in love with another school administrator nine years later. She lived with this woman until the woman's death from cancer in the late 1970s–a painful episode that resulted in her losing an extensive friendship network of gay women. Closest to a lesbian with whom she has been friends for many years, and with whom she travels, a gay man, and her sisters: "my sisters and I are close even though we don't discuss my sordid past."

Jeannine (66): Partnered white woman born in 1930 in southern California, now living in own house. Retired from twenty-year career as a schoolteacher in 1995, now owns and runs real estate business. Some graduate school. Annual income: $100,000. BA and teaching credential. Identified as gay in high school. Lived with one lover from 1948 to 1955, and another from 1955 to 1959. For thirteen years, has had a "secret relationship" with a woman who "lives with somebody else." Is closest to her lover, an ex-lover, and Jan, who took Jeannine to her first gay bar when Jeannine was seventeen. Knows "a lot of gay people. I give an open house every year, and about 300 of my closest friends come." No biological family except an aunt, to whom she is not close.

Julius (89): Single white male born in New England, now living in apartment. Two years of college; no degree. Retired from career in numismatics and accounting in 1971. Annual income: $8,000. Identified as gay in his mid-thirties, when he realized he had fallen in love with a young man who was stationed in Pearl Harbor after he and Julius had become friends, and whose younger brother lived with Julius (Julius considered the younger brother his son). Involved in "boys' clubs" in New York, where he would meet and mentor teenage boys, some of whom he would have sex with when they turned eighteen and asked to stay with him when they were in town, at which point they would often seduce him. Exclusively interested in young heterosexual men: "I always fell in love with straight people. That was why I eventually got to realize this is a losing game." Lived in Europe in early 1950s, then worked in New York for six years; moved to California in 1959–has had few sexual encounters since. Began attending meetings of a group for lesbian and gay seniors because "I was just curious. I didn't know anything much about gay people outside of what I had seen or read," but has "never sought [gay people] out and I still don't seek them out." Has few friends; is closest to a gay man he has known for over forty years.

Lillian (69): Single white female born in 1929 in Brooklyn, living in own house. Annual income: $20,000–$25,000. Two years of college. Retired in 1994 from career in real estate and business. "Got involved in gay life" in early twenties, after fiancé broke off their engagement, and "chose this sort of lifestyle. Truthfully I'm sorry I did, but I did." Soon thereafter, moved to California. Has "two or three very dear friends," all of whom are gay women, but "no family" except for a cousin in New York. Volunteers with children and elders, and attends social groups for lesbian seniors; wants to make more friends "because a lot of my friends have passed away."

Manny (77): Single white male born in 1919 in Canada, living in own house. Semi-retired from career in fashion industry. Annual income: $45,000–$47,000. Left school after elementary education because "it was the Depression years and we were poor." Joined the Canadian Army in 1939, at the age of twenty, and served in England from 1940 until 1944. Identified as gay in the early 1940s. Returned to Canada after the war, trained in "design and pattern making," and worked in New York, Florida, and Atlanta, moving to Los Angeles in 1953. Close to his nieces and to his brother. Has lunch once a week with "some people from my younger days when we used to cruise Pershing Square" (in the 1940s through the 1960s, a notorious gay cruising spot in downtown Los Angeles).

Maria (64): Single Latina born in 1932 in New Mexico and raised in Los Angeles, now living in apartment. Was expelled from school for refusing to wear girls' clothes in sixth grade, and got GED in 1979. Went on welfare and disability when she left job as a barber because of bad back and feet. Annual income: $7,968. Identified as gay in early teens; met "the love of my life" at age fifteen and was with her until she was in her twenties, when her lover stole the money from the bar they had bought and left. Maria could not find work because of her criminal record (she had been consistently picked up for "masquerading" and because of antigay bias) and lived on the streets "for a while" until she moved in with Mary, with whom she lived from 1957 to 1981. Is close to her brother, her brother-in-law, and two or three older lesbians she has known for years, including Patricia and Constance, and attends COOL functions and meetings. Has been seeing a psychiatrist for her depression over her physical disabilities, but doesn't feel she can discuss her depression with her friends.

Mark (72): Single white male born in 1940 in a farm in upstate New York, now living in apartment in a complex for which he had worked for fifteen years. Annual income from social security, disability, and investments: $12,000. Attended college and business school and received degree in business administration. Was ordained as minister in local Christian church when he "came to Christ" in 1989 as a way of coming to terms with his diagnosis of Parkinson's disease that same year. Identified as gay during the Second World War. Returned to upstate New York after the war and attended gay parties, meeting and falling in love with Joe; after he realized that Joe did not love him, he "decided that I was going to give up being gay," and had sex with a woman. When she told him she was pregnant, they married, but had their marriage annulled ("denying my daughter") after their daughter was born (and when she was pregnant with his son) when he found his wife in bed with his brother. He returned to Joe, and drove to California with him. They broke up three years later. Remains close to his daughter, who has two sons; he and his son are "not as close as we'd like to be." Neither of his children know he is gay, "and they never will." Is currently in love with a twenty-three year-old actor who used to be his masseuse, but does not know whether the feelings are requited. Is closest to his daughter; to a gay man he met "when he was younger" and through whom he became involved in the church; and to another gay man.

Michael (78): Single white male born in Wisconsin in 1917, now living in cooperative apartment. Got a bachelor's degree and a law degree. After law school, passed the bar, but found he "hated law"; got a job at a major newspaper in New York, then got a job at CBS, where he "sold two shows," both of which were highly successful, and became a soap-opera writer. Annual income: $100,000. Identified as gay in his early teens. Met lover of thirty-seven years in 1941 in New York, and moved to California with him in the early 1960s; lover died in 1977. Until recently, was active in several AIDS organizations, and is a trustee of a major Los Angeles hospital. Has a large network of heterosexual and homosexual friends in Hollywood, but no family except a cousin in San Francisco whom he visits once a month, and has made a new circle of friends through volunteer work.

Patricia (77): Single Latina born in 1914 in southern California, now living in apartment. AA in business administration. Retired from job as accountant in 1981; has worked part-time as secretary and treasurer for local nonprofit organization since late 1960s. Annual income: $15,000–$20,000. Diagnosed with cancer in 1992, and sold her house because it became too big for her to take care of when she was sick. Identified as gay in late 1930s, when she was in her late teens. Met Deborah in late 1940s and lived with her until the 1950s. Was with a third lover for five years, and has lived alone ever since. Closest to a lesbian she's known for fifteen years; her ex-lover, Deborah; two of her three sisters; and a gay man.

Phoebe (79): Coupled white female born in 1916 in Michigan, now living in own house. Retired from career in social work in 1973, then taught social work at local college until 1980. BA and master's degree in social work. Annual income: $34,000. Had sexual encounters with girls in high school, but her sexuality was "a spaceless mass" until she learned about lesbianism in her first year of graduate school in California, where she had moved with her current lover to "seek our fortunes during World War II," at which point she identified as gay. Was lovers with her supervisor from 1952 to 1989, until her lover developed dementia. Phoebe put her in a home, but visited every day; the woman died in 1994. Has been "committed" to her current lover for five years; closest to her lover and to several longtime lesbian and gay male friends. Considers herself a "political animal" and a "rock-ribbed Democrat," and is very active in her neighborhood organization.

Rhoda (89): Single white female born in 1907 in the midwest, now living in an apartment. Retired since 1984, when she sold the florist's shop she had owned since 1951. Annual income: $7,440. Has had four strokes, the last one earlier that year. Is "a joiner," but has cut her involvement in neighborhood, business, and civic organizations to "five clubs" since her last stroke–attends various meetings three to four times a week. Is on the board of a support group for senior gay men and women. Identified as gay in high school, and was very active in the prewar gay bar life in Kansas City. After high school, she broke up with her girlfriend of five years and worked for the Girl Scouts until the late 1930s, when she and her then girlfriend moved to Los Angeles, where she worked as a florist and was active in the gay culture of the time. Left her lover Ray for a woman named Billie in the 1950s and was about to buy a house with Billie when Ray, hurt by the breakup, circulated a rumor that Rhoda and Billie were gay. To protect Billie's "reputation," Rhoda broke off the relationship. She has not had a lover since. Is closest to Ray, who lives outside Los Angeles in a house they both own. Likes to visit Ray "every Christmas," but lost her driver's license after the last stroke; her friends at the support group for lesbian and gay seniors paid for her recent trip to see Ray. Of all her longtime friends, only Ray is still alive: "They are all gone; I have outlived them. So that makes it hard."

Ricardo (66): Single Latino born in 1930 in Argentina, now living in house with roommate. Retired from job as civil engineer in 1994. Bachelor's degree and some postgraduate training in civil engineering. Annual income: $20,000–$25,000. Identified as gay in his early twenties in Argentina. Immigrated to the United States in 1959 "to free myself from any expectations from my family to get married" and became active in gay subculture in Chicago and Seattle. Has had three lovers in the United States. Closest to his roommate, who is his "favorite person," but otherwise is "not really close to any one particularly in Los Angeles"; is close to his sisters, one of whom lives in Poland and whom he is planning to visit.

Rodney (75): Single white male born in 1920 in Utah, now living in retirement home. Retired in 1985 from career in social work. Annual income: $50,000. Received a master's degree and did doctoral work, but never got Ph.D. Learned he was homosexual in his late teens and had a nervous breakdown at twenty-one due to his sense that was a "misfit," of which his homosexuality was one expression–a self-understanding he still has. Was in therapy from 1941 to 1950 to distance himself from his homosexuality; worked from 1947 to 1951 while attending night school to get his high school and his bachelor's degrees. "Buried [him]self in school twenty-four hours a day . . . to compensate for [his] earlier feelings of inadequacy" and to "fit in socially," something he only achieved when, in 1959, he found a gay subculture in Salt Lake City and "began to socialize with other gay men," at which point he stopped distancing himself from his homosexuality and actively identified as gay. Moved to Los Angeles in 1973 and worked as a caseworker until he retired. Moved into retirement home in 1993. Closest to three gay men, two in San Francisco (one of whom he has known for forty-five years) and an ex-lover in Salt Lake City. Not close to his family, but became close to a gay nephew who contacted him in the late 1980s and who had recently died of AIDS. "I'm not [involved with family] and I wish I were. I feel very stranded, I have a lot of hurt feelings here. I just feel–they know that I'm alone."

Ryan (81): Single white male born in 1915 in Midwest, living alone in own house. Two years of college, received an AA in Human Services. Retired from union job as grocery clerk in 1974. Annual income: $13,200. Identified as gay in his early forties, when he realized that he wanted to connect with men on an emotional as well as a sexual level. Attends gay and lesbian support group at Catholic Church. Has cut back on his volunteer work at AIDS hospices and cancer wards because of heart condition (he had heart bypass surgery in 1987). Looking for a roommate ("because sometimes at night I wonder what'd happen if I got sick during the night, or what I'm going to do with the house and things"), preferably a gay one (because "I think it would be better to have a gay guy than a straight guy. I'd get along with a straight guy but I think it'd be better, we could talk better and enjoy each other better"). Does not think he is "real close to anybody" except for his cousins, who live in the area, and he and his ex-lover are "like brothers."

Susan (75): Single white female born in 1921 in New York, now living in own house. Retired from job as medical receptionist in 1974, "then took some part-time jobs after that." Completed high school. Annual income: $20,000–$25,000. Identified as lesbian in her early forties, during a three- to four-year affair with another army wife. Divorced her husband in 1964, moved to California with her three daughters, and met a woman who became her lover until her death in 1990–a total of twenty-three years. Closest to her daughters, one of whom lives in the area, and to that daughter's twenty-five-year old son. While one of her daughters is a born-again Christian and condemns Susan's lesbianism, "it's not an issue that hurts us." She has some lesbian friends, but not "a preponderance of friends," and feels that she "had the best of both worlds. I really feel even if I don't find anybody else to share the rest of my life with, I've been blessed."

Tony (70): Partnered white male born in 1926 in New York, now living with partner of forty-six-years in house they both own. Retired from job as insurance executive in 1991. Annual joint income: $25,000–$30,000. Identified as gay in late teens. Moved to Philadelphia in late 1940s to escape the gossip and hurtful comments to which he was subjected after his homosexuality became known in the wake of a public fight he had with a lover. Moved to Los Angeles in 1949 and met Bill, with whom he has been lovers ever since. Closest to Bill; a lesbian neighbor he and Bill have known for thirty years; a gay male neighbor they have known for thirty-five years; a lesbian couple in San Diego; a gay male ex co-worker of Tony's who now lives in Las Vegas; and Tony's sister in New York. Bill's recent open-heart surgery has been a significant strain on Tony, who started to cry when he described how worried he was about him and told me that it was "very difficult to watch him suffer."

Val (74): Single white female born in 1921 in Southwest, living in apartment. Retired from Los Angeles Police Department in 1969. Annual income: $15,000 and $19,000 (receives no social security). After high school, worked for the telephone company, then in airplane parts manufacturing during the war. Controls diabetes through diet. Identified as gay in late 1930s "as the next natural step" in her understanding of herself as essentially a heterosexual male. Closest to "a little gang" of older lesbians, none of whom know she identifies as a heterosexual man. Since "almost my entire family has died off," she feels "totally isolated," but is "very close" to her brother, who lives in Florida. "I am one of the last leaves on the tree."

William (76): Single white male born in 1920 in upstate New York, living in apartment; works as a real estate broker. Annual income: $50,000. Moved to Los Angeles from New York in 1967. Identified as gay in 1954 when he fell in love with another man, after his fiancée broke off their engagement. Close to his cousins in California and New York; not close to any other family members. Volunteers at AIDS service organization.

Accredited Identity Cohort

Abby (70): Single white female born in New Jersey in 1926, now living in rented house. Retired in 1989 from job in human resources. Annual income: $10,000. Identified as gay in 1941, but then distanced herself from her homosexuality in the 1980s, when, after alcohol rehabilitation, she began to equate her alcoholism with her lesbianism, since she began drinking when she entered gay life in 1952. Until 1992, when she reconnected with the gay world, she was "living in a straight world, more or less," and "was completely unaware of all the changes that had occurred in gay life, I guess since the seventies, that the centers were evolving and everything." When she attended a Gay Pride Festival in West Hollywood in the summer of 1992, however, she learned of the existence of a group for lesbian and gay seniors and became involved in that group and in the new, post-Stonewall gay culture, through which she now identifies. Volunteers at a local lesbian historical society; closest to two lesbian seniors who are active in that society. Is "very close" to her family on the East Coast, and "very, very close" to her sister. Tries to visit family every two years.

Kate (76): Single white woman born in 1920 in Texas, now living in own house. Retired in 1982 from a career in teaching; works part-time for teacher's organization. BA, some graduate school. Annual income: $28,404. Met Jan in 1944 ("it was love at first sight"), and had a relationship that ended eighteen months later when Kate "hit the panic button and threw [Jan] out" after she discovered other lesbians at a summer camp where she was working as a counselor and realized that her relationship with Jan placed her in the homosexual category. Began to visit doctors and psychiatrists, and to date men, to "cure" herself of her lesbianism, a quest she only relinquished when Jan visited her in the spring of 1955 and they "fell all back in love again." Jan and she lived together until 1964, when they broke up. At the encouragement of a new therapist, Kate began attending NOW meetings in the early 1970s, and became a "born-again lesbian," identifying through the properties of the lesbian-feminist discourse that NOW members were creating. Closest to three gay women; a heterosexual male co-worker; her uncle's wife; her aunt; and a female cousin; and is very involved in her gay temple, where she has "the feeling of family" but feels "very much alone."

Leonard (72): Partnered white male born in 1924 in Los Angeles, now living in own house. Retired from counseling job; on permanent disability since 1979, when he was assaulted by a client.

Some graduate school. Annual income: $14,600. Had sexual encounter with man in air force during Second World War. Was fired from job in State Department in 1954, during McCarthy-era purge of homosexuals and other "security threats," for admitting to same-sex sexual fantasies, even though he identified as heterosexual at the time and was engaged to be married to a longtime girlfriend. Moved to New York and went into therapy to "cure" himself of homosexuality, but identified as gay later that year, when he discovered that the bar he had been patronizing was a gay bar, that the "normal," gender-conforming men with whom he had been socializing were homosexual, and that there was a homosexual identity, based not on gender inversion but on same-sex attraction, which he could embrace. Broke up with his fiancée that same year, and began a series of same-sex encounters with black men, becoming involved in the thriving gay life in Harlem and in the nascent civil rights struggle of the 1950s and 1960s, spending some time in the South in the early 1960s. This involvement caused him to recognize the futility of black men passing as white and, by extension, of gay men passing as straight, and to see his exclusive choice of black men as sexual partners as a way to distance himself from his homosexuality. Leonard was instrumental in creating a gay liberationist discourse based on the open disclosure and celebration of homosexuality, and identified through its properties. Moved to Los Angeles in 1961 and became lovers with Randall; they moved in together in 1966, and lived together until 1989, when Randall died. Works part-time counseling neighborhood youth and running program for gay seniors in downtown housing complex. Close to his current partner.

Marilyn (66): Single white female born in 1930 in California, living alone on social security and pension in a co-op apartment. Annual income: $18,300. Was a librarian's assistant in Los Angeles for thirteen years before retirement in 1995; previously, had delivered sandwiches and worked for a corporation. Lived in New York from 1957 to 1969. Identified as lesbian in the early 1970s, when, after encountering feminists at a NOW meeting, she immersed herself in radical lesbian-feminism and joined a lesbian-separatist collective. Close to her sister; not close to her brother; very close to a cousin in Arizona. Involved in social groups for lesbian and gay seniors, and volunteers at local cultural program for seniors.

Mary (66): Single African-American female born in 1930 in Oklahoma, now living in own house. Some college. Active in lesbian and gay movement–has "been an activist for many years"–and holds a leadership position in a national African-American gay organization, which she helped found. Works as a social worker, a job she secured in 1990 after a five-year retirement, and from which she hoped to retire soon. Annual income: $40,000. "Decided to become gay" in the early 1970s when her husband asked for an "open marriage" and she found that her new relationships with women were more emotionally fulfilling than her relationships with men. After three years of an open marriage, she and her husband divorced. Is "very close" to her two daughters, her son, and her six grandchildren. One daughter and her son live in the area. "My whole family is close. Christmas time, we all had dinner out with my ex-husband and his wife. Thanksgiving they were all here. We just have that kind of a family. Once you're in this family, divorce does not put you out of it. You only get out of this family if you choose to. That's the way it is." Most of her close friends have died; remaining friends include a female ex-lover, with whom she had lived from 1978 to 1986, "a couple of other younger women that have become very close friends with me," and childhood friends from Oklahoma.

Sharon (66): Partnered white female born in 1930 in Florida, now living with female lover in rental house. Is a paralegal employed full-time as a collection manager, although her "real life is a minister." Looking for part-time work so that she and her lover "can enjoy life a little more." Planning on retiring in 2001. Annual income: $40,000. Two years of college, BA in theology, AA from local college. Has had two heart attacks and circulatory problems with legs, being treated "for a heart murmur, but the Lord healed me, I'm sure I'm fine," and problems with her wrists. Identified as lesbian in the 1950s, then moved to California in 1956 and embraced a gay liberationist identity, which she found through the new Metropolitan Community Church in the 1960s. She pursued a career as a minister, receiving her BA in theology in 1979, and opened her own MCC church, which folded in 1984. Closest to her lover of twenty years, her brother, her sister, and a lesbian with whom she's been friends for thirty-five years. Very involved in religious and volunteer work, both within and outside the gay community, and in visiting and helping her lover's family, which lives in the area; had just started a social group for older lesbians. Is concerned about her lover, who is diabetic and is losing her eyesight.

Tex (72): Partnered white male born in 1924 in the Northeast, living with lover of twenty-two years in apartment. Combined annual income: $25,000. Is employed full-time as manager of the apartment building in which he lives. Two years of college, got an AA degree. Takes daily insulin injections for diabetes. Worked for

Lockheed through mid-1960s, then as a home health care worker and a classroom aid for handicapped children. Had same-sex encounters in late 1950s and early 1960s, while heterosexually married, and identified as gay in the late 1960s when he read an early gay liberationist book that told him he "had to be myself." Left his wife in 1966 and divorced her in 1968; had a "good relationship" with his five children "for a while," but then "it all fell apart," and he has only been in touch with them for the last "couple of years." Two have visited, and they were planning a family reunion in the spring of 1995. Is closest to his lover and to a few other gay men his age.

Notes

Introduction

1. With the exception of Maria, who "sneaked in" a few months shy of that age.

2. Adelman goes on to caution against interpreting the comforts that old homosexuals derive from passing as a panacea. On the contrary, she emphasizes that all her subjects, whether passing or not, expressed "frustration and anger" at having to "negotiate between equally demanding extremes," namely, secrecy or the discrimination attendant upon disclosure (1991, p. 22).

3. While traditional sociology views identity as an objective category that can be used to predict or explain social behavior, the interactionist tradition approaches individual and group identities as social products of–and sustained and elaborated in–interaction with self and others. According to this approach, membership in a category relies not on an analytic congruence between an actor's "characteristics" and those typical of that category, but on the actor's own, active identification with that category–in Anderson's (1983) formulation, as an interpretive commitment to an "imagined community." Moreover, identities, while the product of interpretive work, are themselves interpretive resources; actors invoke existing categories of persons–whether they identify with them or not–to make sense of their own and others' actions, and elaborate those categories as new behaviors, interpretations, or circumstances emerge. Through this situated discursive and practical identity work, categories and attributes "of" a particular identity are invoked, enacted, and elaborated by those claiming that identity for self and for individual and group others. Others, such as Barbara Ponse (1978), have understood the term *identity work* to refer only to the work designed to change specific identities, and not to

224   Notes to Introduction

the work that elaborates and/or reaffirms them. Stein (1997, p.
66), citing Ponse, uses the term to "signify the process by which many
individuals sought to make their subjective sense of self congruent
with their emergent social identity and to narrow the experiential
gap separating them from other, more experienced lesbians." This
understanding has more in common with Berger's (1981) "ideological work" than with my application of the term to the process
of producing both taken-for-granted identities and identities with
which the subject might be consciously engaged.

4. The interviews, which lasted anywhere from one and a half
to three hours, were conducted in subjects' homes (one was conducted in mine), and covered coming out, daily routines, relations
with family, friends, and the lesbian and gay communities, attitudes toward these communities, concerns for the future, and gay
aging itself. I coded the transcribed interviews using open cod-
ing schemes, developing a list of issues and concerns the subjects
raised in response to my questions and in the context of topics we
pursued. I then input these coded transcripts into Ethnograph, a
qualitative software program, to generate separate files on each
of these themes (e.g., identifying as homosexual, passing, gender,
harassment, and heterosexual marriage). While analyzing individual narratives allowed me to appreciate the emergence of subjects'
concerns and experiences over time, these files encouraged me to
note differences between and patterns among these narratives, and
to see how the patterns that emerged were linked.

5. No cold calls were made. Instead, I asked if respondents
would call people they knew who fell within the study's guidelines
and ask if they would consent to my calling them. If they agreed, the
initial contacts called me and gave me their names and numbers.

6. Nineteenth-century sexologists such as Havelock Ellis and
Richard Krafft-Ebing, proceeding from the assumption of the necessary and exclusive complementarity of male and female repro-
ductive functions, helped hegemonize a gender-based discourse of
sexuality that associated gender inversion with homosexuality by
describing homosexuality "as violating 'the hidden laws of nature'
by confusing the appropriate roles of men and women" (D'Emilio
1983, p. 17). According to both authors, "the true invert was a being between categories, neither man nor woman, a 'third sex' or
'trapped soul'" (Newton 1989, pp. 288–289). However, while Krafft-
Ebing pathologized homosexuals, deeming them "degenerates" incapable of controlling their sexual urges, Ellis was more sympathetic, locating inversion in "the vast range of sexualities in which
healthy men and women had indulged" (McLaren 1999, p. 95.)

7. Organizations stressing an assimilationist response also emphasized educating heterosexuals about the potential of the "sex variant" for adjustment. This, combined with a desire to understand the homosexual "condition," produced a reliance upon the alleged expertise of professional psychologists and academics, many of whom attended meetings to educate gay men and women on their "emotional disturbance" (D'Emilio 1983, pp. 116–17). (The assimilationist reliance on "experts" drawn from the ranks of dominant society was already a firmly established practice, having been used to settle "the woman question" that virtually dominated public discourse in the late eighteenth to early nineteenth centuries–see Ehrenreich and English 1978.) This reliance, in turn, informed a purposeful condemnation and avoidance of an incipient, politicized homosexual movement, a stance based upon a perceived lack of solidarity and connection between gays, and on the real dangers of publicly identifying oneself as homosexual. Because assimilationists assumed that homosexuals were incapable of understanding their "condition" without the help of science, any form of public organization or activism was seen as counterproductive and dangerous to the safety afforded by assimilation.

8. Published in the first edition of *The Ladder*, its official newsletter, and reprinted in every issue until 1967 (Faderman 1991, p. 180).

9. Note that the variant was cautioned to adapt to "society," not to "heterosexual society." This demonstrates the assimilationist understanding of a distinctive homosexual society as unthinkable or unacceptable, as was a homosexual identity, since homosexuality was, in this middle-class formulation, merely a question of sexual object choice.

10. The Gay Liberation Front, which saw gay liberation as a stepping stone to human emancipation from, among other things, capitalism and imperialism, saw the traditional gay subculture, with its transient and anonymous sex and its use of sexual and gender "role-playing," as an impediment to human liberation, as were the "old-line homosexuals" who embraced it. The Gay Activists Alliance, on the other hand, was formed out of discomfort with this radical line, and devoted itself to protecting this gay world from police harassment by gaining the support of liberal heterosexual politicians.

11. The more radical gay liberationists (the Gay Liberation Front) "portrayed homosexuals as revolutionary subjects who were uniquely situated to advance the cause of sexual liberation as a whole" (Epstein 1987, p. 138), an emancipation that, prefiguring

social constructionism, foresaw the eventual dissolution of sexual categorization itself–including the hetero/homosexual binary upon which both heterosexual and homosexual identities had come to depend. This approach informed lesbian-feminism, according to which "lesbianism became a political stance, a challenge to patriarchal domination" (Stein 1993, p. 13) and to a gay movement that equated the needs and dispositions of gay men and women only by erasing women's unique experiences and political position. Finally, a group of more reformist homosexual activists (the Gay Activists Alliance), having embraced "the language and politics of minority groups" provided by the civil rights movement (Valocchi 1991, p. 217), saw homosexuality as a distinct mode of being whose collective "possession" constituted "a distinct social group with [its] own political and social interests" (Epstein 1987, p. 139) centered on demonstrating and ensuring individual homosexuals' comfort with their identity and subculture and best met through social reform. While the radical gay liberationist and lesbian-feminist approaches had waned by 1973 (see Valocchi 1991, p. 217), the reformist approach produced the dominant homosexual identity today: an ethniclike construction of homosexuality as a source of status–an innate, totalizing identity that should be proclaimed with pride–rather than as a source of stigma.

12. The term itself, of course, had meant very different things even over the past century. Before the 1960s, *coming out* did not refer to identifying as gay to heterosexuals, but to "the private decision to accept one's homosexual desires and to acknowledge one's sexual identity to other gay men and women" (D'Emilio 1983, p. 235). While members of the homophile movement publicly identified themselves as homosexual through their political work, they did not, for the most part, suggest that other gay men and women do the same, since they saw their own public identification as a politically, but not personally, beneficial practice (ibid.). By the 1970s, the term could be used to mean one's first same-sex experience, but, in Chauncey's (1994, p. 8) words, "more commonly referred to announcing one's homosexuality to friends and family. *The critical audience to which one came out had shifted from the gay world to the straight world*" (emphasis added).

13. Admittedly, this formulation elides important differences between the revolutionary and the reformist branches of the post-Stonewall lesbian and gay movements. But the fact that these movements all called for the public disclosure and enactment of homosexuality, and posited homosexuality as a valid and accrediting identity–either because of its revolutionary potential, or because

of its intrinsic value as a valid alternative to heterosexuality—made them individually and collectively distinct from the stigmatizing discourse that they rejected, at least in the eyes of my subjects, none of whom made explicit or implicit distinctions between them in the course of their identity work.

14. In Hewitt's (1994, p. 161) words, identity categories "provide a basis for people to locate themselves and one another in the social order and at the same time to imagine the social order itself."

Chapter 1: "I Didn't Have Identity"

1. When I asked Ryan (81) if he was aware of being attracted to men during his childhood, he spoke of a preoccupation with anal pleasure before the age of two, when "anything I found that was shaped like a penis, I was trying to stick it up my fanny." Discovering that "there was just more pleasure that way than any other way, that's [the way] I went." Phoebe also described becoming aware of her sexual desires during her first lesbian experience, which occurred in high school. While the sexual encounter was both "wonderful" and "scary," it "sort of defined" her previously unsuccessful heterosexual encounters. It was because of the sexual experience with the girl that she "began to know that I was attracted to girls. It was kind of a spaceless mass before that, because I was too busy with music."

2. For some of those whom I interviewed, this ignorance about homosexuality was exacerbated by an ignorance of sexuality in general. Rodney, for example, was "extremely naive about sexuality, I didn't understand sexuality," and his naivete "was such a misery" because "I knew that I was attracted to men but I didn't verbalize it. I didn't understand it, I didn't understand sexuality, reproduction." Jeannine linked her failure to recognize that her attraction to women was sexual to the fact that she didn't know "anything about sexuality *really*, except for a little book that my mother gave me when I started menstruating. Just something about male and female anatomy."

3. Others contrasted the dearth of information in their youth to the relative bumper crop of information about, and discussion and images of, homosexuals that they felt characterized late-twentieth-century America. During his first relationship with a man in his teen years in Argentina, Ricardo "was confused" because he "didn't know exactly what gay meant," and explained his confusion as the product of a general ignorance typical of the times. "Nowadays," he explained, "your generation has more information about these

cases, more vocabulary, pictures, movies, everything. At that time, it was taboo to talk about this." When I asked Henri (67) what he thought being gay was about before he had his first same-sex experience, he answered that he "didn't really know. It may be different today, now that we have gay magazines and all kinds of stories. In those days you just didn't know."

4. Indeed, getting one's hands on printed versions of this discourse in the first place was memorably difficult, even dangerous. Kate described the virtual security measures she had to undergo to take sexological literature out of the University of California in Los Angeles's library, where she went after finding that

> the public library of course had next to nothing. And somebody told me, I figured out for myself: go to the UCLA Library. Do you know I had to fill out a form to get hold of Krafft-Ebing and Havelock Ellis, saying that I was doing research? Now what kind of lie I told them, I was also a teacher and I guess that that was enough, but I had to fill out a form to get the damned things and absolve them. I don't know, what the hell.

5. Rodney was "intrigued" with the magazine for two reasons. First, having suffered through a childhood of taunting, he "wanted muscles of my own," and second, he was "interested in the pictures of the men, which was the nearest thing that was available in terms of pornography in those days."

6. The book, published in 1928, depicted its heroine, Stephen, as a tragic yet sympathetic figure whose lesbianism was an innate trait and who discovered the "true nature" of her desires by reading her father's copy of Krafft-Ebing's works. While Stephen's relinquishing of her female lover so that the latter could return to a "normal" heterosexual life depicted homosexuality as a life best avoided, the book "exploded the notion that lesbianism should or could be either punished or prevented" (McLaren 1999, p. 104).

7. *Trade* is a term referring to men who have sex with men while considering themselves heterosexual. As Manny explained, "Trade meant that he was straight and had sex with another man."

8. These relationships must be distinguished from subjects' use of heterosexuality to test their emergent homosexual selves. Patricia, for example, "tried everything. I've slept with men because I wanted to find out where I really belonged and you couldn't sell me on it. So I knew where I belonged and this is where I stayed." Deborah explained that her relationship with a man was a way to clarify her sexual identity.

Half the time I was thinking, "What the hell do you think you are doing?" There were lots of contradictions. You see, it really cemented it for me, my relationships really made me see what I am. And it seems to me I had to have that as a proof even though I had gone through these two long relationships. I still thought, "Gosh, I wonder if maybe . . ." but it wasn't right. I was living the wrong kind of life [with him].

9. When I asked her how these women were recognizable as gay, she described a range of signs: "Partly because some of them were real butchy looking, partly because there was a lot of talk about it in the counselor meetings, a lot of kidding and joshing–they were quite open. And partly because I became very close friends with Gina who was on the point of getting involved with Franny, and she confided in me."

Chapter 2: "I Picked Up That I was Gay"

1. Coming out as a voyage of self-discovery that needs to be made and that needs to be spoken emerged from the consciousness-raising efforts of second-wave feminism in the 1970s and from the politicization of homosexuality by the Gay Liberation Front in the late 1960s. It has since become routinized and readily available through the vast number of outlets for gay narratives–centers, groups, books, magazines, public appearances, and folklore–that have emerged over the past thirty years. The stories' parameters consist of

> a shift in consciousness in which the emergence of stories plays a crucial part. The awareness of stigma that surrounds homosexuality leads the experience to become an extremely negative one; shame and secrecy, silence and self-awareness, a strong sense of differentness–and of peculiarity–pervades the consciousness. At another point in time, the engulfing stigma gets neutralized through an appropriate tale: the ability to experience sexuality positively comes to exist (Plummer 1995, p. 89).

2. As Maria explained, this was a Spanish (and derogatory) term for hermaphrodite:

> Maria: Well, some of the people yelled *manflora* at me. You know, *manflora* in Spanish is a–you know, that's got both parts?

DR: Oh, *flora* referring to the vagina and *man* referring to the–oh, so it's a hermaphrodite!

Maria: Uh huh, that's it.

3. Rodney also explained, however, that this sense of inclusion and solidarity was short-lived:

I was coming out and, "Oh, I've arrived now, I don't need to be lonely anymore because I found my own, where I belong" and not by any means sexual, but social life and so on. I didn't realize, however, I was still very lonely and very isolated.

4. She continued: "I have to tell you, though, that it wasn't because I couldn't enjoy sex with a man. *Never* the way with a woman, I mean it was never *that*–well, it was not satisfying, but I could have an orgasm with a man."

5. Several subjects, however, mentioned wanting to avoid marriage and children as an *effect* of their gay identities rather than their *cause*, although the causal relationship often got murky in the retelling.

Brian: When I came out of the navy, we were stationed quite a length of time, six months or so, in New Orleans with our ship. And they were converting it and doing work on it, so I lived in the city. And I met a girlfriend *there*, whom I was going with. Now, I got out of the navy and I went back to New Orleans a while to live, and we were going to get married. Then I realized, that was before coming out, that this is not what I want. So I had to break up with her. Didn't tell her why. Don't want to be married. Didn't want to do it to her, the girl. I'm off this. So after we broke up, I came out here. Then I knew I belonged.

DR: So it was being engaged to be married, that was the . . .

I would say that. By then, I knew. I knew, "Don't want to be married to a girl." Don't want children, don't want the responsibility of family. Then I knew I was gay. By then I knew.

DR: Was it because you knew you didn't want to get married to a girl that you knew you were gay, or was it because you knew you were gay that you knew you didn't want to get married?

Because I was gay that I didn't want to get married to her, I would say, yeah. Around that time, when I knew for sure.

6. Which she described as someone with

a basic understanding of the fact that every society on the planet, past and present, is male-dominated for the satisfaction of males. Women have been oppressed, are oppressed, by males. They contribute to their own oppression by having been brainwashed to think that this is their role–that we don't recognize our oppression any more than we recognize atmospheric pressure.

7. A stance she now feels was "impractical" and caused her to lose "part of friendship by being separate from some men."

8. The MCC is the first and largest lesbian and gay church in the world, and is explicitly accrediting, albeit reformist, in its insistence that Christian doctrine abandon its stigmatizing stance toward sexual minorities, specifically homosexuals.

9. This was a not atypical move for politically concerned gay men and women at the time. As Valocchi (1999, p. 217) wrote,

The civil rights movement . . . provided the nascent gay movement with the language and politics of minority groups. Further, the movement for black equality proved quite seductive to many middle class men and women who were captivated by its energy and the attention it received. Some of the members of the Daughters of Bilitis and Mattachine were participants in the black freedom struggles, and these activists used the language of discrimination, civil rights, and equal opportunity in their marches to protest discrimination against homosexuals in the armed services and the federal government.

Chapter 3: Biography and History

1. This account is almost identical to one provided by Henri, who, having been in a heterosexual relationship when he joined his dance company, "always wonder[ed] what would have happened if I [had] not joined the show. I would have gotten married, and God knows what would have happened." Similarly, Ricardo felt that "the basis of my gayness was developed" from the strong yet platonic relationship he had with a priest throughout his childhood; had he not met the man, "I don't think I would have been."

2. Social change is also driven by the continuous ascendance of new generations, each with distinctive generational outlooks with which they seek to replace–inevitably, through conflict–preceding

ones. The newly dominant generation, of course, replaces its predecessor's entelechy with its own, thus introducing a new event to which members of different units will respond according to their habitual patterns (hence more conflict). An historical era's worldview is thus the product of the succession of generations fueled by conflict on the one hand and reproduction on the other.

3. Subcultural discourses such as those used by homosexuals are informed by generations and generation units, but are not reducible to them. Subcultures composed of the stigmatized necessarily engage in a local discourse that, to the dominant culture, is unthinkable and unspeakable: namely, that the stigma in question is a construction and the constructors/oppressors are wrong. Thus the actions and interpretations of subcultural members are not part of "the characteristic social and intellectual currents of their society and period," as Mannheim would have it, although they may be filtered through them. This would explain the ideological distinctiveness of subcultures from the *Weltanschauung* of generations and generation units, to which members of a subculture also belong.

4. People are differently implicated by events based, in part, on their age and life-course position, as when teenagers are targeted by ideological campaigns (i.e., antidrug), or when parents are asked to send their sons to war.

5. For example, the age-standardization of education, which launches men and women into the workplace and/or marriage and the family in their early twenties (although the latter have become less standardized since the 1980s), and the medicalization of the life course, which accords each life "stage" a distinctive medical status (see Rosenfeld and Gallagher 2002). For a summation of how "individual lives have become increasingly structured by separate institutional domains and by the state's regulation of those domains," see Settersten (1999, p. 21).

6. Clearly, this statement exhibits a dependence upon the 1960s-era emphasis on public disclosure that elides the more complex processes of homosexual identity formation and identity work.

7. Those she interviewed who came out before Stonewall did so at a median age of fourteen and understand their homosexuality to be an innate condition, whereas those who came out in the post-Stonewall years did so at a median age of twenty and saw their homosexuality as a choice (Whisman 1996, p. 19).

8. Stein thus "designated [her] cohorts by year of birth" (p. 7), grouping her subjects into those born between 1945 and 1961 and those born between 1961 and 1971.

9. However, identity cohorts as I have formulated them are not the equivalent of "political generations." The latter are the result of a generation's mobilizing and organizing to create or prevent political change (see Braungart and Braungart 1991, pp. 297–300). While certain identity cohorts may indeed engage in this task, it is not an essential feature of identity cohort membership: indeed, some identity cohorts may hold political organization to be unnecessary, irrelevant, or threatening.

10. Although I suspect that contingencies of and constraints on individual lives (degree of isolation, other relationships and commitments) as well as the personal satisfaction derived from homosexual associations in relation to the perceived liability to self of identifying as homosexual had something to do with it.

Chapter 4: "Dangerous Territory"

1. To repeat Hewitt's (1994, p. 165) insight: "Each way of talking about the self and relating concrete thoughts, feelings, and actions to self-conception is also a way of imagining the social order and thus establishing a place for oneself in it."

2. This is clearly in keeping with Goffman's statement that normals limit the life chances of the discredited.

3. This was echoed by Maria, who offered her own life as proof that heterosexuals' "fear that we're going to turn [children] gay" was "crazy": "Of all the boys I raised, I don't have one gay guy. And I came from a straight couple, a straight home. And none of my boys are gay. The two brothers, the little ones I helped raise, I was their only discipline, [and] none of them are gay."

4. That public insults and invasions question the citizenship of harassed actors is underscored by their certainty "that no one–not the perpetrator and probably no official–will think anything of note has happened. Thus, public harassment is a sort of *civic denial*" (p. 4).

5. It is important to note that, although his family's rejection was dramatic, at the time of the interview, Manny felt that the effect of his known homosexuality on his family status had waned. He felt that his homosexuality had affected his relationship with his family only "to a certain degree, not like you hear some stories where they throw you out of the house." While his family's knowledge of his sexuality "estranged the friendships" between them, it didn't sever family ties.

6. Tony (70, D) echoed this theme when he spoke of Carol and her lover, who, after Carol's death, was inflicted with Carol's homo-

phobic relatives' treatment of her as unworthy of recognition or respect by declaring themselves Carol's only authentic relations. Tony's description of their treatment of Carol's lover as irrelevant and invisible, of Carol's possessions as belonging to them alone, and of the couple's home as a space to which they had complete access, suggest images of invasion and plunder. By emphasizing that this insulting and insensitive treatment was not fueled by ignorance of the close relationship between Carol and her lover, Tony underscored the motivatedly different treatment to which the traditional family subjects homosexuals.

We got two gals down in Manhattan Beach, one gal, Carol, died. The sister-in-law came in, with the brother. Overnight: went to the funeral, came back, sister-in-law took boxes of packed clothing and went in and took the jewelry off the counter. [And Carol's] lover was in the house! She just walked in and said, "I'm gonna take," you know, and the brother said, "I'm the relative!" But they knew goddamn well she was homosexual. There shouldn't be the difference, but it is there. Reality is, it's there.

7. Indeed, Maria explained that police harassment of exclusively gay bars made it impossible for them to stay open. As a result, "none of the bars were really strictly straight or strictly gay," and she patronized mixed bars into which lesbians, who functioned as entertainment for heterosexuals, could enter for free.

8. Maria explained that, in the 1960s, after years of police harassment, she hired a lawyer and got a case against her dismissed "because some lesbians had already fought that, and they had gone up to the State Supreme Court. It should have gone off the books then, but they were still picking me up. They liked to see me behind bars."

Chapter 5: Homosexual Competence and Relations with Heterosexuals

1. A cover explicitly referred to by Goffman in *Stigma* (see p. 93).

2. Elsewhere, Lillian explained that when she "was active in business," 'dealing with' heterosexuals "put me in a very awkward position, because a lot of men wanted to date me and take me out," but cited her having told them that she had a boyfriend or that she was married as one example of ways to get around those demands.

3. This resonates with the practice Goffman (1963, p. 94) termed "present[ing] signs of [a] stigmatized failing as signs of another attribute, one that is less significantly a stigma."

4. Jan, for example, remembered a bar called "The Gables," where "they had it separated where the lesbians would sit on one side and the men would come in to [ogle]." Jeannine recalled the "very first lesbian bar I went to was called the Gay Boat in South Central. And that had a segregated dance floor and booths for the women, and a long bar along one side, for straight guys, who would sit and watch." Maria and her friends used to patronize a bar that "had a lattice and we were sitting on that side and over here was the bar where the straight people were here and they were trying to look through the ivy and we were balling it up over there on the other side."

5. This reemerges in Patricia's account quoted in Chapter 6, in which she recounts having distinguished between "private" and "outside" worlds, and having understood that homosexuality was appropriately displayed only in private and that outside worlds therefore required different styles of dress. Here, the emphasis is more on the private/public split than on the degree of openness allowed for by heterosexuals that figures in Marge's talk.

> We would have our little private parties but when it was outside we were the nicest ladies you ever saw. We'd dress up to kill: high heels, hose, silk hose, beautiful dresses, gloves, the hat. I didn't mind dressing, but I never enjoyed anything so much as having our little parties that we had when I could wear my pants.

6. For a similar validating practice, see Wolkomir's (2001, pp. 418–19) description of gay Christian men producing themselves as more tolerant toward Christians who condemn them for their sexuality than these condemners are toward them by "trump[ing] traditional Christian ideology."

7. Yet, while the actor may be "repelled" by this practice, he identifies with these "offenders"; consequently, he "can neither embrace his group nor let it go" (Goffman 1963, p. 108).

8. This theme appeared in other subjects' talk as well:

> DR: Was secrecy a concern of yours?
>
> Jeannine: Oh, God yes. It was illegal to be lesbian, and I could have lost my teaching job.

DR: Were there things that you had to do to maintain that?

Jeannine: Well no, I never did. I just kept my mouth shut and didn't discuss my personal life with people that I worked with.

Chapter 6: Contingencies and Challenges

1. She added that she did this, in part, because "I felt guilty about being queer and I didn't want to be that."

2. As an example of how relatively open the film business was regarding homosexuality, Michael told me of a regular exchange he and a famous producer would have on the film lot. This producer had ruled that

> mail room boys and messengers could wear shorts after April first. I would be sitting there typing and this eighteen-year-old kid, goofy looking, and [he would have an] envelope: "Michael Watson, personal, wait for answer." And I would open it and look at it; it said, "Get a load of the basket on this guy." I looked, and I would write, "Noted," seal it, send it back. We did this all day long. It was fun.

3. Franz echoed this concern when he explained why he would never want to enter a retirement home despite his family's desire that he do so: "A retirement home is like a nursing home, and then there are more women than men, and the women would be 'Ah! He's available, get him!' Because the ladies—everyone can be as old as they are, and they are good looking people and in good shape too, even at retirement homes when I go for a visit, they look. That would bother me."

4. Leonard and Sharon had been discredited during a time in their lives when they understood their homosexuality in stigmatized terms; they were later "reborn," however, through the properties of the accrediting discourse, which is why I don't discuss them here.

5. Manny also described his rabbi doing "a very nasty thing to me" when she told Manny's niece that Manny had been attending her gay temple. When his niece met the rabbi, the rabbi recognized her last name, and asked her if she knew Manny. When she answered that Manny was her uncle, the rabbi said, " 'Oh, from the gay temple?' And my niece came back and tells me this. I was shocked."

6. This can be seen in Marilyn's other comments as well.

> I became involved in NOW. I had good friends who were lesbians but I had different lives, because I never really came out at work. When I was at [my corporate job], I chose particular people who I came out to. At the library I didn't to most of my co-workers, there were some people who knew but I didn't– and this was a bit of a conflict for me too because I didn't want the condemnation and at the same time I could rationalize it. If they can know me as a person they don't need to know my sexuality, it's not an everyday issue that comes up at work and so I just didn't. But at the same time there's a conflict of when a person does come out it is making a political statement to their fellow workers.

In this account, Marilyn distinguishes between herself and other lesbian members of NOW who, having disclosed themselves to all manner of contact, led "different" lives. Marilyn also recasts her past account for declining to come out to her co-workers–that is, they could "know" her outside the context of her lesbianism–as inspired by fear of condemnation, and contrasts her past sense of her lesbianism as something other than "an everyday issue that comes up at work" with her current understanding of coming out as making a much-needed "political statement to the fellow workers."

Conclusion: Challenges and Opportunities

1. If criteria for membership in the homosexual category are unclear, the *age criterion* seems arbitrary. That I only interviewed self-identified homosexuals over the age of sixty-five meant that they had to have been born before 1930 to be included in the sample–hardly a "natural," endogenous category into which to fall. Anyone familiar with gerontology will easily recognize that I chose sixty-five as the minimum age because that is when people in North America are deemed to have entered the ranks of the elderly, and in order to claim legitimately to have interviewed lesbian and gay elders, I felt I had to abide by this number. Although it is problematic to assume that honoring such arbitrary divisions will necessarily yield substantive fruit, more natural divisions having to do with time and its passage emerged in subjects' accounts, specifically, the fact that all my subjects had reached at least middle age before the emergence of gay liberation.

2. See, for example, Boyarin's (1997) work on the transformation of Jewish masculine identity over the course of the late nineteenth and early twentieth centuries.

3. Before gay liberation, "experts" contended that homosexuals, lacking marital and family ties, suffered from accelerated aging. In this construction, the homosexual life course consisted of a promiscuous youth and an old age that began at the age of forty. (For a refutation of this strain of research, see Minnigerode 1976.) Post-gay liberation research reformulated these stresses and burdens into sources of strength. Starting with Kimmel in 1978, researchers suggested that homosexuality involved the mastery of crises throughout the life course (e.g., coming out to self and others, fear of disclosure, rejection by family and friends, and loneliness), or "crisis competence" (see Friend 1980). This made the older gay person more capable of coping with the crises of old age than were older heterosexuals, whose crises (e.g., retirement, children leaving home, widowhood, and role loss) invariably occurred during and as a constituent feature of old age itself. In short, the presumed pain of passing was seen as a successful way to "toughen up" for the equally presumed pain of growing old. In 1987, Lee challenged this concept as a new version of the Puritan adage that suffering pays off in the end. Indeed, his analysis of interviews with Canadian gay men ages fifty to eighty disproved the theory of crisis competence, finding that those with the highest life satisfaction scores reported the *fewest* crises (both generic and gay-specific). This suggests that avoiding crises is more important to adaptation to old age than is managing or learning from them; clearly, one way to avoid crises for those for whom disclosure is a significant fear is to remain in the closet.

4. But see Fullmer et al. 1999 and Shenk and Fullmer 1996 for a more sociological approach.

5. The distinct identity careers of those who "decided" to "become gay" (although, interestingly, not for political reasons, but because new circumstances arose that made this decision seem the best one at the time) did not have any direct implications for identity cohort membership. Two of these subjects entered gay life before gay liberation and lesbian-feminism, via the stigmatized gay subculture, and one entered it in the early 1970s, via the hetero/sexual revolution, and encountered an accrediting homosexual movement through contacts she made there.

Bibliography

Adelman, M. (1987). *Long Time Passing: Lives of Older Lesbians.* Boston: Alyson.

Adelman, M. (1990). "Stigma, gay lifestyles, and adjustment to aging: A study of later-life gay men and lesbians." *Journal of Homosexuality* 20(3–4): 7–32.

Aries, P. (1960). *Centuries of Childhood.* Harmondsworth: Penguin.

Bailey, K. D. (1994). *Methods of Social Research.* New York: The Free Press.

Baron, A., and Cramer, D. W. (2000). "Potential counseling concerns of aging lesbian, gay, and bisexual clients." Pp. 207–223 in Perez, R. M., DeBord, K. A., and Bieschke, K. J. (Eds.). *Handbook of Counseling and Psychotherapy with Lesbian, Gay, and Bisexual Clients.* Washington, DC: American Psychological Association.

Bech, H. (1992). "Report from a rotten state: 'Marriage' and 'homosexuality' in 'Denmark.'" In Plummer, K. (Ed.). *Modern Homosexualities: Fragments of Lesbian and Gay Experience.* New York: Routledge.

Berger, B. M. (1981). *The Survival of a Counterculture: Ideological Work and Everyday Life among Rural Communards.* Berkeley: University of California Press.

Berger, R. M. (1982). *Gay and Gray.* Chicago: University of Chicago Press.

Bergstrom, M. J., and Nussbaum, J. F. (1996). "Cohort differences in interpersonal conflict: Implications for the older patient-younger care provider interaction." *Health Communication* 8(3): 233–248.

Bernstein, M. (1997). "Celebration and suppression: The strategic uses of identity by the lesbian and gay movement." *American Journal of Sociology* 103(3): 531–565.

Boyarin, D. (1997). *Unheroic Conduct: The Rise of Heterosexuality and the Invention of the Jewish Man.* Berkeley: University of California Press.

Brady, S. (1999). "Sexual identity issues in mental health care for older adults." *Journal of Geriatric Psychiatry* 32 (2): 183–194.

Braungart, M. M., and Braungart, R. G. (1991). "The effects of the 1960s political generation on former left- and right-wing youth activist leaders." *Social Problems* 38(23): 291–315.

Cahill, S., South, K., and Spade, J. (2000). *Outing Age: Public Policy Issues Affecting Gay, Lesbian, Bisexual and Transgender Elders.* Washington, DC: Policy Institute of the National Gay and Lesbian Task Force Foundation.

Carr, C. L. (1999). "Cognitive scripting and sexual identification: Essentialism, anarchism, and constructionism." *Symbolic Interaction* 22(1): 1–24.

Chauncey, G. (1994). *Gay New York: Gender, Urban Culture, and the Making of the Gay Male World, 1890–1940.* New York: Basic Books.

Coleman, P. (2000). *Village Elders.* Urbana: University of Illinois Press.

Daughters of Bilitis. (October 1956). "Statement of purpose." *The Ladder* 1(2): 3.

D'Emilio, J. (1983). *Sexual Politics, Sexual Communities: The Making of a Homosexual Minority in the United States.* Chicago: University of Chicago Press.

Devor, H. (1997). *FTM: Female-to-male Transsexuals in Society.* Bloomington: Indiana University Press.

Dorfman, R., Walters, K., Burke, P., Hardin, L., and Karanik, T. (1995). "Old, sad and alone: The myth of the aging homosexual." *Journal of Genrontological Social Work* 24(1/2): 29–44.

Egan, J. (2000). "Lonely gay teen seeking same: How Jeffrey found friendship, sex, and heartache–and himself–online." *New York Times Magazine.* December 10.

Ehrenreich, B., and English, D. (1978). *For Her Own Good: 150 Years of the Experts' Advice to Women.* Garden City, NY: Anchor Press.

Elder, G. J., Jr. (1995). "The life course paradigm: Social change and individual development." Pp. 101–139 in Moen, P., Elder, G. H., Jr., and Luscher, K. (Eds.). *Examining Lives in Context: Perspectives on the Ecology of Human Development.* Washington, DC: American Psychological Association.

Elkins, R. (1997). *Male Femaling: A Grounded Theory Approach to Cross-Dressing and Sex-Changing.* London: Routledge.

Epstein, S. (1990). "Gay politics, ethnic identity: The limits of social constructionism." In Stein, E. (Ed.). *Forms of Desire: Sexual Orientation and the Social Constructionist Controversy.* New York: Garland.

Escoffier, J. (1992). "Generations and paradigms: Mainstreams in lesbian and gay studies." *Journal of Homosexuality* 24(1–2): 7–26.

Faderman, L. (1991). *Odd Girls and Twilight Lovers: A History of Lesbian Life in Twentieth-Century America.* Middlesex: Plume.

Fredriksen, K. (1999). "Family caregiving responsibilities among lesbians and gay men." *Social Work* 44 (2): 142–155.

Friend, R. A. (1980). "Gayging: Adjustment and the older gay male." *Alternative Lifestyles* 3(2): 231–248.

Fullmer, E. M., Shenk, D., and Eastland, L. J. (1999). "Negating identity: A feminist analysis of the social invisibility of older lesbians." *Journal of Women and Aging* 11(2/3): 131–148.

Gagne, P., Tewksbury, R., and McGaughey, D. (1997). "Coming out and crossing over: Identity formation and proclamation in a transgender community." *Gender and Society* 11(4): 478–508.

Gardner, C. B. (1995). *Passing By: Gender and Public Harassment.* Berkeley: University of California Press.

Gershick, Z. (1998). *Gay Old Girls.* Los Angeles: Alyson Publications.

Giddens, A. (1991). *Modernity and Self-Identity.* Oxford: Polity Press.

Goffman, E. (1963). *Stigma: Notes on the Management of Spoiled Identity.* Englewood Cliffs, NJ: Prentice-Hall.

Goodman, M. (1996). "Culture, cohort, and cosmetic surgery." *Journal of Women and Aging* 8(2): 55–73.

Grube, J. (1990). "Natives and settlers: An ethnographic note on early interaction of older homosexual men with younger gay liberationists." *Journal of Homosexuality* 20(3/4): 119–135.

Harding, S. (1991). *Whose Science? Whose Knowledge? Thinking from Women's Lives.* Ithaca, NY: Cornell University Press.

Hardy, M. A., and Waite, L. (1997). "Doing time: Reconciling biography with history in the study of social change." Pp. 1–21 in Hardy, M. A. (Ed.). *Studying Aging and Social Change: Conceptual and Methodological Issues.* Thousand Oaks, CA: Sage.

Hewitt, J. P. (1994). "Self, role, and discourse." In Platt, G. R., and Gordon, C. (Eds.). *Self, Collective Action, and Society: Essays Honoring the Contributions of Ralph H. Turner.* New Haven, CT: JAI Press.

Holstein, J. A. (1988). "Court-ordered incompetence: Conversational organization in involuntary commitment hearings." *Social Problems* 34(4): 458–474.

Holstein, J. A., and Gubrium, J. F. (1995). *The Active Interview.* Thousand Oaks, CA: Sage.

Jenness, V. (1992). "Coming out: Lesbian identities and the categorization problem." Pp. 65–75 in Plummer, K. (Ed.). *Modern Homosexualities: Fragments of Lesbian and Gay Experience.* London: Routledge.

Jensen, K. L. (1999). *Lesbian Epiphanies: Women Coming Out in Later Life.* New York: Harrington Park Press.

Kelly, K. (1977). "The aging male homosexual: Myth and reality." *Gerontologist* 17(4): 328–332.

Kimmel, D. C. (1978). "Adult development and aging: A gay perspective." *Journal of Social Issues* 34(3): 113–130.

Kimmel, D. C. (1979). "Life history interviews of aging gay men." *International Journal of Aging and Human Development* 10(3): 239–248.

King, D. (1993). *The Transvestite and the Transsexual: Public Categories and Private Identities.* Aldershot: Avebury.

Lee, J. A. (1987). "What can homosexual aging studies contribute to theories of aging?" *Journal of Homosexuality* 13(4): 43–71.

Lofland, J. (1969). *Deviance and Identity.* Englewood Cliffs, NJ: Prentice-Hall.

Mannheim, K. (1952 [1928]). "The problem of generations." In Kecskemeti, P. (Ed.). *Essays on the Sociology of Knowledge.* New York: Oxford University Press.

Mason-Schrock, D. (1996). "Transsexuals' narrative construction of the 'true self.'" *Social Psychological Quarterly* 59(3), Special Issue: Gender and Social Interaction: 176–192.

McLaren, A. (1999). *Twentieth-Century Sexuality: A History.* Oxford: Blackwell Publishers.

Minnigerode, F. (1976). "Age-status labeling in homosexual men." *Journal of Homosexuality* 1(3): 273–276.

Nardi, P. M., and Sanders, D. (1994). *Growing Up Before Stonewall: Life Stories of Some Gay Men.* London: Routledge.

Newton, E. (1989). "The mythic mannish lesbian: Radclyffe Hall and the new woman." Pp. 281–293 in Duberman, M. B., Vicinus, M., and Chauncey, G., Jr. (Eds.). *Hidden from History: Reclaiming the Gay and Lesbian Past.* Markham, ON: Penguin.

Plummer, K. (1995). *Telling Sexual Stories: Power, Change, and Social Worlds.* London: Routledge.

Ponse, B. (1978). *Identities in the Lesbian World: The Social Construction of Self.* Westport, CT: Greenwood.

Quam, J. K., and Whitford, G. S. (1992). "Adaptation and age-related expectations of older gay and lesbian adults." *The Gerontologist* 32(3): 367–374.

Robinson, R. V., and Jackson, E. F. (2001). "Is trust in others declining in America? An age-period-cohort analysis." *Social Science Research* 30(1): 117–145.

Rosenfeld, D., and Gallagher, E. B. (2002). "The life course as an organizing principle and a socializing resource in modern medicine." In Settersten, R. A., Jr., and Owens, T. J. (Eds.). *Advances in Life Course Research*, vol. 7: *New Frontiers in Socialization.* Stamford, CT: JAI Press.

Rosenfeld, D. (1999). "Identity work among lesbian and gay elderly." *Journal of Aging Studies* 13(2): 121–144.

Rosow, I. (1978). "What is a cohort and why?" *Human Development* 21: 65–75.

Ryder, N. (1997 [1965]). "The cohort as a concept in the study of social change." Pp. 66–92 in Hardy, M. A. (Ed.). *Studying Aging and Social Change: Conceptual and Methodological Issues.* Thousand Oaks, CA: Sage.

Schutz, A. (1962). *Collected Papers: The Problem of Social Reality.* The Hague: Martinus Nijhoff.

Settersten, R. A., Jr. (1999). *Lives in Time and Place: The Problems and Promises of Developmental Science.* New York: Baywood Publishing Company.

Shenk, D., and Fullmer, E. (1996). "Significant relationships among older women: Cultural and personal constructions of lesbianism." *Journal of Women and Aging* 8(3/4): 75–89.

Sherkat, D. E. (2001). "Investigating the sect-church-sect cycle: Cohort-specific attendance differences across African-American denominations." *Journal for the Scientific Study of Religion* 40(2): 221–233.

Shernoff, M. (Ed.) (1997). *Gay Widowers: Life after the Death of a Partner.* New York: Haworth Press.

Smith, D. (1990). *Texts, Facts, and Femininity: Exploring the Relations of Ruling.* London: Routledge.

Stanley, L. (Ed.) (1990). *Feminist Praxis: Research, Theory and Epistemology in Feminist Sociology.* London: Routledge.

Stein, A. S. (1997). *Sex and Sensibility: Stories of Lesbian Generations.* Berkeley: University of California Press.

Stein, A. S. (Ed.) (1993). *Sisters, Sexperts, Queers: Beyond the Lesbian Nation.* New York: Plume.

Troiden, R. (1988). *Gay and Lesbian Identity: A Sociological Analysis.* New York: General Hall.

Vacha, K. (1985). *Quiet Fire: Memoirs of Older Gay Men.* Trumansburg, NY: The Crossing Press.

Valocchi, S. (1999). "The class-inflected nature of gay identity." *Social Problems* 46(2): 207–224.

Weston, K. (1991). *Families We Choose: Lesbians, Gays, Kinship.* New York: Columbia University Press.

Whisman, V. (1996). *Queer by Choice: Lesbians, Gay Men, and the Politics of Identity.* New York: Routledge.

Whyte, W. H., Jr. (1956). *The Organization Man.* New York: Simon and Schuster.

Widdicombe, S. (1998). "Identity as an analysts' and a participants' resource." Pp. 191–206 in Antaki, C., and Widdicombe, S. (Eds.). *Identities in Talk.* London: Sage.

Wilson, T. C. (1996). "Cohort and prejudice: Whites' attitudes toward Blacks, Hispanics, Jews, and Asians." *Public Opinion Quarterly* 60(2): 253–274.

Wolkomir, M. (2001). "Wrestling with the angels of meaning: The revisionist ideological work of gay and ex-gay Christian men." *Symbolic Interaction* 24(4): 407–424.

Index